In Search of
Security

By the same author

New States, Sovereignty and Intervention

In Search of Security

The Third World in International Relations

Caroline Thomas

Lecturer in Politics
University of Southampton

Wheatsheaf Books

RIENNER   Boulder, Colorado

First published in Great Britain in 1987 by
WHEATSHEAF BOOKS LIMITED
A MEMBER OF THE HARVESTER PRESS PUBLISHING GROUP
Publisher: John Spiers
16 Ship Street, Brighton, Sussex
and in the United States of America by
LYNNE RIENNER PUBLISHERS, INC.
948 North Street, Boulder, Colorado 80302

© Caroline Thomas, 1987

British Library Cataloguing in Publication Data
Thomas, Caroline
  In search of security: the Third World
  in international relations.
  1. Developing countries—Foreign relations
  I. Title
  327´.09172´4   D849
ISBN 0–7450–0124–6
ISBN 0–7450–039–6 Pbk

Library of Congress Cataloging in Publication Data
Thomas, Caroline.
  In search of security.
  Bibliography: p.
  Includes index.
  1. Developing countries—Foreign relations.
2. Developing countries—Foreign economic relations.
3. Economic security—Developing countries.
4. Security, international. I. Title.
JX1391.T48   1987   327´.09172´4   87–4976
ISBN 1–55587–073–2 (Lib. Bdg.)
ISBN 1–55587–074–0 (Pbk.)
ISBN 0–7450–0124–6 (Wheatsheaf)

Typeset in 11 on 12pt Times Roman by C. R. Barber & Partners
(Highlands) Ltd, Fort William, Scotland

Printed in Great Britain by
Billing & Sons Ltd, Worcester.

For my parents

Contents

Preface

This book has been written with the needs of Western students of the Third World in mind. While it is aimed specifically at the requirements of students of international relations, it should be of interest to social-science students in general. For one can no more study the international relations of the less-developed states without explanatory references to economics, sociology, history and psychology, than one can study the international political stands of the developed countries without reference to these other lines of enquiry. Hence, while the stress of the book is always on the position and the fate of developing countries in the international political system, it is necessary to be aware of and to draw upon economic, social, psychological, cultural, ethnic, linguistic, religious and historical factors, plus many others.

Teaching courses on the Third World in international relations is an exciting occupation because of the great range of problems thrown up, the growing literature on the subject and, last but not least, the enthusiasm with which students approach the subject. However, while a few key books, such as those by Calvert, Clapham and Randall and Theobald, have appeared recently on Third World politics, what has been missing is a basic international relations textbook dealing specifically with the Third World. The title of this book stresses the need which developing states, just like developed states, have to enhance their security. People also crave that some feeling of security, and course books tend to make students more secure in their subject as well as enhancing their understanding of it. Hence this book. Using the framework provided by the idea of security, and interpreting the activities and desires emanating from Third World states in the light of that central idea, the author seeks to illustrate and explain some of the problems and positions of these states in the international arena. The study is based on themes set in a South–North context rather than a South–South context. The latter would highlight the politics of intra-Third World relations. Such relations, while very important, are not the focus of this book.

The introductory chapter briefly examines the idea of a 'Third World', the existence of which has come under challenge due to the diversity of the states within the grouping. A case is argued for the utility of the term. There follows an analysis of the concept of security as it relates to the Third World, as used in this book. Together, these provide an explanatory backdrop against which the rest of the book should be read. Then follows a series of chapters introducing particular problems.

Chapter 2 looks at nation-building in Third World states, which are mostly arbitrary and artificial creations of the colonial powers. The success or failure of nation-state-building has great implications for the Third World states themselves, and for regional and international relations and security. The Tanzanian example illustrates a process by which a Third World government worked in the early years of independence to create a national consciousness.

Chapter 3 looks at the attempts of the developing countries to increase their financial security by trying to change the rules of the international monetary game. Particular attention is paid here to their attitude towards and relationship with the International Monetary Fund, which is regarded by them as the guardian of the present unjust system. The current debt crisis is also touched upon, for an indication both of the financial difficulties in which developing countries find themselves and the opportunities for leverage which present themselves occasionally.

Chapter 4 examines the efforts of developing countries to improve their economic security and developmental stability by working for improvements in terms of trade. Their dissatisfaction with the current GATT rules and their desires, as set out in the Charter of Economic Rights and Duties of States, receive special attention. The Lomé Agreements are singled out as an example of a trade-and-aid package which, while superficially improving the security position of developing countries, in reality does little to achieve that. The newly industrialised countries are looked at briefly, to see whether their progress has been the result of developing along free-market lines enshrined in the post-war trading order.

Chapter 5 raises the thorny issues of food and health security in an era when population increases are phenomenal. The Western desire to curb population growth in the South, and the attitude of the developing countries to this 'cultural imperialism', are examined briefly, followed by a more detailed discussion of the availability of food and the control of the world's food supply. The problem is one of distribution, not simply of Malthusian population economics, as Amartya Sen argues convincingly in his book *Poverty and Famines*. Tied in with this discussion of food and population is the international politics of health in the Third World. Also discussed are the efforts of certain developing countries to control the import and use of pharmaceuticals, thereby moving towards a more secure health regime for their peoples, less tied to the marketing techniques of huge multinational drug companies whose only loyalty is to profit.

Chapter 6 looks at the question of nuclear weapons and the search for security by Third World states. Particular attention is paid here to the Non-Proliferation Treaty (NPT) of 1968. This treaty regulates the acquisition of nuclear weapons and is often charged with being discriminatory since it institutionalises unequal rights and obligations. Article VI, which calls on the nuclear-weapon powers to negotiate on disarmament 'in good faith', has been the cause of much annoyance among Third World states who feel that the superpowers are not keeping to their side of the bargain. The basic problem is that non-nuclear Third World states regard the NPT as an arms-reduction agreement, while the superpowers regard it as an arms-control agreement. Hence the superpowers call on other states not to proliferate while rapidly proliferating their own nuclear arsenals. The nuclear-threshold states of the Third World, who have refused to join the NPT, present a great challenge to the treaty and hence to the common designs of the superpowers.

Chapter 7 presents a case study to illustrate the central theme of the textbook; namely, that most of the policies of developing countries can best be understood by reference to their grave need to increase their individual security in an extremely insecure world. While all states, not only developing ones, are concerned to increase their security, for the developing states, it is of acute importance given their general vulnerability in the international system. Their security is threatened on all levels: domestically, by different groups competing for power in a political system where consensus is often totally absent, and by the inability to provide secure systems of food and health care, employment and education for their people; and internationally, by predatory powers (usually, but not always, great powers) and by international institutions and multinational companies eager to make policy decisions for Third World states. The Jamaican example shows how difficult, if not impossible, it can be for a Third World government to take an independent stand and exercise the sovereignty which is the very essence of statehood. It shows the unwillingness of a superpower, this time the US, to come to terms with the right of a small state to follow a non-aligned foreign policy; indeed, it illustrates the denial of such a policy by the world's strongest military and economic power.

The concluding remarks draw together threads running through the book and assess the progress made by the Third World states in their search for security. The influence of the US on this search comes under scrutiny.

No textbook can hope to cover all relevant issues and provide definitive answers to the problems raised. The thematic approach adopted here, in concentrating specifically on the South–North interface, does not deal with some important issues such as the specific role of Third World institutions and movements in global politics, except as they are relevant to particular themes. Also, intra-Third World conflicts are mentioned only where they affect the respective theme under examination. Such areas are vital for our understanding of Third World international relations, but they are the subject matter for other books. What is attempted here is a general introduction for students interested in the concerns of Third World states in global politics. A framework is provided in which to analyse attitudes, problems and actions, and some of the main aspects of insecurity and the search for security are outlined. Detailed bibliographical notes are provided which can guide students who are interested in pursuing various topics covered here (and others which are not) in more depth. If this book helps to stimulate interest in the problems of the Third World among students, then I shall feel that my aims have been more than fulfilled.

The research for, and writing of, this book have been aided greatly by financial assistance from the New Blood lectureship scheme funded by the University Grants Commission, and by the generous Ford Foundation grant for the study of North–South Security Relations, of which my department is the fortunate recipient. I would like to thank my colleagues at Southampton and elsewhere for their encouragement. Thanks go to Ines Bueno, Gordon Jamieson and Celma Salazar, who in their different ways awakened me to the problems of the Third World; and to Aswini, Vanita and Amit Ray, and Matin, Nasreen and Irfan Zuberi, my friends and mentors in India. The students in the Third World option at Southampton 1985–6 have been a source of infinite enthusiasm and empathy. My friends outside the profession deserve a huge thanks, especially Amanda, Carole, Claire, Hilary, Lakshmi, Lynda, Sarah, Shin-Yuan and Sue, and T. John has been a lively source of criticism and encouragement, while my brother, Steve, has been a constant source of moral support. Jo has been a gem with the typing and organisation, and Liz has shown extraordinary fortitude in the face of uncooperative machines and a nagging author. Thanks also to Julian for his last-minute editorial assistance, and to Peter for his painstaking reading of the manuscript and helpful comments. Last but not least are my thanks to Wally, a highly therapeutic fat tabby who is without a doubt the most handsome moggy in Southampton.

Abbreviations

ACP	Afro-Caribbean-Pacific
AID	Agency for International Development
ASEAN	Association of South-East Asian Nations
CERDS	Charter of Economic Rights and Duties of States
CIA	Central Intelligence Agency
COMECON	Council for Mutual Economic Assistance
COPPTECS	Regional Cooperative Pharmaceutical Production and Technology Centres
EEC	European Economic Community
FAO	Food and Agriculture Association
GATT	General Agreement on Tariffs and Trade
IAEA	International Atomic Energy Agency
IBRD	International Bank for Reconstruction and Development
ICA	International Commodity Agreement
ICSID	International Centre for the Settlement of Investment Disputes
IDA	International Development Association
IMF	International Monetary Fund
IPC	Integrated Programme for Commodities
JLP	Jamaican Labour Party
MNC	Multinational Corporation
NATO	North Atlantic Treaty Organisation
NEC	National Executive Council
NIC	Newly Industrialising Country
NIEO	New International Economic Order
NPT	Non-Proliferation Treaty

OAU	Organisation of African Unity
OPEC	Organisation of Petroleum Exporting Countries
PMA	Pharmaceutical Manufacturers' Association
PNP	Peoples National Party
SDR	Special Drawing Right
TANU	Tanganyika African National Union
UN	United Nations
UNCTAD	United Nations Conference on Trade and Development
UNESCO	United Nations Economic and Social Council
UNIDO	United Nations Industrial Development Organisation
UNDP	United Nations Development Programme

1 Introduction: The Third World in Search of Security

This book aims to describe and explain the role of the Third World states in international relations by reference to the idea of a search for security, and to offer some prescriptions for achieving this goal. A basic theme running through the book is that security in the context of the Third World states does not simply refer to the military dimension, as is often assumed in Western discussions of the concept, but to the whole range of dimensions of a state's existence which are already taken care of in the more-developed states, especially those of the West. Several key areas of the search for security are examined; for example, the search for the internal security of the state through nation-building, the search for secure systems of food, health, money and trade, as well as the search for security through nuclear weapons. The book ends with a case study highlighting the interaction of some of these areas and the difficulties encountered in pursuing the elusive goal of security. This brief introduction addresses two vital questions which form the backdrop to the rest of the book: first, whether a 'Third World' actually exists and, second, what the search for security is really about.

In recent years the idea of the existence of a 'Third World' has come under attack.[1] In the early post-war decades it seemed to make some sense to characterise the advanced capitalist states as the First World, the centrally planned states as the Second World and remaining, poor states as the Third World, even though it was plainly a Western-centric view. However, more recently the obvious and important diversity of Third World states has been highlighted. Diversity both within and between them has always existed on cultural, ethnic, religious and linguistic grounds, but recently economic diversity seems to have increased significantly. Now, for example, we read about the oil-producing Third World states, the non oil-producing, the newly industrialising, the least developed, and so on. Moreover, in simple economic terms some of the advanced states, such as Portugal, seem to be poorer than some of the newly industrialising. Despite all these economic and other differentiations, this book is based on the premise that there remain compelling objective and subjective criteria for using the term 'Third World' as an analytic category.

The most important objective criterion is that Third World states generally are ex-colonies, and this provides a vital psychological backdrop to the grouping. No matter how poor Portugal may be, there would be no support from ex-colonies at the present time for ranking her amongst them as a fellow Third World state. For the most part, Third World states are post-colonial states. Even the notion of the modern nation-state is an imported value for much of the Third World. Hence nation-state-building is a crucial concern for them. A few Third World states, such as Iran, have a longer history, but these are the exceptions not the rule. Third World states are artificial constructs, and their governments must strive to hold them together once the first wave of anti-colonial nationalism has passed and ethnic, religious and linguistic differences come to the fore. Characterised by weak and divisive social, economic and political structures, the task of forging loyalty to the state is difficult. In contrast to the industrialisation of the older, advanced Western states, development is expected to take place in Third World states before the unity of the nation is really under way. Unfortunately, the pattern of economic growth in many Third World states militates against unity, as the benefits of development, such as they are, are often differentially enjoyed by particular regions, ethnic groups, political party members and government officials.

A vast array of other social indicators also provide objective criteria for the existence of a 'Third World'. Lack of access to clean water, sanitation, food, health care and education are the everyday problems of life facing the majority of people on our planet. Again, there are specific exceptions. Cubans enjoy the benefits of a well-developed health service. At times, Sri Lankans have enjoyed free rice. These are the exceptions which prove the rule. To the list of objective criteria many more factors could be added, but we shall settle here for one more: the dependence of Third World states on the industrialised states and transnational corporations for technology. This is a key weakness of those states. Some have been able to develop an indigenous capability, but this is usually sector-specific. Others have proved themselves to be excellent at copying northern technology. Most remain dependent.

If we look for subjective criteria for the existence of the Third World, then the most convincing evidence is simply that the Third World is a self-defining grouping of states. Its origins go back to the struggle for political independence, and then for economic independence. Conferences such as those held in Bandung and Cairo enabled common concerns to be highlighted, and underlined common interests between the Latin American states and those of Afro-Asia. The development of the Non-Aligned Movement, the United Nations Conference on Trade and Development (UNCTAD) and the Group of Seventy-Seven all helped forge the articulation of common interests and the perception of unity.

Perhaps the greatest test of Third World unity came with the action of the Organisation of Petroleum Exporting Countries (OPEC) in the 1970s. Yet the most vehement criticism of the oil price rises came not from the poorest states, who were most vulnerable to it, but from the advanced capitalist states. Those states in the Third World which suffered as a result of the action, championed OPEC; the price rises were seen as a victory for the Third World. Moreover, those OPEC states today still classify themselves diplomatically and in official publications as Third World states, on the grounds that they do not yet have completely structured economies and infrastructures that can produce the food, goods and services that they need for trade and consumption. They are mostly dependent on the export of one primary product.

In arguing a case against those who deny the existence of the Third World, it is not being suggested here that the international system is static; far from it, it is dynamic. Yet the changes which have taken place in the last forty years have not yet sufficiently eroded the political, psychological or economic underpinning of the grouping to warrant a reclassification. As a category in international relations the Third World has not yet been rendered invalid. Indeed, the rapid technological progress of the northern states has reinforced the distance and the difference between the older industrialised states and those of the Third World. As new centres of economic and political power emerge, and with the changed psychological environment that this would evince, the term will become less useful, but such projections have yet to be realised.

Having offered a case for the utility of the notion of the Third World, the next question to be addressed concerns the search for security. Third World states, like all other states, are conscious of the need to make themselves secure. The task for Third World states is qualitatively different, however. They are insecure domestically, because of the factors mentioned previously. The process of forging loyalty to the state is still at an early stage in many cases. Political, economic and social structures are weak and often inflexible. The problem of internal insecurity makes the problem of external insecurity all the more acute, and vice versa. These different dimensions of insecurity feed off one another.

Insecurity here refers to the relative weakness, the lack of autonomy, the vulnerability and the lack of room for manoeuvre which Third World states have on economic, political and of course military levels. Third World states suffer from an acute lack of control over the international environment in which they must function, and of all the world's states they are the ones for whom the economic alternatives of survive or perish are the most pressing. Their lack of control over the external environment has great implications for their ability to control the domestic economic, social and political domain. For example, the market which determines the price of primary products on which so many Third World states depend can be highly unstable. Hence, states which are dependent on the export of single commodities, such as copper, sugar, oil or bananas, are extremely vulnerable to the workings of a mechanism which is completely outside their control. They are vulnerable also to the dictates of institutions like the International Monetary Fund (IMF), in which they have no real decision-making power. They are vulnerable, too, because the domestic policy decisions of the leading capitalist power, the United States, can have extremely adverse repercussions on them. For instance, a United States' policy decision which leads to a rise in interest rates can add millions of dollars to a debtor-state's repayment bill. They are vulnerable to changes in the production policies of multinationals. In addition to these vulnerabilities there is of course the problem of the unpredictability of the weather. Floods, hurricanes and drought can play havoc with the production and distribution of agricultural exports and food for domestic consumption.

On top of all these problems, which erode the possibility of autonomous decision-making and action by Third World states, the overarching geopolitical structure of the East–West divide has placed further limitations on the room for manoeuvre. Geopolitics has vastly limited the possibility of indigenous developments and choices. Non-alignment is a privileged policy which few states can realistically follow. The East–West divide has put a heavy price on political freedom of manoeuvre by Third World states, and has intensified the psychological links of the Third World grouping.

In these circumstances of insecurity, Third World states have attempted where possible to increase their room for manoeuvre, to increase their ability to stabilise the environment in which they must function, and to minimise their vulnerability. This is evidenced in their attempts to change the rules of the international game by influencing the regimes governing specific areas such as money, trade, nuclear weapons, pharmaceuticals, and so forth.[2] ('Regime' refers simply to the set of rules and institutions governing a specific area of activity. Such regimes reflect the power hierarchy of states participating in the activity. More often than not, they reflect the overarching power hierarchy in the international political system.) A synoptic illustration from the field of trade will show how Third World states try to make themselves more secure by altering the regime regulating this activity; in other words, how they try to influence the prevailing rules, institutions and power structure which determine international trade.

After the Second World War the United States and United

Kingdom were largely responsible for creating an international trading regime based on the liberal principles of non-discrimination and reciprocity. The leaders of those states believed that the economic nationalism of the inter-war period was responsible for undermining peace; hence they wanted to establish an order based on free trade. They believed that this would lead to greater peace and stability in the world, as well as prosperity. Regarding the colonies, it was thought that if they participated in the free-trade system, economic growth, and take-off would occur, and the logical result would be liberal, anti-communist democratic societies.

It transpires that the states which have grown most within the liberal trading order are far from liberal and democratic in their domestic politics. The newly industrialising states of South-East Asia spring to mind here,[3] as do Argentina and Brazil (which have only recently undertaken movements towards political liberalisation).[4] It transpires also that modernisation does not necessarily bring with it Western secular values as was expected. The Islamic reaction in Iran is testimony to this.[5]

Most Third World states have not fared well. The unpredictability of commodity prices has devastated many a Third World economy. The Third World has not been silent in the face of such problems. Piecemeal changes have been worked for in the existing trading order. The establishment of UNCTAD, a standing conference on trade and development outside the Western-founded General Agreement on Tariffs and Trade (GATT), has been a major achievement for the Third World. This institution, however, has never been given any real decision-making power. It remains a talking shop. The OPEC oil price rises of the early 1970s changed the psychological environment in which negotiations took place. The call for a New International Economic Order (NIEO) at the General Assembly of the UN was rapidly followed by the call for a Charter of Economic Rights and Duties of States (CERDS). The latter was accepted by 120 states, with only six voting against and ten abstentions. Had this charter come to inform the trading order, then the vulnerability and lack of autonomoy of Third World states with regard to the market, and by implication to the disadvantageous workings of the international system, would have been massively reduced. For instance, the price of primary products would have been index-linked to the price of imported manufactured goods. The sovereign right to exclusive state control over foreign investment and domestic natural resources would have been instituted, thus curbing the vulnerability of Third World states to the activities of multinational corporations. The right of primary commodity producers to form cartels would have been internationally legitimated, thus giving them a lawful case for using such means to obtain a higher price for their produce.

The refusal of the Western states to see the Third World's call in political, not simply economic terms, reflects an unfortunate and misguided attitude. The desire to exercise political control over one's destiny is not an extravagant demand for a state to make; it simply reflects national or state interest and gets to the heart of what sovereignty is supposed to be about. The lesson learned by the Third World states regarding the NIEO and the CERDS, and one that has been repeated in so many other fields such as the Law of the Sea, is that no matter how great the majority in favour of changing the rules of the international game, unless the state which wields most power is in favour of the change, then in all probability no change will come about. Moreover, current political reality is increasing the despair of Third World states, for the United States seems to be withdrawing from those very international arenas where up till now the Third World has at least had a voice and has been able to put forward grievances for discussion and negotiation. Her withdrawal from UNESCO, her refusal to accept the jurisdiction of the World Court after a case had been brought against her by Nicaragua, and her failure to take the Libyan issue to the UN all indicate an ebbing of faith in and respect for those international institutions. The Third World needs access to arenas where its grievances can be heard by the hegemonic power, and the current loss of access is a major blow to the Third World's search for security. It means that the environment in which they must operate is even more unpredictable. It means also that their unity as a group, their self-identification, will be strengthened. All this makes for a more unjust, and more unstable, world order.

Nothing has yet been said of those Third World states which

have sought to decrease their vulnerability by leaving the world market and following some form of Marxist or socialist path. Most Third World states still function within the liberal trading order and show little desire to adopt a radical economy outside that. Even the Third World states classified by the Soviet Union as being 'of socialist orientation' usually undertake the majority of their trade with the capitalist states.[6] The People's Democratic Republic of Yemen is an example. Of those that have espoused Marxism, such as Vietnam, most are extremely dependent on Soviet aid and hence have substituted one vulnerability for another, albeit a preferred one. Whether any of these states can modernise to an extent they consider sufficient without operating in the international market system, is questionable. China is a special case because she has such a vast internal market of her own, but even she is now opening up to the international market. Which path will Mozambique take, now that she has been denied entry to the Council for Mutual Economic Assistance (COMECON)? Other states espousing varieties of socialism, such as Tanzania, have, in varying degrees, attempted a withdrawal from the market, yet they have been drawn back in almost magnetically. Indeed, the Soviet Union takes a very pragmatic view of such efforts. It suggests that autarky is not a realistic option for a state with a population which is not very large.

The attempts by Third World states either to alter the trading regime or to opt out of it do not seem to have borne much fruit. Indeed, the gap between rich and poor states is increasing, and with the current debt burden there is a transfer of capital resources from the poor states to the rich. The picture seems quite dismal. There are a few changes, however, which it is within the power of the Third World states to bring about. For example, they can trade more with each other. Delinking from the international economy is not a realistic option, but increasing links with fellow Third World states is. This is already happening. An increase in barter trade (exchanging one product for another, as Brazil has done with Iraq by bartering arms for oil) is a useful pursuit for poor states. It does mean that less foreign exchange goes directly into paying off debts. Such barter trade is admonished by Western banks and governments—but after all, those very Western states have been practising this type of trade despite the GATT rules, especially within the context of the North Atlantic Treaty Organisation (NATO).

This single example of trade illustrates how very difficult it is for Third World states to make themselves more secure in international relations. The environment in which they are trying to modernise and create a better life for their inhabitants is highly unpredictable, and their ability to cushion themselves against this is very limited. It will be shown in this book that these states are pushing over a wide range of sectors and issues for greater autonomy, but their achievement, individually and collectively, has been small. Some have traded one form of dependence for another, but while the particular states concerned may feel that their security has thus been increased in the international arena, the increase will not be sufficient until they can feel they are their own task masters. Security for Third World states remains elusive.

NOTES

1. See the debate in *Third World Quarterly:* L. Wolf-Phillips, 'Why Third World?', vol. 1, no. 1, January 1979; P. Worsley, 'How Many Worlds?', vol. 1, no. 2, April 1979; S. D. Muni, 'Third World: Concept and Controversy', vol. 1, no. 3, July 1979; J. L. Love, 'Third World: A Response to Professor Worsley', vol. 2, no. 2, April 1980; G. McCall, 'Four Worlds of Experience and Action', vol. 2, no. 3, July 1980. See also H. O'Neill, 'HICs, MICs, NICs and LICs', *World Development* 12, 7 (1984), and Alan Thomas, *Third World: Images, Definitions, Connotations*, Open University Press, Milton Keynes, 1983.
2. For an excellent interpretation, see S. Krasner, *Structural Conflict: The Third World Against Global Liberalism*, University of California Press, Berkeley, 1985.
3. G. White and R. Wade, *Developmental States of East Asia*, IDS Report, no. 16, Sussex, 1985.
4. J. H. Merquior, 'Patterns of State-Building in Brazil and Argentina', in J. A. Hall (ed.), *States in History*, Blackwell, Oxford, 1986.
5. G. H. Jansen, *Militant Islam*, Pan Books, London, 1983.
6. See the articles in R. Cassen (ed.), *Soviet Interests in the Third World*, Sage, London, 1985.

2 Nation-Building and the Search for Security

Most Third World states are artificial creations of the European colonial powers. Their territorial boundaries pay insufficient attention to ethnicity, indigenous historical divisions or even at times geography. They are the result of colonial scramble and division. As such, these youthful states must undertake the process of nation-building.[1] They have to work to forge a domestic political and social consensus, to create a nation, so that state and nation become conterminous. The level of success achieved by individual states in making state and nation coincide is of great significance not only for the state concerned and the populace therein but also for the region and even the international system in many cases. The fact that most Third World states do not contain homogenous nations is a major cause of domestic, regional and international instability, as well as being a source of massive human suffering through repression and displacement of persons.

The problems resulting from the artificial nature of the state can be seen all over the Third World. However, it is the African continent which provides the example *par excellence*. Hence the importance of nation-building will be highlighted here first by reference to a broad African example. Leaders of African independence movements accepted not only the legitimacy of the state as the basic political unit but also the legitimacy of the colonial boundaries which had been drawn arbitrarily by the Europeans.[2] The result is that the borders of newly independent African states contain within them various centres of political allegiance (often identified as tribal loyalties). The existence of different centres of authority within a single state can generate social conflict, and this can spill over state boundaries where the latter are cross-cut by these authorities.

The tensions created by diverse allegiances within a single state pose multi-level threats to security. Not only is domestic security and the continued existence of the state as a viable political unit threatened but also the regional configuration of states. A group may aspire to reunification where it is divided by a state boundary, even though this is unacceptable under the charter of the Organisation of African Unity (OAU). Moreover, the problem does not necessarily stop at the regional level but may have international implications. Experience has shown already that the superpowers can be drawn into trouble spots in Africa.[3] Given the prevailing loosely structured bipolar world-power configuration, based on mutual nuclear deterrence, the threat posed to the international political system by a possible superpower confrontation is enormous. As Phil Williams stresses, any attempt to control such a crisis might in fact be 'an attempt to control what may well be uncontrollable'.[4]

The Horn of Africa is a microcosm of the whole range of problems thrown up by the fact that nations and states do not coincide.[5] Somalia is pursuing irredentist policies: it wants to extend its borders to take in land inhabited by ethnic Somalis.[6] This would mean territory being taken from northern Kenya and from Ethiopia in the cause of the creation of a greater Somali state which would incorporate all Somali people. The Ethiopian state is also threatened with the loss of Eritrea, whose inhabitants, while they do not form a single ethnic group, are pursuing secessionist policies.[7] They are attempting to break away from Ethiopia and to form a separate new state. They base their claim on the fact that Eritrea as a colony was a separate entity from Ethiopia, and thus it should now be able to practise self-determination. The situation has been complicated in the Horn of Africa by the involvement of the superpowers, who have at times even switched sides, thus altering the regional power configuration and thereby the outcome of the conflicts.[8]

The position of the OAU has remained firm regarding such problems: there must be no revision of the colonial boundaries existing at the time of independence. It is very well understood that revisions in one case would lead to the opening up of a Pandora's box with most states in Africa suffering from irredentist or secessionist movements. Chaos would inevitably ensue. To date, the OAU has been unwilling to accept special cases: the right to self-determination applies only to areas under colonial rule; it creates the right within pre-existing boundaries and does not give the right to challenge the legitimacy of those boundaries. This policy has had harsh results in some cases, such as Nigeria, where the attempts of the Ibo to secede and form their own state found very little support from other parts of the African continent.[9] It has also resulted in the existence of millions of refugees (not only in Africa but all over the Third World).[10] Nevertheless, the OAU stands by its original position that legitimating boundary revisions would result in even more adverse consequences for a greater number of people.

Nation-building problems exist in the Middle East, with Lebanon being a tragic contemporary example of the troubles emanating from the lack of coincidence of nation and state.[11] In this example, however, the problem is not that of secession or irredentism but rather that of struggle by different religious and ethnic groups to control the state. No sense of a common national identity has been forged in the Lebanon, and demographic changes have underlined the inappropriate nature of the constitution bequeathed by the French colonial power. In other parts of the Middle East, problems arise from the fact that certain nations are stateless, hence the dilemma of the Palestinian people and of the Kurds.[12]

Asia is marked by diversity. India has seventeen official languages plus hundreds of others and it is faced with strong centrifugal tendencies.[13] In the Punjab, Sikhs are calling for an independent Khalistan, and Kashmir remains a disputed area. The majority of Kashmiris are Muslims, and hence if they cannot hope for an independent state of their own, they may prefer union with Pakistan rather than India. Sri Lanka also has nation-building problems which arise out of ethnicity and which pose problems for the South Asian region.[14] The state is torn apart due to the inability or unwillingness of Tamils and Sinhalese to join together in a single nation. The Tamils are fighting for a separate state, while the government in Colombo is opposing this more by force than by accommodation and positive discrimination for Tamils, who fare less well than the dominant Sinhalese in terms of wealth and opportunities. China and the city states of South-East Asia have achieved a high level of success in nation-state-building, but for most of these, common ethnic bonds and a Confucian heritage have been extremely influential.[15]

Central and South America and the Caribbean do not suffer from territorial disputes in quite the same way as the African continent, but even there nation-building is facing serious obstacles.[16] In many of these states there is no domestic social, economic or political consensus, no real sense of common identity and belonging. The basic nature of the state is contested.

These problems are fundamental to the internal development and international interaction of Third World states. The failure of nation and state to coincide stands in marked contrast to the situation in the older industrialised states, where nation-states have evolved over centuries.[17] Even those fortunate states may suffer from regional separatist movements, but these are on a different scale to those experienced in the new states.[18] If the problems associated with nation-building in the Third World are to be ameliorated, with positive effects at the domestic, regional and international levels, then new states must embark on efforts to endow themselves with the attributes of separate, individual nations. Political allegiance must be transferred from lower levels of group identity to the national system, and governmental authority must achieve legitimacy in the eyes of the population. Nation-building must be seen as a valid attempt to consolidate the authority of, and to secure the continued existence of, a new state. Until this is achieved, a new state cannot act as a viable political unit on the international scene. The achievement of nation-statehood depends not only on the efforts of the new states but also on the attitude of the developed ones.

The rest of this chapter will be devoted to explaining how nation-state-building was undertaken by one African state, Tanzania, in the early years of independence. This is offered as a positive indication of the degree of success that can be achieved in certain circumstances. Negative indications are all too common when we consider the huge number of contemporary conflicts, internal and external, which plague Third World states and in which the nation-building problem often plays a key role. While the diversity of Third World states means that there will be no one universal formula for achieving nation-statehood, the Tanzanian example provides an interesting lesson in the utility of indigenous African answers to African circumstances.

There are three main parts to this case study. The first constitutes an enquiry into certain characteristics of African society at the time of independence, the objective being to determine to what extent they militate against nation-building. Special attention will be paid here to political allegiance, for this is at the heart of nation-building. The second part constitutes an analysis of Nyerere's ideas on the aims and methods of nation-building in Tanzania. The third section is devoted to the experience of Tanzania in the early post-independence period of the 1960s. How far did nation-building progress? How can the findings be explained?

Tanzania has been chosen for special study for various reasons. First, information is readily available for this country. Second, Tanzania has rejected the usual approach to development based on a rapid industrialisation through the injection of foreign capital. Instead, emphasis has been placed on developing the rural sector by traditional socialist methods. A question which arises, and to which we shall return much later, is whether such a method, being more in tune with traditional ways, enhances the chances of successful nation-building. Third, Tanzania is not plagued by allegiance to the tribe, which has been blamed both within and outside Africa for strife in new states. A question which arises here, then, is how far nation-building has been facilitated by this factor, and how far it is still a problem in spite of this. The diversity of the Third World makes it dangerous to draw generalisations from a single case study; however, some useful indicators can perhaps be gleaned from this short study of Tanzania.[19]

Before proceeding, it would be helpful to explain the meanings attributed here to some basic terms of reference. For the terms 'nation' and 'state', the definitions suggested by Hugh Seton-Watson are followed.[20] A state can be regarded 'as a legal and political organ with the power to require obedience and loyalty from its citizens'. A nation is 'a community of people, whose members are bound together by a sense of solidarity, a common culture and a national consciousness'. To be of most benefit to the international political system today, nation and state should coincide. Friedrich's definition of nation-building is adopted: 'a matter of building group cohesion and group loyalty for purposes of international representation and domestic planning'.[21] If a new state forms a cohesive unit, the chances of it acting effectively in the international arena and of implementing a programme of development at home are greatly enhanced.

AFRICA AT INDEPENDENCE

Although leaders such as Kwame Nkrumah and Sekou Touré claimed to represent genuinely nationalist movements, the post-independence experience of many African states has cast doubts as to whether these claims had any true foundation in social reality. Common opposition to the colonial presence engendered a relatively high degree of cohesiveness within the indigenous society. Once this presence was removed, tensions within that society, hitherto latent, manifested themselves.

The task of nation-builders is to unify all the disparate elements within a state and to endow the collectivity with a national consciousness. Yet many characteristics of African society at independence appeared to militate against this. The infrastructure was often barely developed and communications were poor. The environment and the climate in many cases posed great obstacles to integration and national development. A large proportion of the population was illiterate and skilled labour was in short supply. Overriding all these difficulties, however, and many more, was that of political loyalty. Usually the society was a traditional one, with only a fraction of the population politically mobilised.[22] Nation-builders had to work to transfer loyalty from traditional centres of authority to the state. (Many of these obstacles still remain in African states today and to this extent the job of the nation-builder remains similar even now.) Since the question of political allegiance is at the heart of nation-building, we shall concentrate on it.

Two major levels of socio-political allegiance may be discerned in African society at the time of independence. The first is that of the traditional society. This is characterised by a variety of ethnic groups existing within different social and political frameworks. To such groups we attribute the umbrella term 'tribe'.[23] The second level is that of the colonial or colonial-derived structures. A third level, that of pan-African aspirations, could be said to exist in rhetoric rather than in reality, among a small group of African intellectuals. A requirement of a nation is a common feeling of belonging. Hence, the question which must be answered is how far these separate levels of community allegiance hinder the process of nation-building by diverting loyalty away from the central authority of the state, thereby obstructing national integration.

Traditional Society
Since independence, there has been a growing consensus among both Africans and non-Africans alike that traditional loyalties, in the form of tribalism, are responsible for the lack of national cohesion with which so many new African states are beset. At the First All-African Peoples' Conference at Accra, in 1958, leaders called tribalism 'an evil practice' and 'a serious obstacle' to the unity, political evolution and liberation of Africa. Tribal loyalties have been blamed for the chaos attending the accession of the Belgian Congo to independence. Stated simply, the problem is commonly perceived as this: a modern European-styled state-system has been imposed on an area where society remains predominantly traditional and where loyalties flow to traditional centres of authority. Nation-builders must transfer loyalties from the traditional tribal base to the new state and its government.

The term 'tribalism' is used widely as a device for explaining many of the political problems of Africa, yet its precise meaning is difficult to construe. The confused literature on the subject seems to suggest that 'tribe' refers to an ethnic or cultural group, while its derivative sentiment, 'tribalism' refers to attachment and loyalty by members to a particular ethnic group. Christopher Potholm, however, argues that in focusing attention on the ethnic element of a group, the most germane factor is overlooked: the nature of the socio-political system in which the ethnic group is expressed.[24] He believes that ethnicity comes into play as an obstacle to nation-building only as a function of the political framework in which it is expressed. What matters is the power distribution within the political framework.

Two broad categories of power distribution can be discerned in traditional African societies. The first is that of diffused power, where a linguistic or cultural nation may exist but political power is dispersed or segmented. There are many variations on the theme of diffused power systems, ranging from the simple band (Such as the Bahi of Tanzania and the Anaguta of Nigeria) to the autonomous village systems (found widely among the Swahili-speaking people of East Africa). In the centralised power systems, all groups owe allegiance to a central political authority. This system can be seen in the diverse monarchies which have flourished all over Africa: the Asante in Ghana, the Shambala in Tanzania, the Mossi in Upper Volta, and many more.

Potholm suggests that nation-building is facilitated if the state includes tribes with segmented political systems rather than centralised ones; for centralised systems imply vested interests and cohesive groups whose tribal loyalties will prove difficult to transfer. Segmented systems, on the other hand, will be more easily incorporated into a single nation-state. The theory is convincing; its practical efficacy will be examined in the study of Tanzania. The task here is to air ideas rather than present definite answers.

While Potholm stresses the power distribution within ethnic groups, Immanuel Wallerstein prefers to highlight what he considers to be the class component of traditional societies. He equates tribal tensions with class conflict.[25] The civil wars in Nigeria and the Sudan are cited as proof of this hypothesis. In the case of the Nigerian civil war, the Ibos were generally far better educated than the Hausa-Fulanis of northern Nigeria. The latter felt great resentment when the Ibos appeared to get all the better-paying jobs which required technical skills. Wallerstein implies that were class differences to disappear, then so too would ethnic or tribal conflict.

There is much truth in the claim that in Africa today, ethnic affiliations are often harnessed for the political achievement of economic ends and for influence in the decision-making apparatus of the state. Numerous examples of ethno-political rivalry can be cited: the Kikuyu and Luo in Kenya; the Bemba and the Lozi in Zambia; the Saab and the Somaale in Somalia. These examples suggest that the Marxist analysis of the African situation has some validity. Wallerstein's approach also presents us with a few difficulties, however. If we accept his hypothesis that class and tribe are basically synonymous, we must accept the context or framework within which he locates his idea: that of the core–periphery theory. Here we must accept that the primary contradiction in African states is between the interests organised and located in the core countries and their local allies on the one hand, and the majority of the population on the other. From this angle, the anti-imperialist nationalist struggle can be seen as an expression of class interest. Yet so often the anti-colonial leaders have been drawn from the ranks of the middle and upper classes, which are supposed to be in league with the core imperialist masters. (Whether African leaders are in league with their former masters *after* independence in perpetuating neo-colonialism is a different question. We are considering here the actual time of gaining independence.)

The widespread nature of ethno-national consciousness is an important element in the cohesion of the state system today. In accepting this system, the people who wield decision-making power in Africa have bound themselves to work towards the achievement of this consciousness within their respective states. To this extent, class consciousness is significant for Africa today on the international level, in the call for a New International Economic Order (NIEO). This is not to say that economic inequalities do not exist within Africa (for they most certainly do); only that to think of traditional African societies in terms of class conflict may perhaps amount to a misapplication of this concept in time and space.

Traditional African society presents many problems for the nation-builder in terms of group loyalties. Entrenched allegiances must be overcome. If we accept conventional wisdom, which blames ethnic divisions for discord, or

Potholm's view, which stresses the necessity of probing behind the ethnic frontage and discovering power distributions within tribes, or if we accept Wallerstein's analysis, which equates class with tribe—one common conclusion emerges. The traditional group is a focus of loyalty which must be superseded if a nation is to be built.

The Colonial or Colonial-Derived Structure

The second level of political community present at the time of independence is the colonial structure. Although the traditional level cited above has transcended the colonial overlay in much of Africa, the latter left important foci for loyalty within African society. These foci can detract from the legitimacy of the state as the sole focus for political allegiance.

Marked differences can be pinpointed in the patterns of colonial rule. The British, for example, chose indirect rule, making use of traditional chiefs and leaders such as those in Barotseland and Buganda. The French preferred a policy of assimilation, of seeing the colony as a province of the metropole. Despite the different patterns of colonial rule, certain generalisations can be made. Traditional African groups, like any other regional groups, were often forming and transmuting in response to external stimuli such as new technologies or ideologies carried by merchants, migrants or conquerors.[26] It was the European conquest that was most influential in the history of African societies, not only by marking off boundaries which paid no heed to ethnic or physical realities but also by vastly expanding the scale of African societies in the process. Moreover, new divisions were created, such as Anglophone and Francophone West Africa. The agents of this change were the missionaries, the merchants and the administrators. In essence, an artificial order was superimposed on the indigenous one.

The colonies tended to develop into plural societies. The dominant European group faced outwards and identified with the metropoles. The traders, often Asian or Mediterranean in origin, formed a middle group who, to the indigenous inhabitants, had all the attributes of strangers. The indigenous peoples were loyal to diverse ethnic groups or tribes. Loyalties were not focused on the national unit, rather they were directed towards racial, economic or ethnic ends.

During the colonial period some traditional African authorities suffered a loss of power. Peoples whose major loyalties had been to chiefs and kings saw their allegiances weakened and subordinated to new identities as members of larger linguistic and cultural groups. The colonisers imposed comprehensive labels such as Yoruba and Mossi on groups which, to them as outsiders, appeared to have some common features. As Skinner has remarked, it was during the colonial period that many homogenous group identities were formed.[27]

However, the impact of the colonisers did not result in any massive social mobilisation. It has been estimated that between 5 and 10 per cent of the indigenous populations were literate on independence. Though the percentage was small, it was these people who formed the core groups which struggled for independence; it was they who were politically mobilised. It followed that after independence was won it was often they that posed the greatest immediate problems for new governments. They constituted the few people capable of effective organisation; for example, through labour unions. The existence of such groups was an anomaly in societies that remained essentially traditional. With the development of dual economies this discontinuity has intensified since independence. The economic, social and political gap between two sectors of the African community widens. It is important to remember, however, that at independence, for the majority of indigenous inhabitants in new African states, the rural existence of subsistence farming remained the norm, and traditional loyalties were still firmly entrenched.

Perhaps one of the most significant colonial legacies in African politics is the high premium put on power. The way this was expressed made for instability in new states. In the colonial situation, the possession of the reins of government became virtually the only issue of politics. Claude Ake has remarked that colonial politics was a 'single-minded struggle for the capture of governmental power'.[28] African leaders were not socialised in an environment that would make them interested in the morality of power or the limits of political obligation, argues Ake. Statism and political authoritarianism could not be ruled out where politics was conceived as a struggle for rulership. In such circumstances misgivings about opponents would be deepened by the heterogeneity of competing élites. This heterogeneity would in some part be a result of their respective experiences under colonialism and the environments in which they had studied, often abroad. It would be expressed in ideological terms, and often with respect to social and economic status. Competing élites struggling for control were not unlikely after independence, and this did not bode well for the political stabiliy of new states and hence for the cause of nation-building.

The factors that militate against nation-building on independence are many and varied. The problem of political allegiance has been discussed at length, for this is central to nation-building. Other factors, however, should not be forgotten. Lack of communications often makes it difficult for the governments of new states to explain their policies to the people and to implement them, and to deal with rebellious elements. Shortage of skilled labour and capital makes it difficult to develop and expand a modern sector in the economy. Poor infrastructure means that essential services cannot always be provided. The lack of a common language often presents enormous problems for national communication. In sum, the problems before nation-builders are enormous. Moreover, they are accentuated where the rapid turnover of leaders[29] (by such methods as palace coups, for example) in states with poorly developed bureaucracies can lead to marked inconsistencies in policy.

The task of nation-builders is great. Having examined some of the problems which confront them, let us turn now to some ideas on how to overcome these problems.

NYERERE ON NATION-BUILDING

Three important works by Nyerere ('The Arusha Declaration', 'Socialism and Rural Development', 'Education and Self-Reliance') make up a coherent body of thought on nation-building. Socialism is to be the guiding principle, rural development the priority, and self-reliance the method.[30] All three are intimately interwoven. To understand these, however, we need to locate them against the background of nationalism and the one-party state.

Nyerere on Nationalism

In the Introduction to *Uhuru na Umoja* (*Freedom and Unity*), published in 1966, Nyerere writes '... although African nations are very artificial creations of man (indeed, of European men), sixty years of history means that they are the basic societies from which our development must now start.'[31] Having accepted colonial boundaries as the basic political divisions of Africa, Nyerere sets about justifying African nationalism as an extension of African traditions. (This harping back to traditional ways is a device used by many African leaders, and not only in the context of nationalism. Seretse Khama, for example, used it to justify the principles of Kagisano).[32] Although the validity of such claims may sometimes be in doubt, the effectiveness of the device is not in question.

It is often claimed that nationalism is an artificial political device to unite the country in the face of a common enemy, colonialism. Nyerere rejects this, claiming that nationalism has its very roots in African traditions, and citing as evidence the traditional tribal practice of 'talking until all agreed'. All tribal elders supposedly had equal influence over decision-making, and decisions were reached on the basis of unanimity. Nationalism, by extension, sees all the members of the nation in agreement on proposals.

Following on from this is Nyerere's advocacy of the one-party system. Given fundamental agreement on national interests, a multi-party system represents an expression of private interests. In *Freedom and Unity*, Nyerere argues that 'the politics of a country governed by the two-party system are not, and cannot be, national politics; they are the politics of groups, whose differences more often than not are of small concern to the majority of people'. The implication is that only a single-party system is compatible with Africa's tradition of arriving at political decisions. (Nyerere was probably influenced in his belief in a one-party state by what had happened on the accession of the Congo to independence. He wanted to kill from the start any chance of regional, economic or ethnic interests flourishing.) His ideas achieved expression when, in January 1963, the TANU National Executive decided that the Tanganyikan Constitution should be changed so that Tanganyika became by law what it already was in fact—a one-party state.[33] Landslide election victories for TANU had convinced Nyerere that when there is political agreement about the ends of the state, democratic elections should mean the choice between candidates who have the same political affiliation. Such electoral competition within the single-party apparatus would increase national participation and cohesion and play a vital role in mobilising the population.

Another important element for nation-building found in Nyerere's nationalism is its non-racialism. Before independence, Governor Twining had advocated a multi-racial government framework based on parity. This was unacceptable to Nyerere, for not only would it preclude Africans from moving into many positions of influence which other races already occupied, but also because he wanted to cultivate the attitude that race did not matter. Loyalty to Tanzania and competence in a job were more important. Such ideas were to cause trouble in the early days of independence, when there was a threatened split in the government partly over the issue of non-racialism. Nyerere resigned and concentrated on strengthening and directing the evolution of TANU.

Nyerere on Socialism
Morton Schoolman has remarked that Nyerere's theory of African socialism 'is the most important dimension of his political thought'.[34] It is on socialism that the Tanzanian nation is to be built. Nyerere believes that while socialism can be expressed and reached in a number of ways, there is a common goal involved: that of human equality and dignity. The road to socialism appropriate to Tanzania is revealed in traditional African society. There, mutual respect and obligation, common property, and hard work for shared benefits were the catchwords of the extended family. These values, having been partially eroded by the impact of an individualistic money economy under colonialism, must be reinforced. Schoolman remarks that it is the task of nation-

builders to engender 'remembering'. Through education, Tanzanians must learn of the African heritage of socialism.[35] Then the ideals of Ujamaa (see below) will be understood, not as foreign imports but as an outgrowth of the traditional lifestyle. Such knowledge will facilitate their acceptance and adoption.

Nyerere on Socialism and Self-Reliance

The adoption of this socialist ethic by Nyerere is much more than a mere harping back to tradition: it symbolises a rejection of conventional development strategies. Nyerere intends to break new ground. The nation will not be built around rapid industrialisation, heavy industry, the export of manufactured goods, or central control and planning. Rather, it will be built on a programme of public ownership of the major industries and infrastructure, and a decrease in foreign investment and aid. Most important, there will be a stress on agricultural activity, vocational education, equity in the distribution of income (even among public officials, whose wages are not to exceed six times the average), popular participation and non-alignment in foreign policy.

In the paper 'Education and Self-Reliance' Nyerere suggests that in the first few years of independence, too much emphasis was placed on money as the vital factor in development, and that aid, where it was forthcoming, was unacceptable due to the political strings attached. The alternative proposed in this paper is an increased concern for the rural areas of Tanzania, where 90 per cent of the population resides and where most of Tanzania's very limited resources are located. Agriculture must henceforth be the basis of development, and it must be the focus of peoples' individual efforts, for the injection of capital will be very limited.

Other African states have emphasised rural development, but Tanzania was the first to officially dedicate her primary efforts to that task in 'The Arusha Declaration' and subsequent policy papers. However, Nyerere goes farther than simply laying down hollow slogans. Tom Mboya, the Kenyan leader who has written prolifically on nation-building, has remarked that 'It's no good telling the peasant scratching away at the soil to be self-reliant, he's been that way since he was born—that's why he is still scratching away.'[36] Nyerere anticipates Mboya's plea, voiced a few years later, for the slogan to be given substance. Peasants must be guided to channel the self-reliant feature of their existence into an improved standard of living. His concern with self-reliance not just for its own sake but for the rewards it can bring, is emphasised in his writings on Ujamaa villages: 'Their community would be the traditional family group or any other group of people living according to Ujama principles, *large enough to take account of modern methods and the twentieth century needs of man.*'[37] Self-reliance is a dynamic strategy which responds to scientific and technological progress and changes in man's expectations. The pervasive socialist ethic will ensure that the rewards of self-reliance are shared.

Nyerere on Socialism and Rural Development

The policy paper 'Socialism and Rural Development' suggests how best the self-reliant strategy may be implemented. The emergence under colonialism of a self-interested rural capitalist class must be reversed by the setting up of Ujamaa Vijiji (socialist villages) in rural areas. Such villages constitute Nyerere's ideal society. In theory these are socialist organisations created and governed by those who work in them. No officials are allowed to enter the village to tell people what to do. The role of the party, TANU, in the context of these villages is 'education and leadership'. This reflects Nyerere's conception of the function of national leadership, which he believes is not to establish particular goals for Africans but to set guidelines. Ultimately, several Ujamaa villages will come together to form a large cooperative. This will be the basis for promoting a more advanced industrial development.

The policies implicit in such self-reliant, agriculturally based socialist villages are very different from those implicit in a growth strategy. The two approaches have different time frames and different attitudes towards inequality. Growth theories stress long-term gain and immediate sacrifice, while the strategy proposed by Nyerere stresses immediate gratification and different types of long-term gains. Whereas growth theories stress the necessity of inequalities, there is an imperative need implicit in Nyerere's strategy for reducing existing inequalities and raising everyone at least to subsistence level.

Two streams of thought can be discerned in Nyerere's proposals. The first is that of practical doubts regarding what the international system will (as opposed to can) offer a less developed country like Tanzania. The second is that of moral doubts about a set of values in which growth is a higher priority than the immediate relief of suffering. Such doubts, and the practical policies put forward to remedy them, are in tune with the realisation that to build a cohesive national unit, 90 per cent of the population cannot be swept to one side and forgotten. As Nyerere himself says, 'While other countries aim to reach the moon, we must aim . . . to reach the village.'[38] In a new state like Tanzania, poor communications alone pose tremendous obstacles to reaching rural areas. These must be overcome before the problem of local allegiance is even encountered. Once the rural population is reached, however, the government must ensure that the people are aware of the benefits it can bring in terms of a higher standard of living. Hence, it is through Ujamaa villages and the self-reliant strategy they imply, set within the framework of the democratic, single-party apparatus, that Nyerere hopes to make the first crucial steps towards integrating the population into a single nation.

THE TANZANIAN ACHIEVEMENT

This section examines the extent of Tanzania's achievement in the process of nation-building in the 1960s.

The Political Framework
A major problem facing the government on independence was that of extending and consolidating its authority. It had to win the obedience not only of the small, politically mobilised strata which had played a vital role in the anti-colonial struggle, but also of the comparatively large rural population. It set about achieving this by synchronising the party and the government, by drawing other national institutions under governmental control, and by encouraging political participation at all levels.

A threatened split in TANU in January 1962 (over questions such as the rapid Africanisation of the civil service, and the setting aside of seats in the National Assembly for racial minorities) led Nyerere to resign as prime minister. He concentrated now on revitalising TANU and blending the government and TANU together. Allegiance to TANU and allegiance to the government were to be one and the same thing. The president and vice-president of TANU were to hold the same positions in the government. TANU's regional secretaries were to be the government's regional commissioners, while TANU's district secretaries were to be the government's area commissioners. The linkage was to extend right down to the local level, where TANU representatives were found on village development committees and where leaders of ten-house cells (see below) were party members.

The government went further than the mere synchronisation of party and government: it attempted to consolidate its hold over the vital instruments of power by extending its control over those mobilised groups which had the potential to challenge its authority. The entire trade-union movement, for example, after the outbreak of illegal strikes on sisal plantations in 1962, was brought under governmental control. All workers were required to join the National Union of Tanganyikan Workers, which was affiliated to TANU. Its secretary-general was the minister of labour.

The greatest threat to the government was posed by the army when in 1964 the Tanganyikan Rifles mutinied. This group was motivated more by specific grievances, such as the Africanisation of the officer corps, than by a general desire to overthrow the government. British marines had to be called in to restore order. This must have been an extremely painful request for Nyerere to make of the old colonial power, which had only recently been removed. The army was disbanded and reformed, drawing half its members from the TANU Youth League.

Having made provisions to cope with challenges to governmental authority by the small politically mobilised strata, the government could then turn to the rural area, where 90 per cent of the population resided. Its policy here was to increase social and political mobilisation through the activities of the party. As Clyde Ingle points out, party efforts did much to encourage political participation in decision-making at the local level, as well as at the intermediate and national levels.[39] This participation was to encourage the integration of rural and national systems. Hence, governmental legitimacy would be increased.

For the vast majority of the peasant population, the primary political system at independence was the immediate or local system. TANU was to provide linkages between the localities and the national and intermediate systems by operation of what Nyerere called a 'two-way track'. This track was to be the carrier of ideas from the government to the people and vice versa. At the local level the track was to be the ten-house cell system, a concept developed by the National Executive Committee of TANU. Every ten houses throughout the country were to comprise a cell, which would elect a leader. A prerequisite was that the leader belonged to TANU. His job would be to facilitate communication by explaining government policies to the people and passing on criticisms and messages from the people to the government. Clyde Ingle suggests that for the decade under review, messages critical of government policy did not work their way up the track.

One way of estimating the government's success in consolidating its authority is to examine national elections. Do people participate, and if they do, does their participation reflect national or some other vested interest? Another way is to look at governmental effectiveness at the local level.

The National Level
During the period under review, participation in national elections increased. In 1962, 20 per cent of the eligible voters registered and voted. By 1965, 50 per cent had registered, and of these, 76 per cent had voted. This increase indicated a growing political awareness and mobilisation, and a willingness to take part in activities concerning the state. In judging the significance of these figures we need to remember that over 80 per cent of the population at this time was illiterate. Political awareness was engendered verbally rather than by the written word, and hence the importance of TANU

activities is underlined. In the absence of other parties, TANU had a monopoly on political activisation.

Not only the amount of participation in elections but also the outcome of those elections was encouraging. In the 1965 elections few constituencies seemed to be decided on tribal grounds. Moreover, a greater percentage of non-Africans were elected to the National Assembly than existed in the country as a whole (e.g. Amin Jamal, the Asian minister of finance). Nyerere's non-racist and anti-tribal pronouncements seemed to be taking root; or at least opposition to them was being muted.

The 1965 election lent credibility to the idea of a one-party democracy, when it is considered that voters defeated so many incumbents. Two ministers, six junior ministers, thirteen districts chairmen and sixteen out of thirty-one MPs who ran, were defeated. It seemed that in the first decade of independence the national political system was not only accepted by well over a third of the population but that it was put to good use by them. At the local level progress was not so promising.

The Local Level
Almond and Powell suggest a developmental view of nation-building: nation-building refers to 'the process whereby people transfer their commitment and loyalty from smaller tribes, villages or petty principalities to the larger central political system'.[40] Rupert Emerson believes that a nation is any group of people who think that they are a nation.[41] If the national policies are adopted at the local level, then using either definition we can deduce that nation-building was succeeding. Evidence suggests that at the local level, however, there was much resistance to, or simple acquiescence in, government policies in the 1960s. The malfunctioning of the 'two-way track' has already been noted. This compounded the problem of peasants disobeying government orders. Clyde Ingle cites several examples in the Tanga and Handeni regions of Tanzania where peasants retreated from roads into the bush to avoid tax collectors, and where they ignored government orders to plant new crops. To questions such as 'What is this nation's biggest problem?' and 'What are the things of which

you are more proud?' peasants responses bore a marked
similarity to the phraseology of the national leadership. Not
even this is totally convincing, however, for the answers could
merely amount to regurgitated propaganda. Whether anything
more than lip-service was paid to government ideas is
questionable. Old habits die hard, and loyalties must be won
over. This process takes time.

Some Problems of Rural Development and Self-Reliance

Time is exactly what the government would not allow. Nyerere
decided on a policy of forced relocation of peasants into more
productive rural units, and the implementation of this policy
had many unexpected side-effects At first, the peasants affected
by the policy were those who did not own smallholdings. The
policy was then extended to those who did, and it met with
much resistance on a personal level. Nyerere himself has
admitted that there were several abuses by TANU stalwarts in
implementing the Ujamaa policy. By 1974, seven million
people—over half the population—had been relocated into
Ujamaa or other villages to form more viable economic units.
This amounted to a massive movement of people. That it was
carried through at all without major disturbances or threats to
governmental authority is no mean achievement.

The policy did not result in immediate success. The loss of
production which occurred on nationalised capitalist farms
meant that basic foodstuffs had to be imported. (The problem
was intensified in the early 1970s by a series of droughts and
shortfalls and the quadrupling of the oil price which affected
the price of fertilisers). The government revived an old colonial
rule which required each peasant family to grow a minimum
amount of food. Yet, if environmental conditions were not
conducive, then no amount of government pressure could
increase yields. It became increasingly obvious that self-
reliance alone was not going to carry Tanzania into the modern
world. Outside help would be needed. Tanzania's foreign
policy would follow the principle of non-alignment. Nyerere
would try to weave a path between the superpowers, without
being drawn into the camp of either, especially not for the sake
of obtaining development aid. Tanzania was a new state and,
as such, eager to assert her sovereignty.

A major problem was the limited numbers involved in the money economy. Though relocated, the population remained essentially traditional. By drawing people into the money economy, political realignment would be made easier and the government could widen its base of support at the popular level. During the 1960s, however, the expansion of the money economy was limited.

The situation was partly accounted for by the paucity of skilled labour. Indeed, the lack of professionals and skilled labour was one of Tanzania's most chronic problems on gaining independence. In a sense it could be argued that rural development at that time was the only feasible option. From the point of view of increasing governmental effectiveness, it was problems such as these more than any discontinuities in language, culture or ethnicity, which posed the major problems for nation-builders.

FACTORS CONDUCIVE TO NATION-BUILDING IN TANZANIA

Several factors of a social, political and economic nature aided the Tanzanian experiment in nation-building in its early years and provided leaders with a basis on which to build unity and to encourage national integration.

An important factor was the relative lack of Europeans and the related factor of little land alienation. Only 4,000 Europeans were permanent residents in Tanganyika on independence. Hence, the residual colonial overlay was less significant here than elsewhere in Africa.[42]

A marked lack of tribal tensions was also conducive to successful nation-building.[43] The largest political community or tribe was that of the Sukuma, which had just over one million members, but there were at least twelve other groups with hundreds of thousands of members; for example, the Chagga, the Hehe and the Haya. Other smaller tribes abounded, making in total well over 120 groups. There was little danger of numerical domination by any one group. This is in great contrast to Uganda, for example, where the Buganda played such a powerful role.

It was not only the fact that no single ethnic group dominated in Tanzania that helped the process of nation-building, but also the nature of the African systems existing there. Traditional groups lacked strong centralised authority. This point brings to mind Potholm's idea that a diffused traditional power structure is more conducive to nation-building than a centralised one. The diffused power structure in Tanzanian tribes aided the growth of non-tribal politics. The contrary is true when we consider the powerful role played by the Asante in Ghana, and the Buganda in Uganda, both of which formed highly centralised kingdoms. Such groups can pose a threat to nation-building by presenting a strong, alternative centre of allegiance and power to that of the state, and one which can mobilise the support of a significant proportion of the population in many cases. When the British tried to institute a process of indirect rule in Tanganyika, they found the area to be highly fragmented: over 120 units existed there. On independence, TANU did nothing to enhance tribal authority, and in 1963 it was abolished with the African Chief Ordinance (Repeal) Act. This is not to say that people of the same ethnic group no longer identified with each other as members of that group. What it means is that the ethnic group was positively discriminated against as a focus for political mobilisation.

The existence of a national language, Kiswahili, facilitated communication between different groups.[44] An estimated 40 per cent of the population spoke it on independence, including nearly all adult males. This made the work of the government much easier: at least, if it could reach the people it would be understood.

Nyerere would argue that the existence of underlying values like communal welfare and the social obligation to work did much to help promote his principles of socialism. If such values did exist, then this would be true.

Henry Bienen has suggested that there exists a correlation between Tanzania's extremely low per capita wealth on independence and her fairly successful attempts in the early years at nation-building.[45] He argues that the low wealth meant that the national system was not faced with many entrenched socio-economic oppositions. The lack of socio-economic differentiation stood Tanzania in good stead in this respect and highlighted marked differences from countries like Nigeria.

Finally, in the Tanzanian case the national leadership can be seen as a factor conducive to nation-building. Nyerere stood out in his country as a leader relatively untainted by corruption and unaffected by power. He was once reported to have said 'ultimately, humanity must not be denied', and this idea runs through all his writings, speeches and actions. Man is the end of all his efforts, and human equality and dignity his catchwords. Despite a few cleaveages, the élite with which Nyerere worked in the early years of independence sustained a fairly high level of internal cohesion (though in later years some people, such as the women's leader, Bibi Titi, were removed from high office). This led to consistency in official policy, which was very useful in a country where there was as yet no common concept of central legitimate authority. Clearly seen by the population, this consistency in central policy facilitated the transference of loyalties from lower-order groups to the state. Unlike so many other new African states, Tanzania was fortunate not to experience rapid changeovers in government, which have a destabilising effect.

In spite of the many factors advantageous to nation-building in Tanzania on independence, the task of engineering a national culture was not easy. The process of transforming a society from a traditional one into a modern one takes time. Developing in Tanzania in the 1960s was what Ali Mazrui has described as a high level of secondary consensus behind Nyerere and his policies of socialism and self-reliance. Once this was secured, nation-builders had to work towards the achievement of a primary consensus, or a consensus on methods, procedures and the sanctity of institutions. Only when this type of consensus is secured can we say that national integration is truly well under way. For Tanzania in the 1960s this remained a goal, yet the evidence of the first decade of independence augured well for the future development of a nation-state of Tanzania.

Conclusion
At the foot of his own statue, Nkrumah wrote, 'Seek ye first the political kingdom and all else will be added unto it'.

Unfortunately, the reality is not so simple. Once the political kingdom in the legal sense is achieved, the problem of integrating it into a single unit must be tackled. This means establishing a national consciousness.

A nation must be built if the internal policies of a government are to be carried through with minimum opposition. Development will be hindered if the state is characterised by divisive centrifugal tendencies. Moreover, even if governmental policies are accepted by the people, external forces can ruin or distort them. The rise in oil prices is an illustration of this. Often, new states depend on the export of primary products for much-needed foreign exchange, and fluctuations in price or demand in the world market can have disastrous results. An example is Tanzania, which suffered badly in the period reviewed due to the fall in the price of sisal. Given the potentially disastrous consequences of external events over which new states exercise no control, it is all the more important that they develop internal cohesion. At least then, problems can be tackled together, without the threat of large-scale internal subversion or political chaos, whether it be externally sponsored or of an indigenous kind, or a mix of the two. Moreover, cohesive societies in new states will enhance regional stability and security and thus produce an environment more conducive to economic development.

Successful nation-building is of great significance for all the other actors in the international political system as well as for the new states for whom the benefit is obvious. Even if a nation is built in a new state, a myriad of further problems remain to be tackled by that state. The economic weakness which characterises most new states, not to mention their relative military and political weakness, places them in an extremely vulnerable position in international affairs. Although it can be argued, after Keohane and Nye, that we live in a world of complex interdependence in which economic power is gaining in importance relative to military might,[46] for the majority of new states this is of little significance. The success of OPEC has not been repeated in other commodities.[47] New states are unlikely to wield much influence in world affairs, except perhaps as moral mentors who touch the consciences of the developed world. However, for the stability of the international system, the importance of nation-building must not be underestimated. Great power intervention is no new feature in Africa or elsewhere in the Third World. It was witnessed in the Congo in 1960, and much more recently in the Horn and Southern Africa. Central America and the Caribbean have witnessed several interventions, most recently the US invasion of Grenada in 1983. Asia has not escaped either, with Afghanistan and Vietnam providing the most blatant examples. It is the potential for superpower intervention or confrontation in Third World states that makes successful nation-building so important for international security. Great powers vie for influence in, and the support of, smaller states. The tension which may result is greatly increased when different groups within a single state are supported by competing superpowers. Similarly, if the authority within a new state is confused, great powers can be drawn into the power vacuum more easily.

In the final analysis, national integrity does not of itself make a state an influential actor in world politics. However, where national integrity is lacking, the temptation for external powers to intervene is greater. A state which has built a nation is at an advantage in the struggle for increased autonomy, economic development and security.

NOTES

1. For a general discussion, see A. D. Smith, *States and Nations in the Third World*, Harvester Press, Brighton, 1983.
2. The charter of the OAU did not discuss borders; it was implicit, however, that the colonial boundaries should not be changed. Self-determination was a right within colonial boundaries. For the charter, see I. Brownlie, *Basic Documents on African Affairs*, Clarendon Press, Oxford, 1971. For more details, see C. Thomas, *New States, Sovereignty and Intervention*, Gower, Aldershot, 1985.
3. See A. Gavshon, *Crisis in Africa: Battleground of East and West*, Penguin, Harmondsworth, 1981. Also, G. Chaliand, *The Struggle for Africa*, Macmillan, London, 1982.
4. P. Williams, *Crisis Management*, Robertson, London, 1976, p. 30.
5. For a detailed study, see I. M. Lewis (ed.), *Nationalism and Self-Determination in the Horn of Africa*, Ithaca Press, London, 1983.

6.   See J. Mayall, 'The Battle for the Horn, Somali Irredentism and International Diplomacy', *World Today*, September 1978, and *idem*, 'The National Question in the Horn of Africa', *World Today*, September 1983.

7.   J. Firebrace with S. Holland, *Never Kneel Down: Drought, Development and Liberation in Eritrea*, Spokesman, Nottingham, 1984.

8.   For Soviet policy, see F. Halliday and M. Molyneux, 'The Soviet Union and the Ethiopian Revolution', in *Third World Affairs*, Third World Foundation, London, 1986; and H. Brind, 'Soviet Policy in the Horn of Africa', *International Affairs*, London, 1984. For US policy, see both Gavshon and Chaliand.

9.   For a detailed account of the Nigerian civil war which was a result of the Ibo's desire to secede from Nigeria and to create their own state, and the response of the central government, see A. H. M. Kirk-Greene, *Conflict and Crisis in Nigeria*, vols. I & II, Oxford U.P., London, 1971; see also S. J. Stremlau, *The International Politics of the Nigerian Civil War, 1967–70*, Princeton University Press, Princeton, New Jersey, 1977; and S. K. Panter-Brick (ed.), *Nigerian Politics and Military Rule, Prelude to Civil War*, Athlone Press for the Institute of Commonwealth Studies, London, 1970. While the OAU sided with the central government, Nyerere stood out among African leaders for championing the cause of the Ibos.

10. On the refugee problem in the Third World, see *Third World Affairs*, Third World Foundation, London, 1985.

11. See B. S. Odeh, *Lebanon, Dynamics of Conflict*, Zed Press, London, 1985.

12. D. Gilmour, *The Dispossessed*, Sphere Books, London, 1982, also G. Chaliand (ed.), *People Without A Country: The Kurds and Kurdistan*, Zed Press, London, 1980.

13. See M. Akbar, *India, the Siege Within: Challenges to a Nation's Unity*, Penguin, Harmondworth, 1985.

14. See R. Goldmann and A. J. Wilson (ed.), *From Independence to Statehood*, Pinter, London, 1984.

15. See G. White and R. Wade, *Developmental States of East Asia*, IDS Reports, no. 16, Brighton, 1984.

16. See M. Manley, *Jamaica: Struggle in the Periphery*, Writers and Readers, London, 1982; also C. Searle, *Grenada: The Struggle Against Destabilization*, Writers and Readers, London, 1983, and P. A. R. Calvert, *Boundary Disputes in Latin America*, Conflict Study no. 146, Institute for Conflict Studies, London, 1983.

17. See M. Mann, *Sources of Social Power: From the Beginning to AD 1760*, Cambridge University Press, Cambridge, 1986; and J. A. Hall, *Powers and Liberties: The Causes and Consequences of the Rise of the West*, Blackwell, Oxford, 1985.

18. See A. D. Smith, *The Ethnic Revival*, Cambridge University Press, Cambridge, 1980.

19. On the diversity of the Third World, see the debate in *Third World Quarterly*, vol. 1, 1979.

20. H. Seton-Watson, *Nations and States: An Enquiry into the Origins of Nations and the Politics of Nationalism*, Methuen, London, 1977.

21. See C. Friedrich, 'Nation-Building?', in K. Deutsch and W. Foltz (eds.), *Nation-Building*, Atherton, New York, 1963, p. 32.

22. See K. Deutsch, 'Social Mobilisation and Political Development', *American Political Science Review*, September 1961, for the relationship between social mobilisation and the expansion of the politically relevant strata of the population.

23. See P. Crone, 'The Tribe and the State', in J. A. Hall (ed.), *States in History*, Blackwell, Oxford, 1986.

24. For an expansion of these ideas, see C. Potholm, *The Theory and Practice of African Politics*, Prentice-Hall, Englewood Cliffs, New Jersey, 1979, pp. 3–33.

25. I. Wallerstein, *The Capitalist World-Economy*, Cambridge University Press, Cambridge, 1979, pp. 165–81.

26. *Ibid.*

27. See Skinner in J. Helm (ed.), *Essays in the Problem of Tribe*, AES, Seattle, 1968.

28. C. Ake, 'Explaining Political Instability in New States', *Journal of Modern African Studies*, 11, 3 (1973).

29. See P. Anyang'Nyong'o. 'Military Intervention in African Politics', *Third World Affairs*, Third World Foundation, London, 1986.

30. This framework is suggested by M. Minogue and J. Molloy, *African Aims and Attitudes*, Cambridge University Press, Cambridge, 1974.

31. For extracts from Nyerere's writings on nation-building referred to here, see Minogue and Molloy, *bid.*

32. See S. Khama, 'Kagisano: A Policy for Harmony', extracts of which appear in Minogue and Molloy, pp. 164–7. Kagisano is a concept which brings together unity, peace, harmony and a sense of community—factors which it is claimed are found in traditional African society.

33. The Tanganyika African National Union was a development of the Tanganyika African Association. TANU was established in 1954, and in 1965 it became the single governing party of Tanzania.

34. M. Schoolman, 'African Political Thought', in Potholm, p. 73.

35. Whether or not traditional African society developed along socialist lines remains contentious. See I. Kopytoff, 'Socialism and Traditional African Societies', in W. H. Friedland and C. G. Rosberg (eds.), *African Socialism*, Stanford University Press, Stanford, 1964. Kopytoff argues that traditional African societies were highly stratified, and that individual ownership and communal cooperation existed side by side. He argues also that the idea of a traditional African socialism is used by leaders trying to accelerate modernisation as an instrument for their political needs. Essentially, he is arguing that the idea of traditional African socialism is fictitious.

36.   See extracts from T. Mboya, *The Challenge of Nationhood*, in Minogue and Molloy, pp. 148–53.

37.   Minogue and Molloy, p. 90.

38.   This sentence is taken from a speech by Nyerere, part of which is reprinted in S. Dryden, *Local Administration in Tanzania*, East African Publishing House, Nairobi, 1968.

39.   C. R. Ingle, *From Village to State in Tanzania: The Politics of Rural Development*, Ithaca, New York, 1972.

40.   G. A. Almond and G. B. Powell, *Comparative Politics: A Developmental Approach*, Little, Brown & Co, Boston and Toronto, 1966, p. 36.

41.   R. Emerson, *From Empire to Nation: The Rise to Self-Assertion of Asian and African Peoples*, Harvard University Press, Cambridge, 1960, p. 102.

42.   The situation in Tanzania stood in marked contrast to that in Kenya, for example, where there were several hundred thousand non-Africans playing a major role in the economy. Moreover, there was intense competition for land in Kenya, which was not experienced in Tanzania.

43.   Again, a contrast can be drawn with Kenya to illustrate the point. There existed in Kenya what Potholm (*op. cit.*) has referred to as 'a veritable tribal mosaic with strong tribal undercurrents to its politics'. The dominant tribe was the Kikuyu, which represented 20 per cent of the total Kenyan population.

44.   A contrast can be drawn here with the situation in Uganda, where the Buganda, the largest tribe, resisted the use of Swahili. They were in a strong position to spread their own language to other groups in the country and hence strengthen their credentials for ruling.

45.   H. Bienen, *Tanzania: Party Transformation and Economic Development*, Princeton University Press, Princeton, 1967.

46.   R. Keohane and J. Nye, *Power and Interdependence: World Politics in Transition*, Little Brown & Co., Boston, Mass., 1977.

47.   See Chapter 4 for details.

3 The Search for Monetary Security

A major and continuous headache for most countries of the Third World, including some of the oil-exporting ones, is how to balance their payments: how to achieve financial equilibrium between the cost of their imports and the money earned from their exports. When imports exceed exports, money must be found to balance the books and to keep the life-blood of those states flowing. The usual method of dealing with such a deficit is recourse to borrowing. The IMF was set up specifically to help states when they were faced with a balance of payments deficit. The relationship between the institution and the developing countries is far from smooth at the moment. Previously, it was socialist or social-democratic states which were most critical of the IMF; currently, the institution is attacked even by the leaders of authoritarian states of right-wing, capitalist inclination. Hence alignments are shifting, and the Third World is appearing more and more as a unified grouping in relation to the IMF.

It has been the experience of many developing countries that the system established at Bretton Woods has failed to enhance their sense of national security; indeed, the operation of that system has seemingly underlined the precarious nature of their position in the international political system. The IMF, as guardian of the post-war monetary order, has come to be seen by the developing world as an instrument of Western domination and as a violator of their sovereign rights. In July 1980 a meeting took place in Arusha, Tanzania, bringing together interested parties from over twenty countries. The topic of discussion was the international monetary system and its need of reform. Recent turbulent relations between the IMF and Jamaica and Tanzania meant that the scene was set for an emotional and penetrating debate on the merits of that institution. Since then, the forces of opposition have grown. The root of the problem is that the IMF, which exerts so much control over the economies of Third World states, was never conceived with their needs in mind. Nor for that matter was the international monetary system, of which it is the cornerstone. Thus Third World states attack the IMF both in general terms and on three specific issues. First, it is claimed that the institution has an underlying political philosophy which determines its economic orthodoxy, and that orthodoxy does not always pay heed to the needs of developing states. Second, it is charged that the voting and the general structure of influence in the Fund reinforce the application of such an orthodoxy and preclude Third World states from exerting any influence. Third, the IMF is accused of violating the sovereign authority of client states, especially those in the Third World, by imposing unwelcome conditions on the loans it makes. Each of these grievances will be examined in turn.

THE IMF: POLITICAL PHILOSOPHY AND ECONOMIC ORTHODOXY

As part of the Bretton Woods system devised in 1944, the IMF was the child of liberal thinkers who believed that economics and politics belonged to two separate worlds; that market forces were the optimal determinant of economic management; and that the pursuit of the freest possible system of trade between nations was a corollary of the pursuit of peace. From the outset, therefore, the institution was established as a primary pillar of the international capitalist system.

This position is clearly reflected in the Purposes, set out in the Articles of Agreement of the IMF.[1] These purposes underline the fact that it is the health of the international monetary and free-trade systems which is the matter of primary concern, while the health of national economies is a matter of concern in so far as it affects the international systems of money and trade. This is not to suggest that the formulators of the agreement did not have the well-being of national economies in mind; rather, they believed that healthy national economies were impossible to develop and sustain without primary regulation at the macro-level.

This stress on the macro-level is not hard to understand. All treaties are a product of the era in which their formulators live and work, and hence of their experiences and perceptions. The stress on the international level is a direct product of their experience of the 1930s, when priority was given to national needs and criteria, and beggar-thy-neighbour policies proliferated. It was widely believed that such economic nationalism was a major contributory factor in the outbreak and spread of the Second World War. Hence wartime planners were anxious that in the post-war era, priority be given to international requirements. Only this ordering of priorities, it was believed, could lead to a peaceful, stable and prosperous world. National security could only be obtained under the umbrella of international security. J. K. Horsefield has written of H. Dexter White and J. M. Keynes, the two main formulators of the agreement, that 'Both men, in the proposals that they put forward, were animated by a belief that the economic distresses of the interwar years could be avoided after the end of World War Two only by international cooperation on a previously untried scale'.[2] Massive deflationary pressures during the 1930s had resulted in states individually attempting to defend themselves by national measures such as stringent import controls, exchange depreciations and multiple exchange rates. States attempted to export their unemployment by undercutting their competitors' prices abroad, and the whole international monetary and trade systems degenerated in a downward spiral. Social costs were inevitably high. The ultimate aim of Keynes and White, therefore, was to bring about the fullest possible collaboration between all states in the economic field. Both regarded Germany in the 1930s as the epitome of what was to be avoided. Multilateralism was to be the saviour of the future economic order, and this system was regarded as the vehicle to obtain the greatest advances in social well-being and world peace.

An examination of the Articles of Agreement reveals that the

IMF is concerned primarily with the smooth functioning of the international monetary and free-trade systems. Here, it is the second paragraph of Article 1 which is of greatest interest. It states a purpose of the IMF to be: 'To facilitate the expansion and balanced growth of international trade, and to contribute thereby to the promotion and maintenance of high levels of employment and real income and to the development of the productive resources of all members as primary objectives of economic policy'. Two interesting issues arise for the developing states. First, the national objective of high employment is seen to be in part the result of the implementation of the international objective, but it is the latter which is given primary importance. System-maintenance is the main focus for concern. The Australian delegation at Bretton Woods entered a reservation to Article 1 as a whole, which it criticised for placing 'too little emphasis on the promotion of high levels of employment'. It will be seen later that one of the grievances voiced by Third World states (and some from the developed world, for that matter), is that implementation of some of the IMF's policies leads to an increase in the number of unemployed.

A second issue arising from this paragraph concerns the special position of developing states which neither this paragraph, nor indeed the whole agreement, acknowledge. India proposed an amendment to the paragraph at Bretton Woods, calling on the IMF 'to assist in the fuller utilisation of the resources of the economically underdeveloped countries.'[3] This amendment was supported by Ecuador but opposed by the UK and South Africa, both of whom believed that development was a matter for the World Bank. In order to circumvent this objection, India then proposed a revised amendment which called for 'the development of the resources and productive power of all member countries, with due regard to the needs of economically backward countries'.[4] This formulation was unacceptable to the states which wielded power at Bretton Woods, namely the US and the UK. The final version, noted above, refers to 'the development of the productive resources of all members as primary objectives of economic policy'. This illustrates both the desire of the Fund formulators to keep strictly separate the issues of short-term finance to correct payments imbalances and that of development, and also their desire to follow a non-discriminatory course of equal treatment for all members without exception. The problem for Third World states, of course, is that their payments imbalances are not short-term but long-term structural problems. Equal treatment of unequal members is bound to have unequal and inappropriate results. But more of that later. In paragraph 2, just as in all the other paragraphs of Article 1, it is the well-being of the macro-system which is stressed, while there is an implicit belief that the well-being of the micro-system (i.e. the individual state) will be enhanced as a positive benefit and direct outcome of the former. There is a dichotomy here. This is explained succinctly by de Vries when she writes: 'The issue of the consistency of economic development—especially in what were only later to be called the less-developed countries—with the international objectives of exchange stability and free trade and payments was still in the wings, rather than on the stage in economists' thinking'.[5] That all national economies would benefit directly from the functioning of the international monetary system in a manner laid down in the Articles of Agreement was almost an unquestioned assumption. It was taken for granted that from a balance-of-payments equilibrium would flow automatically social and economic progress and well-being for all states. This assumption has since been questioned.

The article outlining the purposes of the IMF ends with the statement that 'The Fund shall be guided in all its policies and decisions by the purposes set forth in this Article'. The Fund is committed to the freest possible international economic system, and as such it is concerned with national details only as they affect the international system.

Given this underlying political philosophy, what sort of job does the Fund do in relation to client states? The British delegation to the Atlantic City Conference in June 1944 made the statement that 'so far as possible, we want to aim at a governing structure doing a technical job'.[6] Ever since, this technical quality has been revered. Fund staff and devotees have consistently maintained that the institution is a functional one whose purpose is purely technical. Accordingly, advice is given on how to improve imbalances of payments (at least when the imbalance falls on the deficit side). Money is lent for this purpose and is seen as short-term finance to remedy a short-term, non-structural problem. The overall aim of course is the perpetuation of the free-market system in the most open and consistent manner possible. Short-term problems are overcome by Fund lending until market forces once more do their bit to restore equilibrium.

This claim that the Fund is a purely technical agency is true on one level yet false on another. Inasmuch as it applies standard remedies to economic problems, its job is that of a technician. However, this technical aspect cannot hide the fact that the whole orientation of the institution has political overtones. Even technicians, after all, work within a given understanding of the machine with which they are dealing. Their questions, their thoughts, their opinions and conclusions concerning the machine all spring from the particular understanding or conceptual framework they have of the machine at hand. Hence, in the technical job the IMF employees perform, they are identifying problems and applying economic remedies according to the guidelines of the framework that they adopt for their understanding. That framework is that of the international free market, and hence employees are blinkered in their vision of problems and possibilities by the ideas and ideals of the international free-market economic system. In this sense, they are certainly not performing purely technical functions; rather, they are implementing a political orthodoxy by means of an economic application.

How do the developing countries fare in this respect? For the most part they were not sovereign states at the time of Bretton Woods, and their interests were neither truly championed nor safeguarded. Having thrown off the shackles of their colonial masters, these states were born into an economic structure which worked against them and from which for many there has seemingly been no escape. The rules and policies formulated at Bretton Woods have largely been transferred to apply to these new states as well as to the older industrialised ones. Yet as producers of primary products (excluding here some of the newly industrialised states), they are far more sensitive to the harsh realities of the market mechanism than are the countries producing manufactured goods for export. Also, the governments of many developing countries do not have the means to implement the welfare programmes needed to cushion their populations against the most severe consequences of the market mechanism.

To claim, therefore, that the IMF plays merely a technical role in relation to developing countries is false. That institution is a pillar of the free-market economy. It was suggested earlier that there are two levels on which to interpret the claim of technicality. On the first level the job the IMF is performing is technical. Basically, it involves the maintenance of a machine which is malfunctioning. On the second level, however, and I believe this to be the more important one, the IMF is carrying out the technical implementation of an economic orthodoxy which derives from a political philosophy. The IMF provides developing countries with technical advice and funds, but the problems of those countries are analysed purely within the context of the well-being of the competitive international free-market economy. For as was stressed before, the formulators of the IMF agreement saw this international system as the surest and safest way to develop international prosperity, peace and stability. Hence, the IMF functions with a particular economic orthodoxy, which derives from a political philosophy, and that orthodoxy can sometimes be at odds with the national values of client states. (This point will be examined more closely in the section on conditionality, below.)

This being so, the Fund cannot really claim to be devoid of political colour or preference. In everything it stands for, upholds and implements, it is acting as a political agency. 'Technical' here is used to imply neutrality, lack of prejudice and bias. In its application to the Fund's activities, therefore, it is a rather misleading adjective. To claim this quality for the Fund would be tantamount to claiming that economics and politics bear no relation to one another in the contemporary international political system, and this is an argument that cannot reasonably be sustained. An economic policy is nothing more and nothing less than a reflection of a political preference; priorities within a society derive not from the functioning of a technical economic mechanism but rather from a political choice, whether that choice is made by a single person, an élite or under any one of the varieties of democratic procedure.

The present international monetary system arose in large part as a response to the economic collapse of the 1930s and the Second World War. It reflected originally both the desire of governments to exercise responsibility for the domestic situation of their respective states and for their citizens' welfare, and their concern for the international dimension. It represented a rejection of the gold standard, which had required immediate adjustment when a payments imbalance occurred, and thus intensified human suffering. It is an irony of fate, however, that today, in accepting membership of the IMF, many governments are in fact disclaiming responsibility for the fate of their people and allowing decisions not only of an economic nature but by necessity of a political and social nature as well, to be made outside their states. Social welfare no longer seems to hold as prominent a place in IMF policy as it did in the minds of the formulators of the agreement. In its claim to be a technical agency, the IMF is in fact admitting its championship of a particular ideology—that of the free market.

VOTING AND THE STRUCTURE OF INFLUENCE IN THE FUND

Cheryl Payer has claimed that 'From its inception, the Fund has been dominated by the wishes of its largest member, the US'.[7] From an examination of the distribution of voting power, we may discern whether those who wield power are responsible for imposing their own stamp on the institution. Payer's statement suggests that this is the case.

Voting power within the Fund is intimately bound up with the system of quotas operating there. Quotas are very important for understanding the working of the Fund. A state's quota determines how many votes it has, how much money it must pay into the Fund, and how much it can ask to borrow. Voting is organised on a weighted basis, not on the principle of one state one vote. Under the original Articles of Agreement each member was given 250 votes, plus one additional vote for each part of its quota equal to 100,000 US dollars of fixed gold value. Under the second amendment of the Articles of Agreement, effective since April 1978, the same formula applies except that additional votes are allocated in accordance with the amount of Special Drawing Rights each country holds as its quota.[8]

At Bretton Woods, an *ad hoc* Committee on Quotas was established to determine the quota for each Fund member. It is difficult to identify precisely what factors went into quota decisions. Professor Mosse, a member of the French delegation at Bretton Woods, has remarked that 'quotas were established more or less arbitrarily by the US in a series of deals'.[9] The *ad hoc* Committee on Quotas left no detailed records of the foundations of its work, except for a statement in a report that 'the Mexican delegation agreed to relinquish $10m of its quota in favour of $5m each for Columbia and Chile.'[10] This suggests that a regional distribution was effected, at least in some cases. As far as the US and UK were concerned, Keynes has admitted that an agreement was reached between them on their respective quotas and also on the aggregate for all other members.

Probably the Brandt Report gets fairly near the truth when it states that 'Quotas were distributed on the basis of the perceived economic and political importance of countries rather than on their demand for reserves as such; they were based on trade and international reserves including gold holdings.'[11] As such, five Western industrialised countries have the biggest say in the management of the IMF. For between them, the US, UK, West Germany, France and Japan command 40.9 per cent of the votes. Moreover, if we add to this list the quotas held by Italy and Canada, these Western industrialised countries hold over half the quotas operating in the Fund.

While a review of quotas may take place at five-yearly intervals or less, the current distribution even so does not reflect the reality of economic power in the world today. For example, Britain's quota is still the second largest in the Fund, and this is very much a hangover from her position of perceived relative economic potential and political strength in 1944. In 1978 the total number of quotas in operation was increased by about one-third. Oil-exporting states doubled their share of quotas from 5 per cent to 9.9 per cent. However, the dominant position of the West was unaffected, and more particularly, the pre-eminent position of the US remained. That state is the only one which can unilaterally exert veto power on all major decisions. When the IMF was established in 1944, the US was allotted 31 per cent of the total quota. Although by 1980 her share had declined to just under 20 per cent, this did not result in any significant alteration in her position of preponderance in the Fund in terms of decision-making capability. This is because the decrease in the US's percentage holding of the total quotas has been matched by an increase in the percentage of total quotas needed for key decisions. Thus on the many decisions requiring an 85 per cent majority of total voting power, the US is distinguished as the one country which can alone exercise veto power. Other states may, if grouped together, achieve a blocking vote of more than 15 per cent, but it is only the US that can achieve a veto unilaterally. Even if the veto is not resorted to, the psychological implications of its existence on both the US and all other member states are profound.

It is not only the fact that the Western industrialised states, especially the US, hold the lion's share of the quotas that gives this group so much power in directing the affairs of the international monetary system. Another factor is the actual structure of influence within the Executive Board, where major decisions of the Fund are taken. That board consists as a standard rule of twenty directors and a chairman. The five states with the largest quotas each appoint a director, and the other fifteen are elected for two-year periods by the other Fund members. A provision is made for the two largest creditors, if they are not among the five largest quota holders, to appoint one of the fifteen elected positions or a twenty-first member of the Board. Voting on this Board is not on the one-person one-vote principle; rather the strength of each director's vote varies to match the quotas of the Fund members who elected her or him. This system of weighted voting has been attacked by champions of the developing world who regard a more equitable system of decision-making as a vital component of any reformed international monetary system.

Actual voting is a rare occurrence: decisions are taken more often than not on a consensus basis before the board even meets. The importance attached to a particular viewpoint is dependent upon the weight of votes commanded by the member expressing it. In this type of consensus-seeking decision-making, the orthodox thinking underlying the Fund can be emphasised by the managing director and his staff more easily. A type of 'groupthink'[12] operates which facilitates the director's job of influencing decisions in accordance with the Fund's underlying philosophy. Moreover, since the managing director is invariably a European, and his deputy an American, the orthodoxy of the Fund is more likely to be adhered to. It is often the case too that these men have worked for several years in the Fund, sometimes as executive directors, and hence they are eminently well-suited to champion the economic orthodoxy stemming from the political philosophy outlined earlier.

With the special exception of the oil-producers, therefore, it seems that the developing countries cannot play an influential role in the Fund given its present structure. In the distribution of voting strength, in the type of decision-making process and in the holding of key posts, their secondary position within the Fund is accentuated, while the leading role of the Western industrialised countries is emphasised. They remain the frustrated recipients of decisions made for them.

It is pertinent to note here that the Western industrialised states, in spite of their preponderant role within the Fund, have taken decisions on the international monetary system on their own initiative outside the Fund and to the exclusion of the developing world. Hence the so-called 'Group of Ten' was born in the early 1960s, composed of ten industrialised countries, all of whom belonged to the Fund. Throughout the 1960s it was the main forum for negotiating international monetary issues. Not only did it exclude Third World states from membership and decisions, but at one stage it tried to exclude them from benefits also. This is clearly seen in the Emminger Compromise, which suggested that Special Drawing Rights should be available only to creditworthy industrialised countries. It was surprisingly due to the efforts of the US that this was avoided. Her motives were by no means selfless, however: she had a shared interest with the developing countries in her immediate shortage of national reserves, and as Susan Strange points out, was concerned to develop more friendly relations with that section of states.[13] The developing countries responded to the formation of the Group of Ten with the formation of the Group of Twenty-Four, composed exclusively from among their ranks. That body could wield no influence against the giant of the North.

IMF CONDITIONALITY AND THIRD WORLD STATES

The IMF is largely the creation of the developed Western states, especially the UK and the US. As such, it is tailored to suit their needs, as they perceived them on its foundation. Hence its main function is to provide short-term finance to correct temporary balance-of-payments problems and thereby to facilitate the smooth functioning of the international adjustment process. This function does not embrace the area of structural imbalances, nor that of development finance. If a state falls into balance-of-payments deficit, the Fund is an obvious place to go to for help. While help is usually forthcoming, there is a price to be paid for such aid. This is only to be expected, for no bank will lend money willingly unless it believes there is a fair chance of recouping its loans. The price takes the form of conditionality, which means the policies the IMF attaches to its loans.

If a member wants to borrow up to 25 per cent of its quota, then it may do so without conditions being attached. A member's right to draw upon the next 25 per cent is almost as automatic. It has merely to demonstrate to the IMF that it will make 'reasonable efforts'[14] to overcome its balance of payments problem. Beyond this, however, lie the so-called three upper credit tranches, each of which is equivalent to 25 per cent of a member's quota. It is at these higher levels of borrowing that the contentious question of conditionality raises its head. In order to have access to these upper lines of credit, the state must present the IMF with a stabilisation programme which is intended to rectify the imbalance, usually within a year. Other special lines of credit have been developed at various times, such as the Compensatory Finance Facility and the Oil Facility, and each of these carries with it a specific set of conditions.

The stabilisation or stand-by programme is the most common method of borrowing, so it is this that shall be investigated here in most detail. The usual procedure for negotiating a stand-by arrangement is that IMF advisors, having visited the country requesting the loan, make recommendations and offer guidelines on solutions to the payments imbalance. The state then presents the Fund with a letter of intent, outlining the policies to be followed and performance targets to be met. Essentially, these policies and targets are those that the IMF team has suggested. The IMF has no formal authority to dictate to a member the course it should follow. However, it has both the authority and the power to refuse a loan if a state fails to accept its advice. Moreover, if performance targets are not met, the loan is interrupted and there are no further drawings until conclusive negotiations have been undertaken.

The recommendations of the IMF staff reflect the philosophy which underpins the institution. While Western industrialised countries have usually been able to implement the IMF's recommendations without risking domestic political disorder (even if the political debate has been intense, as was the case in Britain), the same cannot be said of some developing countries. It has sometimes been the case that domestic aims and values have been thwarted by the application of IMF remedies, and political conflict in the domestic setting has been heightened. Jamaica is a good example of this. This has led to the charge by leaders like Nyerere of Tanzania, and Manley of Jamaica, that the IMF is insensitive to their sovereign rights.

What are the aims and content of an IMF stabilisation package? The primary aim is to bring about adjustment, but in a less harsh manner than if no resources were forthcoming. The basic medicine is designed to check imports, expand exports and lower domestic consumption. Problems and solutions are framed within the context of a monetary approach to a balance-of-payments analysis. The IMF team usually suggests hard-currency spending targets to limit imports, and devaluation to stimulate exports, dampen domestic consumption and to check the expansion of the bureaucracy. Performance criteria are often set to constrain government policy in fields such as wages, public spending, prices and reserve levels. The loan is handed over in stages, and this depends upon passing the quarterly tests.

While the application of such policies may be suited to the economies of the developed Western states, this may not necessarily be so in the case of all the developing countries. Apart from the economic arguments which some authors put forward, denying the utility of such policies in the context of economies based on the production of primary products,[15] the social costs of these policies can be tremendously high. As a general rule developing countries do not have sound welfare systems to cushion their populations against the harsh consequences of these policies.

Under the orthodox monetary approach of analysing balance-of-payments problems, it is usual to assume that a deficit is the result of technical mismanagement of the domestic economy. The IMF generally sees itself as offering technical advice for rectifying domestic problems which have domestic roots. However, as the Brandt Report states:

Many developing countries now face many pressures on their balance of payments which are outside their control. The unprecedented rise in the price of oil, grains, capital goods, the slackening of business activity and hence of import demand in the industrial countries, and the protectionism of industrial countries against imports from the developing countries, have all affected their balance of payments. The deficits for which a government can be held responsible should surely be distinguished from those that are due to short-term factors beyond its control . . . external influences impose the need for longer-term adjustments . . . special consideration must be given to the poor countries, since they will experience greater difficulties in undertaking them.[16]

Joseph Gold, the Fund's legal expert, answers this argument quite simply. Referring to the various reasons for payments imbalances, he remarks that 'Some of these forces may be the result of external circumstances, such as the state of the world economy, and not the result of a member's own policies, but the member nevertheless may have to adapt its policies to the situation.'[17] Adjustment has to be undertaken; the cause of the imbalance is often of little significance in so far as the choice of policies to bring about domestic adjustment is concerned.

Devaluation is frequently used as a means of adjustment. While this may result in an increase in exports (and even this is not necessarily the case, where the sale of primary products is tied by quota and price to buyers in the developed world, as with the sugar agreement between Britain and the Commonwealth Caribbean), it can also make the country less able to import equipment and machinery needed for developing an industrial base. What is more, it makes domestic goods dearer. Hence the cost of living rises as food and other essentials increase in price. Add to this wage ceilings, the throwing off of price controls and food subsidies, and the slashing of public programmes in the fields of health, housing, literacy and transport, and the potential for social strife is all too obvious. The political stability of a country can be put at risk.

The Fund has often claimed that if problem-ridden countries were to resort to borrowing from the Fund at an early stage in their difficulties, then adjustment would be less severe and conditionality less stringent. (Hence Brazil was praised in late 1982 for going to the Fund at an early stage in her difficulties, compared with Mexico, which left it until the situation was more critical.) Also, the dislike of conditionality has contributed to an underutilisation of the Fund's general resources in the past. States have preferred to borrow from less-exacting sources such as the low-conditionality oil facility or the private banks.

Borrowing from private banks in the international capital markets has always been favoured by Third World states because funds from these sources usually have no conditions attached. Hence it was reported in November 1982 that President Shehu Shagari of Nigeria would be seeking 2.5 billion pounds sterling in foreign loans from bilateral sources and international capital markets, but not from the IMF. The reason given was that a precondition for stand-by credit from the IMF would be devaluation, and since Nigeria depended largely on the export of one commodity (oil), and relied on substantial imports of raw material and capital goods, devaluation would be counter-productive and would increase Nigeria's balance-of-payments problem. Nigeria is a special case in that her oil wealth allows her to go to the capital markets. However, for many developing countries this is not so. As Gold points out, 'The Fund's endorsement, and the member's observance, of a programme have become, increasingly, conditions for the entry into loan contracts by other lenders or for making resources available under contracts.'[18] In the early days of the intensification of the banking crisis, this applied more and more, and for many developing countries there was simply no alternative source of finance available. While this is often still the case for the least developed, the bigger debtors have found that the IMF has played an influential or even coercive role in getting the private banks to continue lending and to make new money available even when states are considered to be bad bets.

When states join the IMF, they accept that it can apply conditions to loans. However, since these conditions are not made explicit in the Articles of Agreement, many statesmen believe that they have the right to argue with the Fund, not over the acceptibility of conditionality itself but over the content of that conditionality. President Nyerere is one such leader. While accepting that conditions will be attached to loans, he has objected to the nature of such conditions: 'We expected these conditions to be non-ideological, and related to ensuring that money lent to us is not wasted, pocketed by political leaders or bureaucrats, used to build private villas at home or abroad, or deposited in private Swiss bank accounts.'[19] Instead, the conditions laid down by the IMF suggest to Nyerere that 'It has an ideology of economic and social development which it is trying to impose on poor countries irrespective of their own clearly stated policies.'[20] Essentially, Nyerere is claiming that the IMF seeks to impose an ideological solution on a country's problems, regardless of the chosen ideology of the state involved. To all intents and purposes, this is true, in that it provides a monetarist solution for each country's problems, even if the government of a particular country is trying to develop a socialist or democratic-socialist economy. However, to be fair to the Fund, it must be acknowledged that its primary aim is to facilitate the smooth functioning of the international monetary and free-market systems. As such, it is bound to advocate policies which it believes to be consistent with this aim. There is little point in charging an institution whose whole *raison d'être* is the perpetuation of one particular system with inhibiting the development of another type of system when its resources are called upon. Of course it will advocate its own policies and beliefs.

The problem really arises due to the fact that in an ideal situation a state can chose between membership of the organisation (and, by implication, the free-market system) and rejection of it. However, in present circumstances Third World states really have little choice except to join. From their colonial positions many were borne into the system which had the development of the free market as a primary objective, and there is usually no other means of finance open to them. Autarky is the only alternative, and few have chosen this route. They join the IMF not so much because they believe in what it stands for but because membership seems to be a necessity of life. What is more, apart from the immediate need to borrow to meet balance-of-payments deficits, membership of the Fund is a prerequisite for borrowing from the World Bank or the IDA.

This being the case, a more valid charge against the IMF would be that it is insensitive to the legitimate demands of some governments who feel that they have lost decision-making capability within their own theoretically sovereign states and, moreover, that their wishes and goals are being ignored. This charge of insensitivity is a two-sided coin. The IMF is insensitive not only to the legitimate demands of certain governments but also to the political requirements of the system it is trying to uphold. For if the consequence of implementing the IMF's decisions in certain states is to raise the level of social and political strife to unmanageable proportions, the end result is likely to be counter-productive even in the IMF's own terms. Domestic instability resulting from the application of IMF-imposed austerity measures is a fairly common feature in the Third World. Riots in Morocco in 1981 and the Sudan in 1982 are just two examples. In Brazil, IMF policies were directly linked to the unpopular military government, and demonstrators in Sao Paulo chanted, 'IMF go home, direct elections now.'

The basic-needs argument is one frequently alluded to by Nyerere when he states the case for a better deal for Third World states in the IMF. Examples help elucidate the point. 'My government is not prepared to give up our national endeavour to provide primary education for every child, basic medicines and some clean water for all our people.'[21] For anyone living in those countries whose interests the formulators of the IMF had in mind, these provisions are taken for granted. The situation in the IMF today is radically different from that of forty years ago, however, for the membership has been swollen massively by the influx of developing countries. The Fund needs to devote more attention to the specific needs of the majority of its members within the international monetary system. There must be some recognition of basic needs, of a minimum standard of living and welfare in a country before the Fund can expect a state to slash food subsidies and welfare programmes. This is very important for the Fund's dealings and relationship with poor clients.

In another attack on the Fund's policies, Nyerere has claimed that his government 'is not prepared to surrender its right to restrict imports by measures designed to ensure that we import quinine rather than cosmetics, or buses rather than cars for the élite'.[22] The Fund's general policy on imports is that their range should not be restricted by the government but should be left to the laws of demand and supply. If a government does not want people to spend foreign exchange on cars, then it should tax cars heavily. Nyerere's reply to this would be that in a society where there is so little foreign exchange available, any hard currency diverted from the provision of basic services for the population at large to satisfy the tastes of a wealthy élite is unjustified. The reason for this is simply that the average Tanzanian is so very poor. In other words, Nyerere is arguing that policies cannot simply be transferred from a developed to a developing country for the sake of consistency with an economic theory; their relative effect on the population of both states is a factor that must be borne in mind. It is this which the Fund tends to ignore.

In the same vein, he reiterates the point: 'Nor are we prepared to deal with inflation and shortages by relying only on monetary policy regardless of its relative effect on the poorest and less poor.' Also, 'Tanzania is not prepared to devalue its currency just because this is a traditional free market solution to everything and regardless of the merits of our position'.[23] The merits he refers to are not the pursuit of a socialist economy but rather the simple fact that a developing society is so very different from a developed one and cannot be treated in exactly the same way. There is no comparability between envisaging a 10 per cent drop in the standard of living in a developed and a developing state. A fundamental tenet of the Fund is that it should give equal treatment to all its members, and what is being argued here is that equal treatment in the case of unequal members does not call for strictly similar policies. Rather, it calls for a flexibility in approach and hence the advocacy of a particular policy to meet a specific need and situation. Adjustment is the goal in all cases, but the ability of a society to bear the cost of monetarist solutions to effect this is not constant in time and space, and needs to be taken into account.

Nyerere is not alone in holding such ideas. Amir H. Jamal, chairman of the 1980 Annual Meetings of the IMF and World Bank, spoke in his opening address of what adjustment means for the least-developed countries: 'Should they abandon the pursuit of basic needs? Are food and shelter, health and education, any less vital for their well-being?'[24] Jamal has got to the heart of the issue here. Many leaders of the developing world detect a fundamental contradiction between adjustment via the Fund's monetarist policies and the achievement of basic welfare for their populations. They find the different levels of hardship which people in the developing as opposed to the developed world are expected to tolerate very difficult to accept themselves. Are Third World lives worth any less than First World lives?

The Fund has displayed a certain degree of flexibility and creativity in relations with its poorer clients, and this, albeit limited, should be acknowledged. The low conditionality borrowing facilities deserve special attention, for they demonstrate the ability of the Fund to respond to a changing perception of the needs in the international monetary system with the provision of different facilities carrying with them differing conditions. The Compensatory Finance Facility is one such innovation. De Vries has written in the IMF's official history that:

In 1963 a decision on compensatory financing introduced a new drawing policy, chiefly for the benefit of those countries (i.e. less-developed countries).

Under this decision, members can draw on the Fund's resources to meet payments difficulties arising out of temporary export shortfalls, provided that the shortfall is largely attributable to circumstances beyond the control of the member, and provided that the member is willing to cooperate with the Fund in seeking appropriate solutions for its balance of payments difficulties where such solutions are called for ... in other words, there was a recognition that even countries which had difficulty in meeting the Fund's standards should be able to obtain assistance to meet difficulties arising out of genuinely short-term export fluctuations.[25]

While this facility goes some way to mitigating the specific balance-of-payments problems of Third World states, for many commentators from those states it does not go far enough. Hence Jamal makes a plea for 'defining the scope of compensatory financing in terms of what the primary commodities produced can buy to meet development needs such as energy, transport, equipment, education, medical and agricultural inputs, and intermediate products needed for steady industrialisation, not simply in nominal terms whose true value sinks monthly.'[26] Such a definition is unlikely to be acceptable to the Fund, since development finance is not considered to be one of its functions by those who wield power there.

Like the Compensatory Finance Facility, the Oil Facility of 1974 also catered specifically for the needs of developing countries. The conditions attached to loans were minimal. A year later, however, it was replaced by another facility, which was more demanding. These oil facilities were not born of any real desire to alleviate domestic hardship in developing states; rather, they grew out of the concern that those countries suffering most from the oil price rises might take measures detrimental to the functioning of the international monetary system. Whatever the motivation, however, the fact remains that the Fund chose to deal with developing countries in a special way.

The problem of conditionality is not new. Even before the Fund was set up formally, there was a heated debate about whether drawing on Fund resources should be conditional or automatic. While the Fund's position today is that conditionality is justified because it facilitates the operation of the international adjustment process and minimises welfare losses, and because it ensures the revolving character of the

Fund's resources and increases the confidence of the private banks and makes them more willing to lend, conditionality in practice remains a grey area. The IMF has been unable to provide a convincing response to leaders, like Manley and Nyerere, who claim that the institution rides roughshod over their domestic political ideology and aspirations. Even though an Executive Board decision of March 1979 suggested that henceforth 'the Fund will pay due regard to the domestic social and political objectives, the economic priorities, and the circumstances of members, including the causes of their balance of payments problems',[27] there has been no significant change in the level of insensitivity shown by the Fund in its dealings with Third World states. Either the Fund came under pressure from its most powerful member, the US, not to do so, or it undertook a very transparent public relations exercise or, as is more likely, it is confused about the limits of its own action. While the question of conditionality has always been a thorny one, more recently, with membership including clients whose domestic ideologies are at odds with the ideology underlying the Fund, or simply clients who are keen to hold on to their new-found sovereignty, the question has taken on a new importance and become riddled with greater difficulties.

Despite their dislike of the Fund and its methods, developing countries have had little choice but to go to it in time of need. Though leaders like Nyerere may claim in moments of anger that 'When an international institution refuses us access to the international credit at its disposal except on condition that we surrender to it our policy determination, then we make no application for credit',[28] the reality of the situation is that this choice does not exist. Access to foreign capital is essential for development. The Tanzanian case illustrates the fact that states do not seem to be able to break out of the international monetary and free-market systems; or at least, when they do break out, their success in achieving this is only partial and the system demonstrates a magnetic ability to suck them back in. Thus, for all Nyerere's claims, Tanzania had to go back and renegotiate with the IMF. With the deepening of economic difficulties world-wide, it is increasingly the case that the procurement of foreign capital is necessary not simply for the fulfilment of development plans but rather for the provision of

basic needs and for debt repayment. Third World states are
becoming more rather than less dependent on healthy relations
with the Fund of their simple day-to-day survival. Such
relations depend on the acceptance of an IMF analysis of, and
solution to, a state's problems, and this inevitably means the
acceptance of conditions which reflect monetarist ideas about
finance and development. This leaves no room for a
philosophy of basic needs, and certainly it discounts the
possibility of socialist policies and goals within the domestic
economy. Policies and priorities, therefore, are being decided
outside the state, and the state is compelled to accept them
because it perceives itself as having no other choice.

While up till now the developing countries have been unable
to influence the Fund, their very weakness at present in terms
of their debts can in some sense be seen as a weapon which they
may be able to wield in defence of their own interests.[29] In the
Fund's own terms, the well-being of the international
monetary and free-trade systems can only be sustained while
states are prepared to forego nationalistic economic policies
for the sake of the overall system. States must perceive
themselves to be deriving some benefit from those systems, or
they will have no incentive to follow the rules of the game. The
threat of default by the major debtors makes the developed
Western states as much a hostage to the present crisis as are the
debtors.[30] Now, perhaps more than ever before, there exists a
real mutual interest between the states of the Third World and
those of the developed West to work out an international
monetary regime more acceptable to both.[31] Apart from the
monetary instability experienced by both, the debt crisis has
highlighted the interdependence between economics and
politics and the grave instability that may result in domestic
politics, with spillover effects for the international political
system when governments cannot meet the aspirations of their
peoples, however limited these may be. Political unrest—in
some cases even riots—attributed to the harsh effects of IMF
policies, have been witnessed in Jamaica in the 1970s, Morocco
and Sudan in 1981 and 1982 as mentioned previously, and in
the last few years in the Latin American debtor states.[32] In a
single three-month period, April to June 1984, purchasing
power fell by two-thirds in Bolivia as a direct result of

implementation of the Fund's austerity package.[33] The IMF pushes the Bolivian government one way, and the Bolivian unions push it another; the potential for social and political strife soars, and the threat of a military coup intensifies. Chile is a test-case for IMF austerity packages and so far has been a glaring failure.[34] It has usually been the case that authoritarian governments are far more capable of implementing IMF policies than democratically elected ones, for obvious reasons. Interestingly now, however, even some authoritarian governments of the right are finding it politically infeasible to carry out such policies. Nationalistic fervour in Brazil has led to the direct linking of the IMF with dictatorial rule by the domestic government, and an anti-IMF front composed of people of all different political persuasions has come into being.[35]

To date, Third World states have not used their debt as a lever in international politics to its full extent. While the Peruvians have put an upper limit on the amount of their GDP which they are willing to use for debt repayment per annum, other debtors have not been quick to follow this path. There has been a lack of unity between the largest borrowers (partly born of the divisive tactic of individual, *ad hoc* rescheduling by Western lenders) which has weakened their leverage both individually and collectively. No changes have come about in the structure of the international monetary regime, except those which the US has desired, such as the increased collaboration between the IMF, private international banks, central bankers and governments.[36] Such changes have done nothing to enhance the decision-making power of Third World states in the international monetary regime. If anything, they have demonstrated the preponderant and decisive role of the US government, to the detriment of Third World sovereignty.[37] The international monetary system is in a state of flux, and this is extremely threatening to the security of the entire international system, both to developed states and to the less developed.[38] The Third World states have not yet used the pressure which is potentially at their disposal; the intransigence of the leading capitalist states, in further excluding the Third World from participation in managing the international monetary system, may well compound international insecurity. Third World states have lost faith in the IMF and the monetary system it champions, claiming that international security has been enhanced at the cost of national insecurity in the less-developed states. Given the entrenched power of the existing monetary regime, its major institution, the IMF, and its major champion, the US, it is uncertain whether even widespread default by Third World states (currently an unlikely occurrence) would create a climate favourable for the establishment of a monetary system more in keeping with their priorities of greater participation and justice. In the realm of international monetary relations, the call of Third World states for change goes unheeded.

NOTES

1. See *Articles of Agreement of the IMF*, IMF, Washington DC, 1978.
2. J. K. Horsefield, *The IMF 1945–65*, IMF, Washington DC, 1969.
3. *Ibid.*, vol. 1, pp. 93–4.
4. *Ibid.*, p. 94.
5. *Ibid.*, vol. 2, p. 20.
6. *Ibid.*, vol. 1, p. 86.
7. Cheryl Payer, *The Debt Trap*, Penguin, Harmondsworth, 1974, p. 217.
8. In the early 1960s a shortage of liquidity was seen as a crucial problem for the international monetary system. In 1962 the UK proposed the creation of a new international reserve asset. In 1965 the US adopted the idea, and multilateral negotiations took place over the next few years between the Group of Ten. On 28 July 1969 an amendment to the Fund's Articles of Agreement became effective, and the Fund was empowered to allocate Special Drawing Rights to its members. These were seen as a supplement to existing reserve assets. They were artificial international reserve units created by the IMF. These SDRs amounted, in effect, to 'paper gold'.
9. Horsefield, vol. 1, p. 97.
10. *Ibid.*, p. 95.
    1980, p. 211.
12. The key book on this is I. L. Janis, *Victims of Groupthink: A Psychological Study of Foreign-Policy Decisions and Fiascoes*, Houghton Mifflin, Atlanta, 1972.
13. Susan Strange, *International Monetary Relations*, Oxford University Press, Oxford, 1976, p. 115.
14. *Annual Report*, IMF, Washington DC, 1959, p. 22.
15. See, for example, Ismail-Sabri Abdalla, 'The Inadequacy and Loss of Legitimacy of the IMF', *Development Dialogue*, Sweden, 1980, no. 2, pp. 25–54; or N. Girvan, 'Swallowing the IMF Medicine in the Seventies', in the same issue, pp. 55–74.

16. Brandt Report, p. 216.
17. J. Gold, *Conditionality*, IMF Pamphlet Series, no. 31, Washington DC, 1982, p. 31.
18. *Ibid.*, p. 14.
19. *Development Dialogue*, Sweden, 1980, no. 2, p. 7.
20. *Ibid.*, p. 8.
21. *Ibid.*, p. 7.
22. *Ibid.*
23. *Ibid.*, pp. 7 and 8.
24. *IMF Survey*, IMF, Washington DC, 13 October 1980, p. 308.
25. Horsefield, vol. 2, pp. 33–4.
26. *IMF Survey*, p. 309.
27. *Annual Report*, IMF, Washington DC, 1979, p. 137.
28. *Development Dialogue*, p. 8.
29. There has been much talk of debt being used as a lever by Third World states in their relations with the developed states of the West. See, for example, R. Roett, 'Latin America's Response to the Debt Crisis', *Third World Quarterly* 7, 2 (April 1985).
30. See, for example, J. Kaft, *The Mexican Rescue*, Group of Thirty, New York, 1984, which illustrates the acute anxiety of banks and Western governments when a major debtor threatens default. The problem is a joint one, not merely a problem for the debtors.
31. See H. Lever and C. Huhne, *Debt and Danger*, Penguin Special, Harmondsworth, 1986.
32. See M. Manley, *Jamaica: Struggle in the Periphery*, Writer and Readers, London, 1982; see also *Banking on the Fund: The IMF*, Case Study no. 9, Open University Press, Milton Keynes, 1982; *Keesings Contemporary Archives*, Bristol, 1981, p. 31377 and 1982, p. 31443.
33. For a discussion of the debt problem and its social economic and political implications, see 'Latin American Debt: Bolivia', Radio 4, 29 May 1984. See also, J. Petras and H. Brill, 'The IMF, Austerity and the State in Latin America', *Third World Quarterly* 8, 2 (July 1986).
34. See C. Fortin, 'The Failure of Repressive Monetarism: Chile, 1973–83', *Third World Quarterly* 6, 2, (April 1984); and R. French-Davis, 'The Monetarist Experiment in Chile: A Critical Survey', *World Development* 11, 11 (1983).
35. See 'Latin American Debt: Brazil', Radio 4, 4 June 1984. Also, R. Gonçalves, 'Brazil's Search for Stabilisation', *Third World Quarterly* 7, 2 (April 1985); and L. Alcorta, 'The Brazilian Economic Crisis', in the same issue.
36. See J. W. Sewell, R. E. Feinberg and V. Kallab, *US Foreign Policy and the Third World: Agenda 1985–86*, US–Third World Policy Perspectives, no. 3, Overseas Development Council, Transaction Books, New Brunswick and Oxford, 1985.
37. S. Strange, *Casino Capitalism*, Blackwell, Oxford, 1986.
38. See R. Dornbush, 'Dealing with Debt in the 1980s', *Third World Quarterly* 7, 3 (July 1985); see also C. Payer, 'The World Bank: A New Role in the Debt Crisis?', *Third World Quarterly* 8, 2 (April 1986).

4 The Search for a Secure Trading System

Trade is essential for survival and development in the modern international system. A few states, such as Burma, have tried to follow an autarkic path, withdrawing from the international system, but experience has shown that that system has a magnetic ability to draw states back in. This chapter looks at the place of Third World states in the international trading system.[1] The grievances and demands put forward in the Charter of Economic Rights and Duties of States are used as a starting point to illustrate how developing countries perceive the situation. The establishment of the rules of the international trading game in the General Agreement on Tariffs and Trade are outlined, as are developments aimed at affecting those rules, notably the setting up of the UN Conference on Trade and Development, and the activities of OPEC. The special trading relationship between the European Economic Community and the Afro-Caribbean-Pacific states is examined, to see if the latter have benefited from this special trading relationship with a limited set of Northern countries. The newly industrialising states are looked at briefly to see whether their progress has been the result of working within a liberal free-trade regime. The chapter ends with a note on recent developments in international trade negotiations which are taken as an indication of the future direction of Western policy, and hence of Southern security—or lack of it—in trade.

THE CHARTER OF ECONOMIC RIGHTS AND DUTIES OF STATES

This charter followed closely on the heels of the call for a new international economic order; the latter was passed as a

General Assembly Resolution in April 1974, the former in December.[2] The charter gave substance to the complaints voiced in the earlier resolution and made explicit the changes that the developing countries sought to bring about to make the international economic system more just and more responsive to their needs.

Many of the grievances voiced by the Third World states concerned the international-trade regime: those rules, conventions and institutions governing international exchange of goods. There was a strong feeling throughout the Third World that international trade was biased heavily against the poor countries.[3] In very broad and simplistic terms, they saw their position thus: they produced primary products which they sold at low prices to developed states, which in turn processed them and often exported them at comparatively high prices, thus reaping a far greater profit. Moreover, as the years passed by, the price differential between these two types of product increased, to the disadvantage of the poorer states. More and more coffee, cocoa, sugar, tin, bauxite, and so forth, had to be exported to pay for just one tractor. This is what developing countries referred to when they complained of the terms of trade being stacked against them. Deteriorating terms of trade meant that they had to keep producing and selling more and more just to stand still. On top of these problems was the perennial problem of price instability, which made development planning a hazardous task. In the face of intransigence on the part of the developed countries, who were unwilling to take on board these inherent problems of developing states, the formation of producer cartels seemed to be the only hope for the producers of primary products to get a fair price for their goods. Even then, however, there are huge problems involved.

The Charter of Economic Rights and Duties of States was the brainchild of President Luis Echeverría of Mexico, who voiced the idea at the third UNCTAD conference in Santiago, Chile, in May 1972.[4] His ideas were shaped by the fact that Mexico was heavily dependent on the market in the US, and that over 80 per cent of foreign investment in Mexico came from the US. He felt that Mexican sovereignty was infringed by this position, and he recognised that the position his country was in was by no means unique in the Third World even though it is the only Third World state to share a land border with the US. The vertical sphere of influence that Mexico was locked into by the pattern of her trade and investment was commonplace in the developing world. The charter was envisaged as a vehicle for establishing greater national control over Southern economies and as a means towards accelerated development. It was drawn up under the auspices of UNCTAD. While it was carried in the UN General Assembly by a vote of 120 to 6, with 10 abstentions, without the support of the Western industrialised countries it was virtually a dead letter. Those states would not give it their support; the reasons for this will become clear as the goals of the charter relating to trade are outlined below.

The fundamental principle governing the charter was that all states have an inalienable right to choose the type of economic system they want to operate within their territorial boundaries, without interference from outside powers. Three articles which the developing countries saw as an expression of this right proved to be particularly contentious when put to the developed Western world, and all three pertained to trade.

The first issue of contention concerned the exercise of permanent sovereignty over natural resources, as seen in Article 1. This problem arose because so many of the natural assets of developing countries were (and still are, for that matter), owned by foreign companies. The charter outlined the right of all states to regulate foreign investment and to exercise authority over it in the national domain in accordance with national laws and national priorities. Multinational companies were, and are, regarded by Third World states as threats to their sovereignty, and hence the charter was intended to offer some protection against them. Full national control of resources was imperative if Southern states were to grasp their economies out of the control of neo-colonialist clutches.[5] Emphasis was placed on the primacy of national laws, since international law was seen largely as a product of, and a tool of, the Western industrialised powers.

The response of those powers to Article 1 went a long way to legitimising the expressed fears of the poorer states. For the Western states, respect for international agreements and a recognition of international obligations was far more important than the value of exclusive national control of foreign investment and of domestic natural resources. Yet for the majority of Third World states, international agreements and obligations thrust on them when they were in a position of extreme weakness and vulnerability amount to unjust obligations, and such illegitimate agreements need not command respect and need not be considered binding. The fierce opposition of the Western states, especially France and the US, was seen by those Third World states so affected as an attempt to deny poor states their legitimate sovereign rights, to justify intervention by strong powers in the weak states to protect business interests, and to uphold an inequitable status quo. Interestingly, Canada, despite being the recipient of a huge amount of foreign investment, stood squarely in the camp of the Western industrialised powers on this issue. In stressing the importance of international law and obligations, Canada was in fact championing the smooth functioning of the international free-market system founded on economic liberalism. While in theory this system was based on equality of treatment, it was the belief of many Third World leaders that its practice led to the progressive impoverishment of their countries and a widening of the gap between rich and poor states. This will be discussed later.

The next contentious issue relating to trade raised by the charter concerned the question of cartels. Article 5 dealt with the right of primary-commodity producers to form associations. The idea of a producer cartel, whereby the price of a product can be artificially set, goes against the idea of the free market dictating the price of a particular commodity. The successful OPEC action of 1973 demonstrated what could be done by developing states if they got their act together—at least that is how it appeared at the time both to the Western industrialised states, who were horrified, and to the poorer Southern states, who were overjoyed. The OPEC action made the rich states fearful of a demonstration effect, with the policy being repeated with other commodities.[6] They were afraid of the West being held to ransom. Such cartels were not a new feature. Indeed, they date back to the 1930s in the cases of coffee and sugar. OPEC however represented unprecedented success. Article 5 stated clearly that the formation of producer cartels was a sovereign right of states, and they could not legitimately be prevented by other states from forming producer associations. Any attempt by a state to prevent another, by political or economic means, from forming an association was illegal.

Developing countries saw cartels as a means of obtaining a fair price for their products, while the developed states of the West saw them as a major threat to their economic, political and military security. The latter relied on a cheap and secure supply of raw materials for energy and the production of manufactured goods. As far as these states were concerned, the operation of the free market determined a fair price. Supply and demand was the key to this. Cartels threatened the operation of that law, and to the rich Western states this appeared as an unfair distortion of prices. The US in particular found the clause totally unacceptable. The UK opposed it, but in very slightly milder tones, stressing that a mutual interest existed between producers and consumers and arguing that the article failed to recognise this. The Third World states argued that if they got a better deal, then the world economy would be more prosperous and the growth would be beneficial to all concerned. In other words, it was not only them who would prosper. Clearly, though, they saw the formation of cartels as a sovereign, not simply an economic right, and this is very important in understanding the popularity of the policy across the Third World. The economic bargaining power which the operation of cartels represented increased more than economic security for poorer states; it increased their political security also by enhancing their self-image and esteem.

A third demand in the charter was the call for indexation of prices, as outlined in Article 28. Under this policy the price of primary products would be directly related to the price of manufactured goods. This was seen as necessary to counter the deteriorating terms of trade mentioned previously. It would have the effect not only of aiding development but also of making development planning a more worthwhile pursuit. The insecurity created by fluctuations in the price of primary products would be ameliorated. Again, the US opposed the clause, as did most of the Western states. Japan, herself following an economic course which ran contrary to free-market principles, was adamantly opposed to the developing countries. A few states in the industrialised West, however, were in agreement with the Third World. Norway and Sweden are noteworthy here for arguing that the terms of trade should be substantially improved in the name of fairness and equality.

Through the charter, the Third World states hoped to establish new rules in the international trading game; their overall objective was to make their position in the international trading regime more secure. To this end, they sought to exert permanent sovereignty over those natural resources which were found within their territorial boundaries, and to place obstacles in the way of multinational exploitation. They wanted to obtain a fair and secure price for their products through the medium of producer cartels. Also, they wanted to make development planning more worthwhile by indexing the price of primary products to the price of manufactured goods.

The demands set forth here rest clearly on the belief held by Third World states that their trading position, with its inherent weaknesses, is the result of an international economic structure and process which has been imposed on them from outside, without their consideration or consent. Their role in this structure is extremely insecure; yet it is only when understood within this Western free-market context that their present economic existence makes any sense. Participation in this system is seen by them as a necessity of life, not as something highly desirable. Unequal trading is a fact of life for them, but the political imperative for development dictates that trade they must, and so they battle not to leave the system but to improve their lot within it.

Both in 1974 and since, the Western states have mostly been opposed to the charter; in contrast, the Eastern bloc states have been a source of constant support, albeit for self-interested reasons. The states with centrally planned economies have long championed the cause of full national control over natural resources. They interpret the Western powers' opposition to the charter as being totally consistent with the desire of market-orientated states to maintain international capitalism and their powerful role. Third World states and those of the socialist bloc are in agreement that the international trading system is being maintained at the expense of the welfare and sovereignty of the poorer states.

In order to see why that system, which in the liberal view is supposed to operate fairly and efficiently, has been the cause of so much contention, attention will be turned now to the GATT, which has been governing trade relations since the early post-war period.

THE GENERAL AGREEMENT ON TARIFFS AND TRADE

In the last chapter it was shown how the IMF was established as part of the Bretton Woods system to regulate the world's money. International monetary security was aimed at, and it was believed that national monetary security could only be achieved within a secure international context. Hence the security and smooth functioning of the international system was the primary goal, with the security of individual states taking second place. The same was true of the regime established to deal with international trade. The international level achieved highest priority. Just like the IMF, GATT, too, flattered poor countries by treating them on the basis of equality with the older, established industrialised states. Just like the IMF again, the GATT system was in fact disadvantageous to the poor states, because it treated in an equal fashion states that were not equal. Such inequalities demanded different treatment in order to be equal and fair. This was not forthcoming under any part of the Bretton Woods system. The result of equal treatment of unequal parties was the perpetuation and exacerbation of the inequalities built into the system at the outset.

The problem for the liberal post-war planners in thinking about trade was how to dismantle the beggar-thy-neighbour policies established in the inter-war depression years, while at the same time recognising that states may need to take defensive measures to cope with balance-of-payments deficits or to help get infant industries off the ground. The conflict between domestic politics and international management was acute at this interface.

The US had advocated the creation of an International

Trade Organisation (ITO), which was in trade terms what the IMF was in money terms. However, this plan for an institution to oversee the world trading system came to nothing. There were too many strong conflicting claims. The UK, for example, was keen to maintain an Imperial Preference System. Some European countries wanted special provisions for safeguarding balance-of-payments difficulties. Some less-developed countries wanted provisions for economic development. Negotiations continued from 1943 to 1947, ending not with an ITO but with a compromise: the Havana Charter. The Truman administration felt that the new charter would not pass the newly-elected Republican Eightieth Congress, so, rather than face inevitable defeat, it decided not even to submit it. Without support from the US, the charter was a dead letter.[7]

The upshot was that GATT, which had been drawn up in 1947 as a stop-gap measure to operate until such a time as the Havana Charter got off the ground, by default became the accepted wisdom on international trade. However, whereas the Havana Charter would have helped developing countries specifically, GATT made no special provision to meet their needs. Like the IMF, which made no provision for developing countries to play a formative role in the management of the international monetary system, GATT offered them no chance to play a formative role in the management of the international trading system. Both regimes had been drawn up by the developed Western countries with their own needs in mind. The needs of developing areas, many of which were still colonised, were not entering the decision-makers' equations. The regimes established were the equivalent of rich, white men's clubs.

GATT was based on three principles: the legal equality of states; reciprocity, which meant that in any trade negotiations, mutual concessions would be granted; and the most-favoured-nation principle, under which negotiated concessions were extended not only to the negotiating states but to the whole group of states party to the GATT. Such an effort to liberalise trade would, it was hoped, lead to a more peaceful world. Soon the push for free trade was to take on a new significance, when in the context of the Cold War it was seen in the US as 'a key to a prosperous West and to Western security in the face of Soviet aggression'.[8] Unfortunately, though, in those early post-war years the US concerned itself almost exclusively with economic recovery in Western Europe and Japan, and the developing world was largely ignored.

The wave of decolonisation that swept through the developing world in the late 1950s and early 1960s brought in its wake a surge of criticism from the leaders of those new states of the international trading system. Development had become a political imperative, and the GATT failed to pay any attention to this. Southern states were not undergoing the 'take off' anticipated in Rostow's theory of the stages of economic growth.[9] With deteriorating terms of trade, and a falling share of world trade, it was clear by the late 1950s that the system was not working to the advantage of Third World states. They could not simply be ignored and expected to develop by the magic of the market.

By the early 1960s, hand in hand with the growing political confidence of the new states, demands were being voiced for reform of the international trading system. Third World states perceived themselves to be locked into the Western economic structure; they were at the mercy of certain problems which seemed to be endemic in the operation of that system, and while this situation persisted, political independence would continue to be negated by economic dependence. While the Western states espoused a free-market system, in practice such a system was not in operation. Early efforts had been directed towards series of tariff-cutting which hardly affected the poor states. When they tried to export their products to the developed world, protectionist barriers often denied them access, and cascading tariffs meant that the benefits of processing primary products for export were offset by the higher tariffs such processed products would meet on gaining access to Western markets. Unstable commodity prices hindered national development efforts. The Western European and Japanese states reaped the benefits of the GATT in the early years, not the Third World states. The US pushed for regional liberalisation of trade in Europe, and accepted Japanese protectionism, while largely ignoring the challenge of development in the Third World.

Aware of the dissatisfaction felt in the Third World, GATT sponsored the Haberler Report, published in 1958. It stressed particularly the trade barriers confronting Southern goods as they entered Northern markets, and the deterioration in the price of exports from the less-developed countries. While the report led to the formation of a committee in GATT to deal specifically with the problem of Southern trade, that committee's recommendations did not have a binding character and were not acted upon by the Western states.

The Soviet Union was not a party to GATT, and, ever aware of an opportunity to promote its own cause and to discredit that of the West, it had been proposing since the mid-1950s an international trade conference outside GATT. With the huge caucus of new states admitted to the UN by 1963, it did not miss the chance to link its own cause to that of the developing countries. Faced with a united front composed of the Soviet Union and the Third World, the Western states bowed to the pressure and lent token agreement to the holding of trade discussions outside GATT. They never intended to give up any of their managerial control of the trading system, however. For them, it was tied up with national security; for the developing states, it was tied up with national insecurity.

In 1964 the first meeting of UNCTAD was convened in Geneva. Under the leadership of its chairman, Raul Prebisch, the Third World increased criticism of the post-war system.[10] Problems were analysed in structuralist terms. Southern states were identified as peripheral actors in the world economy. They sold their primary products cheaply to the metropolitan countries of the centre of the system, and those core countries sold them back at an enormous profit as manufactured goods. Southern states were dependent on the metropolitan states for markets, finance and technology. The Southern states rejected the orthodox Western thinking that the poor states would develop by domestic reform and participation within the international free-market economy. They began to champion the idea that only an alteration in the structure of trade itself could lead to a genuine and sustained improvement in their position.

UNCTAD's tangible achievements have been few;[11] perhaps its most notable achievement came in 1970 with the negotiation of a General System of Preferences (GSP).[12] This gave preferential treatment to the manufactured and semi-manufactured goods of all Southern states as they entered the markets of the developed states. Even the Haberler Report commissioned by GATT had paid scant attention to the problems of access of manufactured goods into the Northern markets. But while the GSP was important in principle, in practice its significance was limited. It was not until 1975 that all developed Western countries had put preferential schemes into operation, and even then individual countries applied their own respective policies, rather than there being one unified system. The US has taken a particularly harsh line, exempting from preferential treatment OPEC members and any state which has nationalised or expropriated US property without adequate compensation.

The fact that, in principle, all developing countries were included was very significant, for recent years had witnessed a growing tendency to negotiate regional or selective preferences.[13] This practice was in some respects harmful to Southern unity. It was believed that the unity engendered in UNCTAD would infuse strength into the bargaining power of the Third World. Indeed, this unity has been one of the most beneficial intangible achievements of UNCTAD. Northern intransigence has been able to frustrate reform of the international trading system, but it has been unable to stifle debate. UNCTAD has become a 'poor nations' pressure group'.[14] What's more, the unity established there has been transferred to other international negotiating forums, as was demonstrated in the negotiations on the Law of the Sea.

While the developed Western states have been dragging their feet in the context of UNCTAD, their record in GATT has improved slightly. In 1965, Part IV of GATT came into operation. This dealt with the problems of developing states by, for example, eliminating the reciprocity rule in trade negotiations, and by providing for a stabilisation in the price of commodities. However, this part of GATT is not binding on members, so really it amounts to little more than lip-service to the idea of developing countries having special needs.

The history of the South's quest for security in the field of trade reveals all too clearly that the Western countries are moved mostly by considerations of power and necessity, and hardly at all by considerations of justice and equality. Having failed to acknowledge the special requirements of developing states in the establishment of the post-war international trading regime, those developed states then systematically ignored the facts of their case as they arose. In spite of deteriorating terms of trade, a fall in the South's share of world trade and the failure of the Southern states to take off through import-substitution or trading in the international free market, the states of the industrialised West continued to ignore the plight of developing states and refused their demands for reform of the international trading system. Western participation in UNCTAD amounted to a sop to the developing countries; power was still firmly entrenched in the hands of the developed Western states, especially the US. Indeed, it is noteworthy that that state took a much harsher line than several others on issues important to the South. It was not until commodity power burst onto the international political stage in the early 1970s, shattering previously entrenched notions of security and insecurity, that the South had some bargaining power to use in its negotiations with the North.

THE IMPACT OF OPEC

In light of the little progress that had been made by developing countries in improving their position within the international trading system, the new-found power of the oil-producing countries represented a godsend. It provided hope where previously there had been nothing but despair.

Before 1973 the oil industry was securely tied up by an oligopoly of major oil companies, which kept the industrial world fed with cheap oil. The less-developed countries also benefited from cheap oil, but they consumed very little in comparison with the developed. Few people in the developed world ever questioned the continued availability of cheap oil. The quadrupling of the price of oil in 1973 came as a great shock. It was not only the price rise that led to the shock, however; equally it was the political implications of what had happened.

First, it indicated that developing countries could, in certain circumstances, use commodity power as a lever to affect the market in their own interest, and of course the demonstration effect of oil could have potentially far-reaching effects in the case of other primary products.[15] Thus, developed states could no longer turn a blind eye to the grievances of their poorer neighbours, or at least if they did then they must suffer the consequences of such politically and economically imprudent behaviour.

Second, the shock of oil power thrust the whole question of economic relations between developed and developing states into the realm of high politics, as a group of developing states seemed to exercise control over a commodity that was vital to the West. The question of reform or restructuring the economic system would certainly not go away.[16]

Third, the political profile of developing countries, and more particularly of the oil-producing states in the international arena, was raised in an almost revolutionary way. The psychological environment in which bargaining would take place had suddenly altered fundamentally. Perceptions of power, of bargaining strength and weakness, had undergone a profound transformation. The perceived vulnerability of the West gave the Third World a negotiating position infinitely stronger than an appeal to altruism or long-run enlightened self-interest, the like of which had not got them very far in the past.

Expanding on the points above, two themes need further elaboration. The first is the implication of the oil shock for a cartelisation of trade in primary products. The second is the crystallisation of the North–South debate around commodity trade. Each of these will be addressed in turn.

Oil provided an example to other commodity producers of how prices could be raised unilaterally. The West saw all too clearly what a cartelisation of trade would mean for the industrialised powers. The West became fearful of being held to ransom. Kissinger proposed the setting up of a counter cartel of consumers, believing this would negate the bargaining strength of the oil producers. The European countries and

Japan were far more dependent on oil from the Middle East than was the US, and hence they were less willing to risk upsetting the apple cart even further; thus they pleaded caution. Moreover, they regarded US dominance as a threat in itself, and they were not so concerned about the Arab–Israeli war as was the US. The Western powers therefore limited their action to the establishment of an International Energy Agency to work on emergency oil-sharing measures and to investigate alternate forms of energy.

The prospect of the oil cartel's action being repeated successfully in the case of other products turned out to be unwarranted. A short commodity boom, from 1973 to 1974, was soon followed by economic recession in the West in 1975. Moreover, after the initial shock and horror in the West, and exhilaration and confidence in the South, it was soon realised that the oil example was something of a special case, and that the same story could not easily be repeated with other commodities. Oil had a unique position in the economies of the industrialised countries; there were no effective substitutes; the industry was vertically integrated, with production concentrated in a few countries; there was political cohesion amongst the oil producers. No other commodity to date has shown itself to be as amenable to cartelisation as oil. None enjoys such a strategic position as oil in the economies of the industrialised powers, and few other commodities can be manipulated so easily by the suppliers. For example, whereas the amount of oil produced can be increased or decreased according to the wishes of the producers, this is not so in the case of bananas. A banana cartel has been tried out, unsuccessfully. One of the reasons contributing to its failure was the fact that production cannot be slowed up; once the fruit is ready, if it is not picked and transported then it will rot. In the case of other commodities, the political unity on policy has been lacking. For example, the attempt to cartelise tin collapsed when one of two major producers decided to undercut the price of the other in the market-place. The workers' unions were much stronger in Bolivia than they were in Malaysia, and they demanded higher wages. Bolivian tin was therefore more expensive to produce than Malaysian tin. Hence the demand for Malaysian tin increased at the expense of Bolivian tin. The cartel was ineffective. These examples can be multiplied. Only the producers of oil have been able to stand up to the status-quo powers in international trade and wield some political and economic clout.

Perhaps the major result of the demonstration of oil power in 1973 was the changed focus of the demands made by Southern states in the international economy. While in the 1950s those states had advocated increases in the level of aid to spur development, in the 1960s the debate had shifted and security in the trading system was perceived in terms of improved access to Western markets for semi-manufactured goods from the South. This was to be achieved by the removal of tariff barriers. The impact of oil power was to change the focus of the search for trading security yet again: now the concentration was to be on commodity power. This had both global and regional implications. Here the global implications are examined briefly. Later, the EEC–ACP relationship will be examined as a regional example.

Following the demonstration of oil power, 1974 was a year of hectic activity at the UN. Third World states sponsored first the Declaration and Programme of Action on a New International Economic Order, and then the Charter of Economic Rights and Duties of States. Developing countries were using their new-found bargaining power to push for a new international commodity regime as part of an improved North–South economic relationship. Of course, there were divergent interests and priorities at work here. For the developing states, distributive justice was the key; for the Western states, security of supply, phrased in more general terms of international economic security and the requirements of a stable world order, was the key issue.

What sort of trading regime did developing states want to see instituted? They wanted a set of rules and institutions that were more responsive to the needs and interests of commodity exporters rather than commodity importers. In line with this, they wanted a system that worked efficiently for the producers, not merely the consumers, and hence one that did not lead to declining terms of trade and price instability. What they craved was simply a certain amount of security so that development planning could be undertaken in a serious manner and with certain expectations of continuity. In this context UNCTAD put forward proposals in 1974 for an Integrated Programme for Commodities.[17]

The IPC was conceived originally with the interests of exporters and importers of primary products in mind; it put forward plans to ensure a more secure supply by buffer stock facilities, and balanced this with proposals for stabilising export earnings for producers of non-stockable products. Within UNCTAD, as negotiations took place this mix was lost, and the idea of a Common Fund to guarantee additional finance for international stockbuilding arrangements came to the forefront.[18] The Algerians insisted on indexation, on linking the price of their raw materials directly to the price of manufactured goods. Many in the Third World saw this as the only way to counter effectively the declining terms of trade and to obtain a fair price for their products. The Western states could not support a policy which they felt stood for price increases by market intervention. It went totally against the grain of the free-trade philosophy. Moreover, they stood to lose out financially by it. In these circumstances, they could not be expected to provide the funds necessary to put such a scheme into operation.

No new commodity scheme is imminent as a basis for restructuring the international economic system to the advantage of developing states. A prerequisite is increased cooperation in the South to bring the policies of various producers into line. The enunciation of far-ranging general principles in UNCTAD is not enough; real unity is imperative so that piecemeal improvements can be made on specific details and limited issues. The West has never been interested in any meaningful way with a complete overhaul of the trading order; now, in time of recession, it is even less interested in making concessions. Unfortunately, despite efforts like the Brandt Report, the situation is still perceived by those with economic and political power in the West as a zero-sum game: any concession represents a loss from a finite pie of wealth.

It is understandable that with the shock of oil power, developing countries have focused on the role of commodities both in bringing about a new international economic order which they believe would provide them with more security in an insecure world, and in forming a core element of that new order. In doing so, however, other issues and grievances, also important, have tended to get left by the wayside. The transfer of technology is a case in point. The current debt crisis has tended to reinforce this, since exports are looked to as a means of debt repayment. Whatever the stand adopted by the Third World states, however, Western intransigence remains the major obstacle to the creation of a more secure global trading system for the majority of states participating in it.

THE LOMÉ REGIME

The EEC countries have developed a special trading relationship with certain states in the African, Caribbean and Pacific (ACP) regions, and this will be examined here to see if a particularist as opposed to universal trading arrangement can help Third World states to fare any better.[19] This special arrangement represents a random growth of the former colonial ties. Critics call it a continuation of the former colonial policy of divide and rule, since it treats the developing world differentially and not as a unified whole; supporters, on the other hand, hail it as a real step forward in creating a more secure trading environment, albeit only for a limited group of developing states.

Economic relations between the EEC and ACP countries hinge on the Lomé Régime, first negotiated in 1975 (Lomé I). Since then the regime has been modified and extended in agreements labelled Lomé II and III. The regime is a trade-and-aid package, which has grown haphazardly out of French and later British relations with their respective former colonies. Also included in the ACP entity are a few states that were previously colonies of neither, such as Ethiopia. Added to this, certain countries which are not members of the ACP group, such as India, have become party to certain aspects of the agreement.

In 1975 the forthcoming Lomé regime was hailed as a major breakthrough in relations between the developed and the developing world. It was based on negotiation rather than imposition, and this was a novel aspect in the trade negotiations between rich and poor. However, while high hopes have been held out for it, the substance of the agreement has been disappointing. Here three main parts of the regime will be examined as they relate directly to trade, and briefly a fourth facility which is really the cornerstone of the agreement, but which relates less directly to the question of trade security, which is our main area of concern.

Lomé provided a scheme called 'Stabex' to stabilise the export earnings of ACP states on a limited number of commodities, such as bananas, coffee, cocoa, cotton, groundnuts. The eligibility of a state to seek help under the scheme depended on the passing of two tests called thresholds.[20] The first test was that a state had to have a minimum level of dependence on a particular commodity, in terms of a proportion of its total exports to all places. The figure was set at 2.5 per cent in the case of land-locked, island and least-developed states, and 7.5 per cent for the rest. If this dependence threshold was passed, then the next test was the trigger threshold. Under this test, earnings from the export to the EEC of an eligible commodity must be less than the average yearly earnings of that product over the previous four years, by 2.5 per cent for the least developed, and 7.5 per cent for the rest. The operation of this mechanism was difficult, and its results were highly variable in that some countries, such as Mauritania and the Ivory Coast, found that over 65 per cent of their exports were covered, while others, such as Zambia, found that none of theirs were covered. For those that do benefit, however, the scheme provides interest-free loans to the developing states, and grants to the least developed. It is therefore preferable to drawing upon the compensatory finance facility of the IMF.[21]

Stabex was revised in 1979 to include more products such as lentils, peppers and prawns. Lomé II brought in an additional facility, namely Minex or Sysmin, which was an earnings stabilisation scheme for a limited number of minerals including copper, tin and bauxite.[22] Its application is even more complicated, relying on a 10 per cent drop in productive capacity or export earnings by accident in order to come into operation.

Although admirable in principle, Stabex has major shortcomings. Apart from those noted already, its funds are grossly insufficient for dealing with the problem of smoothing out the export earnings of ACP commodities. In 1981, for example, the fall in the price of primary products meant a loss for the Ivory Coast of 1,000 million US dollars in revenue. To have dealt with this would have required almost twice of the whole allocation of funds to Stabex for a five-year period![23]

The second facility to be investigated here is the Sugar Protocol.[24] Sugar is a major export of several of the ACP states, and when the Commonwealth Sugar Agreement expired in 1974, the EEC followed it with a sugar protocol which was then attached to Lomé I in 1975. The facility was a reciprocal arrangement dealing with the supply and purchase of set amounts of raw cane sugar at fixed prices. The EEC agreed to buy 1.4 million tonnes of raw sugar, indexing the price to nearly that received by European farmers for their sugar beet. Again, while the arrangement was radical in principle, in practice it did not work out so well. When the price of sugar plummets on the world market, the ACP countries gain on that sugar sold to Europe. However, half of their sugar is not bought by the EEC states, and has to be sold on the world market. There, the dumping of subsidised surpluses of EEC beet has at times had a very depressing effect on the world market price. In other words, what is given in one hand is taken away in another. Also, states are heavily penalised for failing to deliver the full extent of their quota; such failure results in the quota for that particular state being slashed. Kenya discovered this to her cost in the late 1970s. Moreover, the protocol has caused much aggravation between developing states, since those countries like Cuba which are not party to the agreement lose out on all fronts (although in some cases they may have their own agricultural price arrangement).

The third facility in the Lomé regime relating directly to international trade facilitates preferential access to the European market for products from the ACP states. Whereas a basic principle of GATT was reciprocity—that is, any concession granted by state A to state B must also be granted by B to A—under Lomé, ACP states have been allowed some access to Europe without having to return the favour. Despite this, the ACP share of the European import market has fallen, and perhaps more importantly, the protectionist policies being pursued by the EEC have meant that the ACP states have been unable to make any inroads in the European market for manufactured and semi-manufactured goods. They are forced to remain exporters of primary products. Some of the harshest EEC measures relate directly to those manufactured products which the ACP states find it most easy to produce: leather goods and textiles. Even where access to the EEC market is theoretically allowed, it can be blocked on whim by the application of so-called 'safety measures', or the 'rule of origin' procedure as McQueen argues cogently in his *Lomé Briefing* (no. 10). In other words, there is *no* security of access to the EEC market to exports from the ACP countries—despite appearances to the contrary.

While Stabex, the Sugar Protocol and the access facilities to EEC markets are all encouraging in theory, representing real steps forward in the remaking of the rules governing international trade, in practice they hold out little hope in terms of securing the position of ACP states or diminishing inequalities. All are constrained in their implementation and results by the self-interest of the European states, not only individually but as a group as well. This is highlighted also in the painful operation of the European Development Fund, designed as the cornerstone of the whole regime, but something of a white elephant in reality.

The EDF was conceived as a multilateral aid instrument to which all the member states of the EEC would contribute.[25] Its operation has been plagued by both national and international accountability and conditions. The degree of bureaucracy attached to its operations has made the disbursement of funds interminably slow, and this of course renders other facilities such as Stabex inefficient, since they rely on drawing on its resources.

The spirit in which the Lomé regime came into being has been lost.[26] Asymmetries of power have manifested themselves in the traditional way, with the ACP states having to accept whatever crumbs are thrown from the European table. Per capita incomes in the ACP states have declined, and not one is anywhere near the stage of becoming a NIC. Over 90 per cent of the population of the ACP states live in Sub-Sahara Africa, a region of the world that is actively declining.[27] To a certain extent, Europe has lost interest in these areas, since she perceives little political or economic gain in courting them. Jean Pierre Cot, former French minister for overseas development and cooperation, has warned against a return to 'simplistic Machiavellianism' by EEC states in their relations with the poor ACP countries.[28] But in a sense his warning has come too late. Even if the EEC states were to throw themselves into the task of cooperation for development, it is the case that a regional initiative is really not enough. While it would be better than nothing, what is required is a global effort, with global concessions, to alter the structure and functioning of the international trading system, with a view to making the states of the developing world more secure. Better terms of trade, with more secure, predictable returns, and greater access on a non-reciprocal basis to the developed states' markets are primary requirements, and hand in hand with these should come a role in the management of the international economic system. In their unwillingness to concede on any of these issues, the Western states are pursuing a self-destructive path, for perceptions of injustice such as those that charge the arguments of the Third World states cannot make for a stable world order. The insecurity felt by the developed states in this situation is spelled out all too clearly by, for example, the proliferation of articles planning for a possible takeover of the Gulf oil-fields.[29] Clearly, public statements like these fire the case of the developing world even more. Even if the West has the military capability and political will to take what it wants from the South, the diversion of resources required in training, preparing for and implementing such a security system must have adverse side-effects in economies which are undergoing recession, all be they 'rich'. In the long run, helping the Southern states to feel more secure must make for a more secure international political system. Thus the South's insecurity is ignored by the North at the latter's own peril.

THE NEWLY INDUSTRIALISING COUNTRIES

The NICs are hailed by advocates of the neo-classical free-trade economic order as living proof of what developing states can achieve if they follow a policy of minimal government intervention and participate in the free-market. It is often claimed that the states of Asia and Latin America which are actively and successfully industrialising are doing so because of their liberal economic policies and their participation in the free-market international trading system. While it is true that some of these states, most especially the East Asian four (Hong Kong, Taiwan, Singapore and South Korea), have undergone a phenomenal and sustained rate of growth and development over the past few decades, the reason for this is not as clear as advocates of the free market make out. Briefly, therefore, the task here is to ask how these NICs have managed to transform their economies so successfully in so short a space of time, and thereby to suggest whether the liberal free-market model of growth and development should be uniformly applied to the rest of the developing world as the magic key to improve the lot of their people.

Adherents of the free market believe broadly that export-led industrialisation will be the salvation of the Third World. Doubts are now being cast, however, on the validity of this claim, for while the East Asian four mentioned above portrayed themselves, and have been portrayed by others here in the West, as models of free-market development, several researchers are explaining their development in another light. Robert Wade, for instance, unravelling the secret of the Taiwanese success story, comments that 'the two key conditions in the neo-classical explanation of Taiwan's success—an open economy and a small public sector—. . . have not been present in anything like the degree they are taken to be present in the neo-classical accounts'.[30] He claims that the Taiwanese government has followed a policy of 'guided markets' and has intervened in the process of industrialisation to this end. It has taken measures to promote particular industries and to change industrial development in the direction it thinks is appropriate. Wade argues that the state managers of such countries realise that forward planning by the state is necessary to limit the vulnerability which comes from dependence on trade. They are already hurt by the protectionism of the West, and to leave entrepreneurs to produce whatever there is a comparative advantage in at present will increase the state's vulnerability in the future. Security necessitates a certain amount of state intervention and regulation of production and trade.

These East Asian states have worked hard to develop the image that they are free-traders precisely because it is in their national interest that this is how they are perceived; if they are seen to be following protectionist policies, then they cannot easily call for free entry of their goods into other states. Wade argues that the myth has been sustained in the West because of the existence of a large constituency that wants it that way, given the hostility towards communism and the perception of these East Asian states as being vital to the defence of the 'free' world. White and Wade remark that:

the bipolar view of the world which dominates US foreign policy, especially since recovering from the 'loss' of Vietnam, makes it all the more likely that those who are patently against the Communist regimes in power over territory which they themselves claim, and who have a critical position in the Western defence perimeter, will be seen as essentially 'like us', 'us' for this bipolar purpose being understood as the embodiment of liberal principles of free markets. This helps their own propagation of the liberal image to be effective, because there is a powerful constituency which wants to believe it.[31]

Apart from arguments such as Wade's, which say that the four NICs of East Asia have *not* got where they are through following staunch free-market practices, the industrialisation of China and North Korea goes some way to cast doubt on, if not defeat, the liberal argument. For these two states, with their planned socialist economies, could also be classified as Asian NICs. Indeed, Wade and White have demonstrated the myriad of similarities between the capitalist NICs and the socialist ones in East Asia:

They share a common Confucian heritage, a historical legacy of strong and economically active states; traditions of social and political hierarchy and strong nationalist sentiment underpinned by cultural homogeneity and reinforced by external threats. These factors have conditioned the degree and forms of state intervention and the demonstrated developmental success of East Asian states ... in each case the developmental impact of the state extended beyond economic policy to include ideological mobilisation, pervasive political controls and social engineering. Each state has sought to define and implement its national economic priorities through varying forms of strategic planning. Both types of regime have been politically authoritarian.[32]

To this extent there may be more similarities between these states of Asia, with their differing ideologies, than between the commonly regarded four NICs of East Asia and the four of Latin America (Argentina, Brazil, Mexico and Colombia).

Latin American NICs require attention here for a very specific reason: their debt.[33] In contrast to Hong Kong, Taiwan, South Korea and Singapore, the Latin American NICs have accumulated huge debts which they are unable to repay. Repayment requires foreign exchange, and this can only be obtained through new loans or from increasing exports. The problem faced by a country like Brazil is that when it produces a product such as steel, which it can export at a very competitive price, it finds the doors of the developed Western states, who profess the value of competition and the free market, closed. A vicious circle is in operation. To repay Western banks, these states must increase their exports; the Western states erect barriers against the imports of the very goods that the Latin Americans can competitively sell to them. Hence the debts stand little chance of being repaid. Even though the West in theory stands for a free, liberal trading order, in practice the developing states find that the West's actions belie its words. The Western states, just like the South-East Asian NICs, are saying one thing and doing another. In many respects, Europe in particular is a closed market. Western policies are not motivated only by liberal trading principles; rather, they are often the result of domestic pressures and problems. The US is as big a culprit as the Europeans on this.

A final point to be made here regarding the NICs is that while a few states have been able to achieve phenomenal growth rates, albeit at a high social and political cost, it is questionable whether the system could sustain many, let alone all of them doing so. For, as it has been shown above, they are not real free-traders; they have relied on a high degree of intervention and protection to achieve their current status.[34] Moreover, states like Hong Kong and Singapore are in fact very vulnerable to the idiosyncracies of the world market, since having few resources they are completely dependent on trade for their economic survival. In the short run, they have made themselves far more secure in the international trading system than those states which have not reached the status of a NIC, but in the longer run, who can predict their fate? What the South-East Asian states have on their side at the moment, however, is strong, centralised state institutions and relatively united populations. These factors alone must greatly enhance their security.

In conclusion, it seems that the efforts of the Third World states to create a more secure trading system have not resulted in any really significant improvements. Prospects for piecemeal reform of the existing trading regime look bleak; the chances of overhauling that system are non-existent. Even in the most recent negotiations on trade in Geneva in July 1986, the US, which portrays itself as the primary champion of the free-trade order, disappointed Third World states by closing her market still further to imports of their textiles. Given that textiles are relatively easy for Third World states to manufacture, unlike so many other products, this action is particularly hurtful. Moreover, the US has added to the list of textiles receiving this treatment. Thus China will suffer due to the inclusion of ramie.[35] This is just one example, but it is a sign of the times. The insecurity in trade experienced by the Third World states since their independence shows no sign of being alleviated; if anything, the increasingly protectionist policies of the developed states are making the trade of the Third World states even more insecure. Given this, any increase in intra-Third-World trade is to be welcomed and encouraged as a small move towards decreasing their vulnerability on the developed Western states.[36]

NOTES

1. For a good general introduction, see J. Spero, *The Politics of International Economic Relations*, George Allen & Unwin, London, 1982.
2. For these General Assembly resolutions, see *Yearbook of the UN*, 1974; or *Keesings Contemporary Archives*, Bristol, 1974.
3. See, for example, S. Amin, *Imperialism and Unequal Development*, Monthly Review Press, London, 1977; L. Roxborough, *Theories of Underdevelopment*, Macmillan, London, 1982; C. Leys,

'Underdevelopment and Dependency', in P. Limqueco and B. Mcfarlane (eds.), *Neo-Marxist Theories of Development*, Croom Helm, London, 1983; for a short case study, see T. Petch, 'Dependency, Land and Oranges in Belize', *Third World Quarterly* 8, 3 (July 1986); and for a contemporary analysis of the general problem, see D. Avramovic, 'Depression of Export Commodity Prices of Developing Countries: What Can Be Done?', *Third World Quarterly* 8, 3 (July 1986).

4. See *Kessings Contemporary Archives*, Bristol, 1973, p. 25903.
5. See J. Faundez and S. Picciotto, *The Nationalisation of Multinationals in the Peripheral Economies*, Macmillan, London, 1978.
6. Not everyone had this fear. See, for instance, S. Krasner, 'Oil is the Exception', *Foreign Policy* 14 (Spring 1974).
7. See M. van Meerhaeghe, *International Economic Institutions*, Longmans, London, 1966, pp. 157–9.
8. Spero, p. 69.
9. W. W. Rostow, *The Stages of Economic Growth: A Non-Communist Manifesto*, Cambridge University Press, Cambridge, 1960; and for a critical appraisal, see R. Aron, *The Industrial Society*, Weidenfeld & Nicolson, London, 1967, especially ch. 1, 'Development Theory or the Ideological Problem of our Time'.
10. Prebisch is remembered for developing the structuralist school of thought on international economic relations in UNCTAD.
11. On the inherent weaknesses of UNCTAD, see R. L. Rothstein, *Global Bargaining, UNCTAD and the Quest for an NIEO*, Princeton University Press, Princeton, New Jersey, 1979; and C. Raghavan, 'UNCTAD and the Group of 77 at Twenty-one: Hope or Uncertainty?, in *Third World Affairs*, Third World Foundation, London, 1985.
12. For the EEC and the GSP, see, for example, A. Weston, 'Who Is More Preferred? An Analysis of the New Generalised System of Preferences', in C. Stevens (ed.), *EEC and The Third World: A Survey*, ODI/IDS, London, 1982.
13. For example, the EEC relations with former French colonies.
14. J. S. Nye, 'UNCTAD: Poor Nations Pressure Group', in R. Cox and Jacobson, (eds.), *The Anatomy of Influence: Decision-Making in International Organisations*, Yale University Press, New Haven, 1973.
15. C. Fred Bergstein, 'The Threat is Real', *Foreign Policy* 14 (Spring 1974).
16. Indeed, oil power was the catalyst for the call for an NIEO and for the sharpening of the whole North–South debate which has been ongoing ever since.
17. The IPC was adopted by the 1976 meeting of UNCTAD in Nairobi. It contained two elements: international commodity agreements were to be established for between ten and eighteen products; and a common fund was to be set up to pay for the buffer stocks on which the operation of the agreements would depend. For a critical analysis of ICAs and the Common Fund, see The Open University, *Third World*

Studies: The International Setting, block 4, parts A–C, Open University Press, Milton Keynes, 1983. The IPC and individual ICAs have been criticised for concentration on price stabilisation rather than price rises.

18. For a critical interpretation of the Common Fund, see *ibid*. Rather than being central to a more secure system of trade for Third World commodity producers, the Common Fund is seen as being largely irrelevant. If the theory behind ICAs is wanting, then so too must be the rationale for the centrality of the Common Fund.

19. The Catholic Institute of International Affairs, London, has published a series of very useful pamphlets on a whole range of issues related to the establishment and operation of the Lomé Regime. The '*Lomé Briefings*' are sponsored by the Liaison Committee of Development NGOs to the European Community.

20. See A. Hewitt, 'Stabex: Time to Overhaul the Mechanics', *Lomé Briefing*, no. 6, London, 1983.

21. See Chapter 3 for details of the compensatory finance facility. Also for the relative merits of the Stabex scheme, see A. Hewitt, 'Stabex: An Evaluation of the Economic Impact over the First Five Years', *World Development* 11, 12 (1983), 1005–27.

22. For an assessment of minex or sysmin, see E. Mulokozi, 'ACP–EE Cooperation Wha Future?' *Lome Briefing* no. 7, London, 1983.

23. J-P. Cot, 'Lomé: An Achievement to be Consolidated and Transcended', *Lomé Briefing*, no. 2, London, 1983.

24. See K. Laidlaw, 'The Sugar Protocol: Room for Improvement', *Lomé Briefing*, no. 12, London, 1983.

25. On the EDF, see T. Hill, 'Lomé II Is Dead, Long Live Lomé III', *Lomé Briefing*, no. 22; London, 1985.

26. See T. Hill, 'The Lomé III Negotiations', in *Third World Quarterly* 7, 3 (July 1985).

27. On the crisis of Africa, see T. Rose, *Crisis and Recovery in Sub-Sahara Africa*, OECD Development Centre, Paris, 1985; and C. Allison and R. Green, 'Sub-Saharan Africa: Getting the Facts Straight, *IDS Bulletin* 16, 3 (July 1985).

28. J-P. Cot.

29. See General Hackett, 'Protecting Oil Supplies: The Military Requirement', in C. Bartram (ed.), *Third World Conflict and International Security Security*. IISS/Macmillan, London, 1982.

30. G. White and R. Wade, (eds.), *Developmental States in South East Asia*, IDS Reports, no. 16, Sussex, 1985, p. 8.

31. *Ibid.*, p. 5.

32. *Ibid.*, p. 18.

33. There is a vast and growing literature on this problem. For a concise account, see H. Lever and C. Huhne, *Debt and Danger*, Penguin Special, Harmondsworth, 1986.

34. For an excellent account, see S. Strange, 'Protectionism and World Politics', *International Organization* 39, 2 (Spring 1985).

35. *The Financial Times*, 2 August, 1986.

36. Barter trade between Third World states has increased significantly recently. See, for example, J. C. Griffin and W. Rouse, 'Counter-trade as a Third World Strategy of Development', *Third World Quarterly* 8, 1 (January 1986). On increasing intra-Third-World cooperation more generally, see A. Gauhar (ed.), *The Rich and the Poor*, Third World Foundation, London, 1983, Part 3; and D. Avramovic, (ed.), *South–South Financial Cooperation*, Pinter Press, London, 1983.

5 The Search for Security in Food and Health

For the great majority of people inhabiting our planet, the most fundamental cause of insecurity is the lack of fulfilment of their most basic needs: food and health. Thus this chapter looks at why so many people in Third World states are starving, and what can be done about it; it looks also at the related issue of health care.[1] While the lack of adequate food and water are primary causes of poor health in these states, attention is directed in the second part of the chapter to the problem of relations between Third World governments and pharmaceutical multinationals. If prevention is unlikely, then cure is important. In this context, increased security in health depends to no small degree on the extent to which governments can decrease their dependence on these external actors.

FOOD SECURITY

Famine in the Horn of Africa has once again thrust the food problem on to the international stage, and the question of whether it should be cast as a political, a climatological or a technical problem has been raised.[2] Enough food is produced in the world to feed everyone, yet millions of people die of starvation and related problems each year. The problem is that the people who *need* food do not always *get* food. The reasons for this are wide-ranging. There may be domestic roots, such as the vested interests of governments who refuse to push through land-reform policies effectively. There may be external causes, including the machinations of both state and non-state actors, with the former using food as a weapon, and the latter, in the form of agribusiness, pursuing profit. There may be trans-national or trans-cultural reasons, such as the patriarchical nature of our world which ensures that females are consistently discriminated against when the distribution of scarce food supplies becomes an issue; or the nature of capitalism; or the evolution of culture; or even racism. In discussing the search for food security by Third World states, the initial and continuous problem the student or analyst is faced with is that attitudes of various governments are highly divergent. What is attempted here, therefore, is an outline of the causes of starvation in the developing countries, with implict suggestions for how the situation may be alleviated. No attempt is made to discover a 'Third World view' on how to achieve secure systems of food; indeed, it is suggested that unlike the problem of monetary or trade security, food security is something that is more within the independent grasp of many individual developing states if their governments chose to make it a priority.

The Traditional versus the Contemporary Analysis of the Food Problem

Traditionally, the problems of famine and starvation have been conceptualised in Malthusian terms: rising populations overtake the growth in the food supply, and hence with population outstripping food availability, shortages result. Starvation therefore is the result of too many people and a finite amount of food. Famine would even out the imbalance between population growth and food supplies, and an equilibrium would be reached once more. Such ideas have held sway in the West until very recently, and vestiges of them remain.[3]

At the first United Nations International Conference on Population, in Bucharest in 1974,[4] the US delegation told the developing countries in no uncertain terms that they must control their population growth if they wanted aid. Sadly, the idea that people in developing countries breed too much is not an uncommon view among various sectors of Western society. It is an attitude born of total ignorance of the social structures and cultural values of those societies, and probably smacks of racism as well.

A decade later, at the Second UN Conference on Population in Mexico City,[5] the US completely changed its position. Senator James Buckley, leading the US delegation, argued that there was no population problem; if all states adopted a free-market economy, the population question would resolve itself. Buckley announced that population growth is 'an asset or a problem only in conjunction with other factors, such as economic policy, social constraints, need for manpower, and so forth'.[6] For Buckley, population growth was a problem in countries where governments implemented policies which ignored the need for economic incentives and where achievement and merit were not rewarded. In other words, a country which did not follow a free-market path, but practised some variety of a socialist economy, would be heading for population problems of its own making. What Buckley seemed to forget was that one of the states which has perhaps most urgently and most successfully been implementing population controls is China, and this has been achieved by both positive and negative inducements for small families in a socialist society. China's achievement is summarised succinctly by Davis and Wilsher:

China, with 1.1 billion people to feed, clothe, house and offer some hope of life-improvement to, set out in the mid-1970s to reduce its annual birth rate, then standing at 34 for every 1,000 inhabitants and threatening the country's future. In less than a decade, thanks to a systematic and often ruthless insistence on smaller families—first a limit of two children per couple and since 1979 only one—it cut that figure to 20.[7]

Moreover, it is certainly not the case that the African continent, whose population is expected to rise from 535 million in 1984, to 874 million in the year 2000, is characterised by staunchly socialist regimes who deny economic incentives to their people; neither is that the case in India, where population is expected to go from 747 million to 962 million over the same period; nor in Latin America, where the anticipated rise is from 395 to 547 million. Indeed, these states and regions are characterised by vastly different political systems. The contention of the US representative does not seem to be borne out by evidence from the developing countries.

This attitude is representative of the general malaise

afflicting some developed states when they assess the population question of the Third World countries: their pronouncements are characterised by arrogance. Yet, as Krishna Roy remarks, 'The population policies of North and South are, in fact, more or less carefully reasoned derivatives of complex historical, ideological, political, social, and economic considerations.'[8] To expect attitudes to be the same is naïve. After all:

population policies historically have been tied to social and political ideologies and have shifted from one base to another . . . it is worth recalling Plato's élitist tendencies to justify a limited population; the mercantilists' interest in cheap labour and its commercial exploitation for the benefit of the state; Malthus' rationalisation of conservative economic policies; John Stuart Mill's acceptance of birth control as part of a liberal social order; Marx's subordination of population growth to the proper economic organisation of the means of production[9]

Hence the attitudes of particular Third World states to the population question differ according to the respective ideology, social structure, cultural values and history of the state involved. Some states, such as India and the NICs of South-East Asia, advocate population control; others, such as Peru or the Gulf states, are less interested in it. Indeed some wish to promote population growth. In Roy's words, 'the widely disparate economic and social conditions of the developing countries are reflected in the varying states of programme planning and development in the area of population policy.'[10]

The Malthusian idea which lays the blame for starvation squarely on the fact that population increases outstrip increases in food production has been challenged in recent years by several researchers. The seminal work of Amartya Sen stands out here. Other authors, such as Susan George, have done much to popularise the attacks on Malthus. Sen, in his book, *Poverty and Famines: An Essay on Entitlement and Deprivation*, charges that famines occur not due to a lack of overall availability of food but due to the lack of access of certain sectors of the population to food.[11] In other words, whether one eats or starves is a function of one's entitlement to food. Can a particular person grow enough, or earn enough, or own or inherit enough, to eat? George, on the other hand, looks

less to the micro-details of entitlement within a particular
society: her interest lies in challenging the Malthusian notions
by demonstrating the vast potential for food production at our
disposal, and by highlighting the machinations and
manipulations of agribusiness which controls so much of the
world's food production.[12]

All these criticisms are highly important, for they suggest
that the achievement of food security is a political problem.
Starvation cannot be easily explained away by pointing to
graphs of population growth; lack of food can no longer be
represented as a technical problem. In Sen's words, 'ultimately,
the food problem is not concerned just with the availability of
food but with the disposition of food. That involves
economics, politics and even law. Starvation and malnutrition
relate ultimately to ownership and exchange in addition to
production possibilities.'[13] Hunger, then, is not the result of an
unkind nature but is a special phenomenon, a man-made
situation. Likewise, feeding hungry people can be achieved by
man-made policies. Sen points out that reliance on the
Malthusian explanation of these matters would lead to a false
feeling of comfort in the present international situation. For if
consideration is given only to the ratio of food supply to
population, there appears to be no cause for concern. But such
an average bears no relation to the political, economic or social
context; indeed, it stands completely in a vacuum, and to this
extent it is meaningless. The thrust of Sen's argument is that
hunger and famine is not necessarily—indeed, not usually, as
far as his research suggests—caused by a decline in the
availability of food per head but rather by the inability of
certain groups to have access to food through their lack of
entitlement, their lack of exchange or purchasing power.
Certain groups are particularly well placed, while others are
particularly disadvantaged in this respect, argues Sen.

Sen presents care studies of various famines. His cases show
that starvation is caused primarily by lack of entitlement to
food. Thus, in the case of the Bangladesh famine in 1974, food
prices did not even rise. Many rural labourers lost their lives
because floods destroyed their means of livelihood, hence they
could not purchase food. Indeed, Sen argues that 1974 was a
year of peak food availability in Bangladesh. Likewise, in the

case of famine in Ethopia in 1973 and 1974, the problem did not stem from a decline in availability per head but rather from a decline in the ability of certain people to pay for the food.

If the argument is transported to the international level, the same threads are borne out. Even if national food production lags behind population requirements of food, ample food is produced internationally to make up for a national shortfall. However, much of what is produced goes to feed livestock, for example, and is outside the range of financial feasibility for many of the states in need. Food, of course, is also used as a weapon sometimes by those with a surplus. A noteworthy case here is the American decision not to send food to Bangladesh while the latter persisted in selling jute to Cuba.[14] On the international plane, therefore, the same principle applies: entitlement is the key to understanding which states go hungry and which grow fat.

Indeed, entitlement is at the heart of the North–South debate, and it is central to the search for, and achievement of, security for Third World states in the contemporary international political system. Moreover, entitlement is a prerequisite not just for food security but for security over a whole range of issues. Internationally, Third World states suffer from the same lack of entitlement as the rural landless labourer in Bangladesh suffers in the national context.

Against this general backdrop, three tiers of reasons contributing to hunger will be briefly investigated below: the domestic level, the international level and the transnational level.

The Domestic Level
While some governments, such as that in Sri Lanka, have at times actively promoted policies aimed at feeding all their people, many others have fallen short of such an aim. Here, a few key problems will be addressed.

Land ownership constitutes a major obstacle to combating hunger within many Third World states.[15] Property rights of course are a highly sensitive political issue, and many governments are unwilling to lose the support of landowning élites by promoting land-reform policies. Indeed, in many cases, governments are drawn from those landowning élites.

The unwillingness to redistribute land is very significant, for it has been shown not only by committed authors such as Susan George but also by a World Bank Report that the smaller the landholding, the greater the productivity.[16] The reason for this is clear: need. Hence Lappe and Collins remark, 'Farming for the peasant family is not an abstract calculation of profit to be weighed against other investments. It is a matter of life and death.'[17] The huge latifundia of Latin America are generally far less productive per hectare than much smaller landholdings. Their owners do not need to farm them exhaustively in order to survive. Hence the World Bank reported that small plots were three to thirteen times more productive than the latifundia.

All over the Third World, millions of landless peasants would benefit from a policy of land reform. If people are to secure food for themselves and their families, land must be in a majority, not a minority, of hands. In certain cases, external patrons have encouraged the domestic élites to push through land reform policies, but this has not always been for the most benevolent of reasons; nor has it always had the desired result. The US has been instrumental in influencing certain Central American governments to implement land-reform programmes. In Guatemala and El Salvador the benefits of such reform have been seen in terms of countering the growth of support for leftist opposition groups. However, in several instances the land has been redistributed to members of death squads and other people who support the government in power, rather than to the neediest landless peasants. Successful land reform requires a truly committed government. All too often members of a government have a vested interest in maintaining the status quo. An attack on land ownership is an attack on privilege and power, and that often means an attack on members of the government or at least on their power base. Few people would willingly implement a policy which will result in an erosion of their support base. Moreover, external actors, whether states or multinationals, may shore up local vested interests for political or economic reasons.

Despite this, there are several examples in the modern state system of successful land reform projects. China is noteworthy here. Land in China is held by the 'production brigade', which may include one or more villages. The brigade makes the land over to the villagers who till it. The central government taxes the produce according to the fertility of the land. Recently, incentives have been offered to peasants to increase production within their individual households. Croll points to two methods used in connection with this. First, the rural responsibility system, and second, domestic sidelines. Croll states that the aim of the former was 'to reduce the size of the labour group and link reward more directly to performance and thus simultaneously both promote production and increase peasant incomes.'[18] Under this scheme the production brigade contracts out land to smaller units, often households, and these units pay a levy to the production brigade. Croll reports that production has been increased by this scheme, and that the standard of living of peasants has also increased. The land is still retained in the hands of the production brigade and is not owned by the family households. The second scheme identified by Croll as a means to increase peasant production and wealth is that of the rural sidelines. Once they have given a stipulated amount of labour and produce to the collective, peasants are being encouraged increasingly to raise livestock or cultivate small plots or produce handicrafts.

The problem with the rural responsibility system, and to a lesser extent with the domestic sidelines policy, is that the larger the household in terms of number of people, the more it may potentially benefit—at least up to a certain point. Hence there is an in-built tension between these policies to increase production and income of peasants, and the governments's goal of limiting population growth. However, in terms of simple food productivity, land reform in China, both in its earlier and more recent forms, has contributed significantly to feeding China's rapidly increasing millions.

Land reform carries with it a multiplicity of connotations. In some cases, such as Kampuchea under the Khmer Rouge, it has taken on a horrific face. However, in most cases where it has been genuinely undertaken, peasants have benefited. Governments which come to power either in the name of the people or with the support of the people, often advocate landholding reforms, on a rhetorical level at least. It will be interesting to see in this context what reforms, if any, President Cory Aquino implements in the Philippines. Her family is a major landholder in the island of Luzon, employing over 2,000 landless peasants for half the year on the cotton plantations. Having taken power in the name of the people, she has not yet shown any inclination to implement land reform—indeed, she has been hostile to the idea.[19] After all, it will require not only the will and determination on her part but the acquiesence, if not cooperation, of powerful vested interests too.

This raises the spectre of other domestic obstacles which can hinder the hungry from eating in certain developing countries at certain times. Such reasons often cluster around the fact that in many of the developing states, the notion and the reality of the state as being there to serve the populace as a whole is not well developed. Particularist interests can dictate who eats and who starves. Many examples spring to mind. In the Bangladesh famine in 1974, food aid went primarily to feed the army and the urban populations. The reason is all too clear: it was these sectors of the population on which the government was most dependent for its continued existence. Likewise, in the ongoing famine in the Horn of Africa, the Ethiopian government has been accused of failing to distribute food aid to certain parts of the state which deny the legitimacy of its rule and control. Hence little food gets through to Eritrea. What is more, the government is using the excuse of drought and famine to move people from such areas into areas which are more strongly within the grip of the Ethiopian government. In the case of Nigeria, food was used as a weapon by the central government when the Ibos tried to form a separate state of Biafra back in 1969. The distribution of food can have an ethnic dimension even when there is no ostensible conflict between different groups; and when conflict becomes explicit, differential access to food, whether it be on ethnic or religious grounds, will inevitably intensify. Governments will feed those groups on whom they can count for support.

A final point which must be mentioned here is the trifling amount paid to peasants for producing food.[20] Unfortunately, because of the nature of the international economic system in which Third World states are seeking to develop, they must trade in order to earn foreign exchange. Thus the pattern developed in colonial days, when the best land was taken for plantation production of export crops, has persisted, and with each year that passes the repercussions of this practice become more devastating. Subsistence farmers are pushed onto marginal and unsuitable land, and soil erosion, often irreversible, proceeds rapidly. Third World states often export crops at the expense of food for domestic consumption. Indeed, while the rise in oil prices in the early and then late 1970s has been blamed by many governments in the developed Western countries for wrecking the development plans of Third World states, World Bank statistics show that in several cases Third World countries spend more per annum on the import of basic foodstuffs than on oil imports. Thus in the mid-1970s, food imports constituted 50 per cent of Sri Lanka's imports, while oil constituted 17 per cent; food accounted for 36 per cent of Egypt's import bill, with oil standing at 7 per cent. Moreover, the figures for 1960 show the increasing proportion of national expenditure being devoted to importing food: 39 per cent in the case of Sri Lanka, and 23 per cent in the Egyptian case.[21] The more land is taken up with cash crops, the more insecure peasant farmers become. They are dependent for their food on the vagaries of the international market on which their cash crops are sold, on the vagaries of their currency's fluctuations, on the vagaries of the price of food in the international markets and their own government's taxation and pricing policies. Just as in the case of the establishment of the IMF, where we saw that international security was sought to a certain extent at the price of national insecurity in the poor states, so in the case of food, the search for national security through greater participation in the world market has, for many peasants in the Third World, resulted in greater personal insecurity. There is arguably no form of insecurity more acute in such countries than the denial of the ability to be in charge of one's own subsistence. Clearly, though, the choices which the governments of Third World states have to make as a matter of routine policy are monumental in their moral, political, economic and social context.

The International Dimension to Hunger

State and non-state international actors can contribute both positively and negatively to the problem of hunger in the Third World. Here the concern is chiefly with the negative aspects, since the task, after all, is to attempt to explain why so many millions of people are hungry in a world where there is more than enough food to feed everyone. The range of possible illustrations is great; here we shall concentrate on two examples. First, the activities of the World Bank will be assessed in relation to the Green Revolution, and second, the basic nature and characteristics of agribusiness will be outlined. The theme running through these examples is that such international actors, which are often praised in the popular press for attempting to feed the starving, swelling masses of the Third World, do as much harm as they do good. In fact, the harm in some instances far outweighs the good, and these international actors can be seen to increase the insecurity of the food procurement systems of Third World states. The literature on the way food is used as a weapon by state actors in the relationship between developed and Third World states is large and growing. Rather than focus specifically on that here, the reader is asked instead to think of the larger implications of the fact that the US exerts such a massive control over international agencies like the IMF, the World Bank and the IDA, plus countless other UN organs. Hence it exerts a great influence on the food issue. Also the developed states of the West, especially the US, are the home of so many of the world's multinational companies. Moreover, the US is a key producer of grain. The influence of the US on Third World food security extends far beyond any direct and overt state-to-state relationship.[22] Her position as the foremost capitalist power and the strongest military power in the international system is crucial in the regime governing food, as it is in all other regimes governing international interactions.

The World Bank is the most important development organisation working in the Third World, at least in terms of the amount of money made available under its auspices.[23] As such, it is only natural that it should address the problem of hunger. In its support of the Green Revolution, the Bank was portrayed by its admirers as an agent of positive change in the poorer parts of the world. However, opponents see this policy as contributing to the misery of millions of landless peasants throughout the Third World. The Green Revolution represented an attempt to increase food production in the

South by using new, high-yield varieties of seeds, chemical fertilisers, pesticides and mechanisation. In order that growers could utilise these, loans had to be made available to them. The World Bank undertook to provide credit facilities. While in principle all this seemed admirable, in practice it resulted in increased food production coupled with increased misery in developing countries. As Lappe and Collins remark, 'For the majority who are hungry, "miracle" seeds are meaningless without control over land, water, tools, storage and marketing.'[24] Loans which facilitate Green Revolution techniques reach only those who have a decent plot of land in the first place. The poorest sectors of society in the rural areas are completely bypassed. Moreover, mechanisation in the countryside throws millions out of work each year. Much of the increased food produced is exported to the rich countries, often to feed livestock, not even people. Sen's arguments seem to be borne out here. Hunger certainly does not necessarily result from population growth outrunning production of food, but rather it has social origins. Some critics of the World Bank, such as Ernest Feder, have depicted its support for the Green Revolution as support for 'a new phase of capitalist expansion'.[25] It appears that agribusiness benefited hugely from the sale of fertilisers, machinery, pesticides, and so forth, while the people whom the project theoretically was meant to help have suffered from its implementation.

A word on agribusiness seems fitting at this point.[26] The term refers to the highly developed, integrated system of farming under which a single corporate interest may produce seeds, sell them or grow them on land which it owns, often in developing states, produce fertilisers, pesticides and machinery, and undertake the packaging, transportation and marketing of the produce. Multinationals may engage in some or all of these activities with regard to a particular product, the deciding factor being the profit margin. Such activities are detrimental in the context of the hunger problem in poor states, because land which could be used for subsistence production is turned over to produce export goods. Agribusiness practises do not make use of the human resources that abound in these countries; they make use only of the land. Mechanised farming means thousands of job losses. The pesticides used in production can be harmful to local populations and cause ill-health—even death.[27] Moreover, the profits gained from these activities usually find their way out of the country, aided of course by the usual multinational techniques such as transfer pricing. Susan George sees agribusiness as being instrumental in the creation of a 'uniform food system model which guarantees Western-style standards of living for some just as surely as it does hunger for others',[28] with the latter, of course, outnumbering the former in a dramatic way. Thus Mexican strawberries reach the North American market, Latin American beef products go the same way, and so do fish exports from the South Pacific and South-East Asia.[29] Even if multinational corporations engaged in the food industry intend no harm to the people of the Third World, the consequences of their activities are clear. They do not contribute to the alleviation of hunger; indeed, they often intensify it. Their aim has nothing to do with feeding the hungry in the developing world; rather, it is maximisation of profit. It is the international institutions and the governments of the West, especially that of the US, which paint a picture of a beneficial agribusiness increasing food production and hence aiding the fight against world hunger. What counts is distribution, not simply production.

Transnational Factors and Third World Hunger
Here the aim is simply to outline a few factors which cut across states, be they rich or poor, and possibly contribute to the hunger of certain groups of people. The ideas are suggestive rather than substantive, but are well worth consideration.

First, there is the concept of patriarchy. All over the world, but especially in the poor countries, women have a secondary status to men in society. This means that when food is scarce, it is females who go without first. Indeed, it is often the case that even when there is enough to go round, women eat what men leave.[30]

Second, there is the question of race. While it is difficult to argue that rich countries consciously deprive poor states of food because their populations are of a different skin colour, it is equally difficult to deny that as a rule, white people eat while brown starve. If the UK was suddenly overtaken by famine, one wonders if the response from the other Western states would be different to their responses to the famine in the Horn of Africa.

Third, there is the question of the nature of capitalism. Can capitalism have a human face? The clash of interests between the needs of the people in the developing countries and the motivations of big business and of capitalist states, seem irreconcilable. The pursuit of the greatest possible corporate profit cannot be in line with the fulfilment of basic human needs.

Fourth, there is the question of state interest. States are motivated primarily by perceptions of national not international interest; there is no well-developed sense of community among states. While rich states may not positively desire the populations of poor states to live a life of degradation, they are generally unwilling to take positive action to remedy the situation because they will perceive their own position as being under threat by this action. State interest is a powerful and selfish force.

Finally, and perhaps most importantly, for food security in Third World states, there is the problem of élites which everywhere are content to feather their own nests at the expense of the population in the state concerned. While corruption in the Western countries is surely not so rampant as it is in notable developing states, it does exist; but in the developed states, where most people have access to basic needs, its consequences are not so devastating. However, the story is entirely different in the Third World. There the tiny rich élites eat up huge proportions of the national income, while the majority are hungry.[31]

The answer to the problem of providing more secure systems of food for the people of the developing countries lies in distribution not production. The problem would be solved in many states if peasants were given land and were allowed to be self-reliant in food production. Then a real step forward would have been taken in the search for food security. Greater sensitivity to the international causes of hunger on the part of the developed states would enhance the North–South dialogue significantly.

THE SEARCH FOR SECURE HEALTH SYSTEMS

The past decade has witnessed the emergence of the health and related drug issues on to the international political agenda. The Third World states have been largely responsible for this. With the promulgation of the 'Health for All' strategy launched by the World Health Organization in 1981,[32] health has been identified as a fundamental human right in the international community of states. The year 2000 has been set as a target date for the achievement of health for all people everywhere. Clearly, access to clean water and sanitation, and improved nutrition, are fundamental to healthier living in the Third World.[33] It is socio-economic factors, rather than a transformation in medical science, which offer the most hope— and the most obstacles—for improved health in the Third World.[34] However, the causes of ill-health are not likely to be eradicated in the near future. Thus the concentration here will be on the relations between the governments of the developing states and the multinational drug companies, on the basis that, while prevention is better than cure, in the absence of the former the latter is extremely important.[35] This relationship has recently come under scrutiny in international forums in a highly politicised manner, as governments try to use to better effect the scarce resources at their disposal for drug procurement. Pharmaceutical manufacturers are motivated by profit, not necessarily by the desire to create a healthier world. Hence they often come into conflict with governments and/or pressure groups who have the interests of people in mind.[36] Surendra Patel, of UNCTAD, has remarked that 'The drug question from now on will never be the same—buried beneath the clichés of the sanctity of the free-market and private enterprises, and hidden under the umbrella of patents and trademarks. The drug question is now in the mainstream of active world concern.'[37]

Mrs Indira Gandhi, as prime minister of India, highlighted some of the problems which face developing countries when dealing with pharmaceutical companies, at the WHO session which adopted the Health For All strategy in 1981:

drug manufacture has become a powerful industry, subject to the same driving considerations of other big industries, that is, concentration on profit, fierce competition and recourse to hard-sell advertising. Medicines which may be of the utmost value to poorer countries can be bought by us only at exorbitant prices, since we are unable to have adequate independent bases of research and production. This apart, sometimes dangerous new drugs are tried out on populations of weaker countries although their use is prohibited within the country of manufacture. It also happens that publicity makes us victims of habits and practices which are economically wasteful or wholly contrary to good health[38]

Faced with over 30,000 (some estimates go as high as 80,000) brand-name drugs on the international market, and given the constraint of limited precious foreign exchange to spend, many governments in the Third World have come to realise that the purchase of pharmaceuticals must be streamlined. Such governments see the achievement of secure health systems as being dependent on the provision of a small number of essential drugs at acceptable prices to a wide spectrum of the population. Such a situation is directly at odds with the colonial legacy in many developing states, where the health system reaches only a small proportion of the population, mainly in the urban areas, and where the range of drugs available is totally haphazard, relying on the whim of individual doctors who often take commission from drug manufacturers. Several Third World governments are now attempting to devise more rational, cost-effective and secure systems for the provision of drugs, and with this end in view they are promoting national production of simple drugs where possible, and fostering regional cooperation on drug issues and policies in the Third World. Greater self-reliance, decreased dependence, are seen as keys to more secure health systems in the Third World.

Third World states are faced with a myriad of problems when confronting the pharmaceutical industries of the developed countries. First, their markets are often flooded with thousands of products, many of which are therapeutically useless, or even harmful. Drugs banned in developed countries find their way into the markets of the less developed. Developing countries usually have insufficient trained manpower and resources to keep up to date with banning orders in the industrialised countries and to erect trade barriers to such products in their own countries. Often, brand-name drugs are purchased at prices far in excess of their generic equivalents, and this problem is intensified where drugs are purchased privately rather than through a state trading corporation. Given the limited funds available, such waste is senseless. A related problem is that developing countries often spend 50 per cent or more of their health expenditure on drugs (far higher than the proportion devoted to drug purchases in developed states), and these drugs reach only a very limited segment of the population—the urban-based. Given the lack of technology, expertise and resources, disentangling this situation is a forbidding task for the government of any developing country which simultaneously faces a host of other equally demanding and equally pressing tasks. Health is by no means the only area where rationalisation is required. It would probably be true to say that in most post-independence developing countries most areas need this kind of attention; it would indeed be a difficult task to identify areas which do not. While even a willing government will find the development of satisfactory relations with the pharmaceutical manufacturers an uphill task, the problem for some peoples in the developing world is that their governments do not seem keen to revise the situation. A main reason for this is that multinationals sometimes buy the support of political figures to ensure themselves a particular market. Health can go by the wayside for a variety of reasons. The government may lack the will to effect change; it may possess the will but lack the means; or it may simply decide to give priority to other equally urgent areas such as trade or education. With such a small national pie to divide, choices are extremely difficult.

When procurement of drugs remains in mostly private hands, the pharmaceuticals question is barely addressed. Thus, in a state like North Yemen, as recently as 1978, less than 2 per cent of the total money spent in one year was devoted to drugs for use in treating the main killers: malaria, tuberculosis; bilharzia.[39] On the other hand, substances as ineffective as cough mixture and tonics received as much as 18 per cent of the total expenditure. A major drawback with the private purchasing system is that price differentials are enormous and bear no relation to the quality of the product. Referring to the

Cuban experience, Capo remarks that 'Before the Revolution, quality control was considered to be a superfluous expense which would only diminish the producers' profits.'[40] Since the Revolution, a central agency has been established to acquire drugs of a stated quality at reasonable prices. Medicura is responsible for both importing and exporting drugs. Capo explains that since 1958 Cuba has moved from an 80 per cent dependence on imported drugs to a 19 per cent dependence in 1980. He regards the 'establishment of a multisource procurement system by the Government or public agencies'[41] as imperative in states where the resources are strictly circumscribed.

Other developing countries have followed similar policies, sometimes more rigorously. Sri Lanka is noteworthy here. A National Formulary was established as early as 1959, specifying a certain number of recognised drugs for use. However, when Mrs Bandaranaike's government came to power in 1970, pledged to make Sri Lanka a sovereign, independent republic based on social-democratic ideals, the scene was set for more far-reaching reforms. This being so, state agencies were created to run plantation industries and heavy capital goods industries, and state trading corporations were established. In 1972 the Sri Lanka Pharmaceutical Corporation was set up as part of this overall policy.[42] One of the main functions of this corporation was to acquire non-brand-name drugs at lower prices than brand-name drugs favoured by private importers, and to ensure that these products were of at least as great efficacy as the brand-name products. An UNCTAD study has shown that the private sector paid twice as much for drugs as the state trading corporation, and that there was little if any difference in quality. For example, Roche's price for Diazepam tablets was one hundred times higher than the alternative supplier's price; similarly, Hoest's price for Tolbutamide was twelve times greater than an alternative supplier's price.[43]

Since gaining independence in 1975, Mozambique has developed a health security system far more responsive to the needs of all Mozambicans than that left by the former colonial power. (Indeed, in the colonial era health care for the majority of the population was non-existent). Primary health care is stressed, and there is a central procurement system for essential drugs. This stands in sharp contrast to pre-independence when 'The colonial health "system" was a set of uncoordinated medical services, curative in orientation and discriminatory in character. More than two-thirds of the population lived out of reach of modern health care.'[44] Within a few years, the health-care system has been made infinitely more secure, based on 'strict drug registration, an effective national formulary, and an exclusive state system of drug procurement through international tenders'.[45] Marzagao and Segall suggest that the main problem for Mozambique to date is probably that no pharmaceutical industry has yet been established, and in this sense no real step has been taken towards becoming self-reliant. However, the achievements of a decade have been remarkable, and much progress has been made towards creating a rational, secure system of drug procurement.

While several developing countries have edged their way towards greater rationalisation in drug procurement, it was Bangladesh that achieved most acclaim when in 1982 it launched a highly controversial (internationally, not nationally), National Drug Policy. This policy will be examined in some detail, for it illustrates what Third World states can do on the drugs question if determined.

The Bangladesh National Drug Policy
In 1982 Banladesh was classified by the World Bank as the third poorest state in the world.[46] It was characterised by the lowest life expectancy, the highest infant mortality rate and the lowest per capita income of all developing countries. At that time, an estimated 60 per cent of the health expenditure was devoted to the purchase of drugs, yet only 15 per cent of the population has access to such drugs.[47] Even more appalling was the fact that over 70 per cent of the annual sales of drugs inside Bangladesh consisted of pharmaceuticals which were categorised as therapeutically useless by the British National Formulary or the Federal Drug Authority in the US. The government of Bangladesh wanted to impose some order on the drugs situation. It wanted specifically to cut expenditure of valuable foreign exchange by streamlining the import of drugs, and by promoting domestic manufacture of simple drug

preparations. It wanted to make a few essential drugs available to more Bangladeshis.

With these aims in view, an eight-person expert committee was established to look into all the registered drugs available in the country and to outline a National Drug Policy more in tune with Bangladesh's health needs and limited resources. The committee acted quickly, and just a few months after its establishment in April 1982 it presented its findings to the government in a report. The report revealed that in 1981 Bangladesh had spent about 75 million US dollars on over 3,500 brands of drugs. Of this, it was felt that at least a third had been spent on useless items such as gripe waters, cough mixtures, vitamins and tonics, and so forth. The committee stated categorically that 'It is a responsibility of the Government to protect the consumers from being hoodwinked into spending their scanty resources on useless, unnecessary and at times harmful drugs.'[48] Sophisticated advertising techniques presented misleading information about the efficacy of certain products. This needed to be controlled.

Bangladesh had its own drugs industry, but while there were 166 licensed manufacturers of drugs in the country, 75 per cent of production was concentrated in the hands of eight multinationals operating there. The nature of local production was very limited, and even the multinationals produced simple, often useless items (vitamins, gripe waters, etc.) rather than sophisticated, essential drugs. Those large producers were motivated by profit alone, and they followed all the usual multinational practices to maximise the profit margin, such as transfer pricing. Vital, sophisticated drugs still had to be imported as finished products and this cost around 15 million US dollars in 1981.

The guidelines suggested by the committee were exacting and far-reaching. They dealt with imports of drugs, multinational behaviour inside Bangladesh, local production, marketing and pricing of drugs, and the traditional medicines (e.g. homeopathic). In essence, the whole drugs industry was to be regulated. There was to be no local production or import of cough mixtures, tonics, restoratives, codeine, combination drugs, multivitamins, preparation chemicals not cited in the British Pharmacopoeia, and no import of drugs for which there was a locally produced close substitute. Of the 1,700 brands of drugs on the market in Bangladesh at the time of the report, it was recommended that 1,450 be withdrawn and banned from the country. The report identified 150 drugs that it believed were essential. Of these, forty-five were earmarked especially for primary health care, with a further twelve being identified specifically for use in rural areas. Another 100 were chosen for use by specialists in the tertiary health sector. Of the 1,450 to be withdrawn, 237 drugs considered dangerous were to be banned immediately, with the remainder to be removed from the market over the next six months by the end of 1982.

Multinationals received special attention in the report. Apart from the ban on many of the products which they both imported and produced in Bangladesh, their behaviour was to be closely circumscribed. Henceforth they were to concentrate their efforts on the production of sophisticated items not easily produced by small local companies. This was to aid the development of self-reliance in simple preparations.

The report recommended replacing the outmoded 1940 Drugs Act with new legislation which would cover a range of principles, including the registration of all medicinal products; control of packaging, labelling, advertising and pricing of medicines; technology transfer regulations and licensing agreements with foreign companies; the revision of patent laws which resulted in artifically high prices; the restriction of ownership of retail pharmacies to professionals only; and control of production and sale of traditional medicines.

The recommendations of the committee were accepted on 12 June 1982. Predictably, the National Drug Policy was met with hostility from the multinational pharmaceutical producers whose vested interests were threatened with erosion. These companies urged the US government to protect their interest, and a debate ensued in the US over the trade in products designated as harmful and unavailable for sale within that country.

The Multinationals' Reaction and the Response in the US
The Pharmaceuticals Manufacturers Association, representing the interests of several American multinational companies affected by the Bangladeshi ban on certain drugs, urged the US

government to press the government of Bangladesh to reconsider its new drugs policy. These companies were worried not simply by Bangladeshi policy for its own sake, but because of the demonstration effect it might have on other less-developed countries. Such states spend over 30 billion US dollars per annum on drugs purchases. While developed countries account for much larger sales, sales to the less developed are not insignificant. Accordingly, the US government asked the government of Bangladesh to review its decision.

On 18 August an official US spokesman remarked that 'The State Department has a statutory right for assisting American interests abroad. In this particular case, the US government is also concerned that these regulations may inhibit future foreign investment in Bangladesh'.[49] Not everyone in the US was of a like mind on this matter, and several charities and consumer groups spoke out against US policy. Dr Sidney Wolfe, director of the Public Citizens Health Research Group, called the government action 'unconscionable', and criticised the encouragement given to the sale of drugs deemed worthless in the US to unsuspecting people in developing countries. It certainly smacks of a double standard that the US government can object to a Bangladeshi ban on, for instance, Clioquinol, which is prohibited in the US itself. The US companies Pfizer and Squibb had nineteen and twenty-two products, respectively, on the list of 237 drugs immediately prohibited by the Bangladesh government, and some of each of their products contained Clioquinol.[50] This substance had been banned initially by Japan, as it was known to have detrimental effects on the central nervous system. The pharmaceutical companies had withdrawn it of their own volition from the US market, but they had continued to offload it onto the markets of the developing countries. The decision of the US government to request a reconsideration of the ban was seen by many consumer groups as an unethical protection of the interests of business.

Trade policy is a highly political issue, as was evidenced in the last chapter. The erection of barriers to trade goes against the grain of belief in the free-market, which the US so adamantly, but selectively, espouses. The erection of barriers to the entry of certain pharmaceuticals into Bangladesh was interpreted by the Washington administration as an attempt to promote local industry by eliminating competition, thus fostering national production. While this was in part true, it was equally the case that the ban was seen as a safeguard against the harmful products which multinationals, motivated only by profit, freely pump into sometimes unsuspecting Third World states. The Bangladeshi policy was aimed at creating a safer and more secure system of health care that would reach a majority of the people and cost less; a system that was less dependent on external agents. There is a direct conflict of interest here between the government of Bangladesh, which believed in national rationalisation, and the US government and the multinationals, which called for international rationalisation and enhanced profits for big business.

The Bangladeshi National Drug Policy found much support from international organisations. At the WHO South-East Asia Regional Committee Meeting held in Dhaka in September 1982, Dr Hafdan Mahler, the director, said, 'I take this opportunity of congratulating our host country on its courage in starting to put its drugs house in order along lines recently endorsed by the WHO'.[51] Surendra Patel, director of the technology division of UNCTAD, remarked that 'The new Bangladeshi initiative can be expected to have a decisive influence on future drug policies throughout the world, but particularly in the Third World.'[52] Certainly, such a policy appeared to be in the best interests of developing countries who cannot afford to waste precious foreign exchange on a multiplicity of brand-name drugs when a limited number of generic-name products will have the same medicinal results.

International Third World Initiatives
The pharmaceuticals issue has featured in several international projects,[53] conferences and reports over the past decade, and from these certain salient issues have emerged. The Non-Aligned Conferences have been a major locus for discussion of the drugs question. In 1976 the Colombo meeting of Heads of State and Government adopted Resolution 25, which addressed two main areas. The first concerned the national arena. It called for the formulation of lists of drugs vital for

each individual developing country and recommended the setting up of national buying agencies to purchase drugs; it called for the denial of patents for pharmaceuticals and the adoption of generic rather than brand-names; national drug production was to be fostered; and regional cooperation was to be promoted through the establishment of COPPTECS— Regional Cooperative Pharmaceutical Production and Technology Centres. (A limited amount of regional cooperation in the drugs field had been established already, for example in the Andean region and also between the Arab states).[54] The second area dealt with under Resolution 25 was the role of relevant international organisations, such as UNCTAD, WHO and UNDP; these institutions were called upon to help in the realisation of the first set of objectives. Again, given the limited resources of developing countries, it was important that there was no unnecessary wastage through a duplication of effort.

The Havana Meeting of the Non-Aligned Heads of State and Government in 1979 reiterated the message of the 1976 meeting, and underlined the need to institute COPPTECS as a means towards rationalising the research into and production of pharmaceuticals in the Third World, by the Third World and for the Third World. Several regional bodies have since proposed initiatives on drug cooperation; for example, ASEAN ministers of health agreed on a Declaration on Collaboration in Health in July 1980. However, while several regional bodies have been established, little progress has been made. K. Balasubramaniam claims that that is not surprising, since 'a regional pharmaceutical centre cannot fully satisfy all the political aspirations, economic, financial and logistical considerations of all the member countries'. What is needed, he argues, before any real progress can take place in cooperative action, is 'a breakthrough in the constraint of history, customs, political relations and private interests'.[55]

In 1979 the WHO published a revised version of its 1977 list of essential drugs, which made the task of the developing countries much easier. In Patel's opinion, such rationalisation is of extreme importance; after all, it alters power configurations and places Third World health on a much more secure footing: 'The acceptance of the idea that a limited number of drugs can cater to over 90 per cent of the pathological problems in developing countries, has, with one bold stroke, swept away the very carefully cultivated (and promoted at high cost) and often spurious justifications for the large number of brand name drugs.'[56]

Responding to the elevation of the pharmaceutical question onto the international political agenda, the International Federation of Pharmaceutical Manufacturers' Association (IFPMA) published in 1981 a Code of Pharmaceutical Marketing Practice. As the title suggests, this code of behaviour suggested regulations for marketing drugs. In the Supplementary Statement, for example, the IFPMA offered free to all governments of developing countries the most recent reference texts used in the Western states. This was to offset the charge that developing countries are often unaware of the side-effects and contra-indications of particular drugs. While in principle the admission of their responsibilities in the field of marketing was a step forward, in practice there were several other areas in need of regulation which the pharmaceutical manufacturers ignored. Hence, in reply to the IFPMA code, the consumer group Health Action International came up with a very different draft code for discussion.[57] It was wide in scope, ranging from definitions of drugs, through registration, packaging, advertising, pricing, sales, technology, research and development and implementation. The aim of the code was 'to enable consumers, particularly those in developing countries, to procure safe and effective pharmaceuticals essential to their real health needs, at costs they can afford.' This goal directly contradicts the goal of the manufacturers'—the search to maximise profits.

In the field of health, just as in every other field of activity, if the states which are most powerful in the international system and in the international regime in question choose not to alter the rules of the game, even if the weight of international opinion is calling for alteration, then little can be achieved. While the attitude of all the Western industrialised states is important,[58] the attitude of the US government is crucial, and often, unfortunately, detrimental to the Third World cause. An excellent example concerns the marketing of breast-milk substitutes. Discussions at the WHO Assembly in Geneva in

May 1981 resulted in the adoption of an international code of conduct for the marketing of these products. The guideline advised that any advert which suggested that these substitutes were more beneficial for babies than breast milk should be banned, and also that free samples of powdered milk should not be allowed. One state voted against this motion: the US. This was no surprise, since Reagan had made it known in advance of the vote that he believed the motion interfered with the right of the manufacturers to free and unhindered commercial activity. An offical of the Agency for International Development (AID), Dr Stephen Joseph, resigned in protest. On 16 June a motion was carried by 301 votes to 100 in the US House of Representatives condemning the government's stand on the issue, and this was followed two days later in the Senate by a vote of 89 to 2, urging the president and the manufacturers of baby food to adhere to the WHO code of marketing practice.[59]

Any attempt by the Third World states to alter the international regime governing health, especially those parts of it relating to the pharmaceutical industry, are likely to meet great obstacles. US government policy can be a fundamental factor determining the success or failure of these efforts. However, as the Bangladesh example has shown, more rational health policies and drug procurement can be achieved even against the wishes of the state which is most powerful in the regime. The Third World state has to decide whether the benefits of rationalisation in terms of money and health care outweigh the costs of incurring the displeasure of the leading state(s). More secure health care is a real possibility for Third World states.

NOTES

1. For a general discussion, see T. Hayter, *The Creation of World Poverty: An Alternative View to the Brandt Report*, Pluto Press, London, 1983.
2. Several recent works deal with the food and famine problem. See, for instance, P. King, *An African Winter*, Penguin Special, Harmondsworth, 1986; L. Timberlake, *Africa in Crisis*, Earthscan, London and Washington DC, 1985; C. Allison and R. Green (eds.),

'Sub-Saharan Africa: Getting the Facts Straight', *IDS Bulletin* 16, 3 (July 1985); E. Clay and E. Everitt, 'Food Aid and Emergencies: A Report on the Third IDS Food Aid Seminar', *IDS Discussion Paper* 206 (July 1985); F. D'Souza and J. Shoham, 'Famine in Africa: Avoiding the Worst', *Third World Quarterly* 7, 3 (July 1985); J. Firebrace with S. Holland, *Never Kneel Down: Drought, Development and Liberation in Eritrea*, Spokesman Books, Nottingham, 1984. For an interesting article concerning the 'interplay of moral and political processes and the ways in which they affect institutions that regulate access to food in South Asia', see A. Appadurai, 'How Moral Is South Asia's Economy?', *Journal of Asian Studies* 43, 3 (May 1984). For a very brief synopsis of the food problem, see 'Muddle and Misery in the Third World', *The Economist*, 12 July 1986, pp. 67–8.

3.   See T. R. Malthus, *A Summary View of the Principle of Population*, in D. V. Glass (ed.), *Introduction to Malthus*, Watts & Co, London, 1953. For a critical assessment of Malthus, see E. A. Wrigley and R. S. Shofield, *The Population History of England, 1541–1871*, Edward Arnold, London, 1981.

4.   See *Yearbook of the UN*, United Nations, New York, 1974, vol. 28, pp. 550–64. Also, for a comment on this conference and the population question in general, see Mahbub ul Haq, *The Poverty Curtain*, Oxford University Press, Oxford, 1983.

5.   See *Keesings Contemporary Archives*, Bristol, 1984, pp. 33312–3.

6.   Quoted in *India Today*, 15 September 1984, p. 84.

7.   See S. Davis and P. Wilsher, 'Five Billion and Births Still Rising', *The Sunday Times*, 13 July 1986.

8.   Krishna Roy, 'Population Policy from the Southern Perspective', in G. F. Erb and V. Kallab (eds.), *Beyond Dependency*, p. 110.

9.   *Ibid.*, p. 96.

10. *Ibid.*, p. 98.

11. A. Sen, *Poverty and Famines: An Essay on Entitlement and Deprivation*, Clarendon Press, Oxford, 1982.

12. S. George, *How the Other Half Dies*, Penguin, Harmondsworth, 1983. Also by the same author, *Feeding the Few: Corporate Control of Food*, Institute for Policy Studies, Washington DC, 1981.

13. A. Sen, 'The Food Problem: Theory and Policy', in A. Gauhar (ed.), *South–South Strategy*, Third World Foundation, London, 1983, p. 103.

14. See. J. Faaland (ed.), *Aid and Influence: The Case of Bangladesh*, Macmillan, London, 1981.

15. For a concise discussion, see A. Kohli, 'The Politics of Land Reform', in *Third World Affairs*, Third World Foundation, London, 1985. For an interesting country analysis, see C. Kay, 'The Monetarist Experiment in the Chilean Countryside', *Third World Quarterly* 7, 2 (April 1985). This article shows how the land reform implemented by the Allende government, 1970–3, has been undermined.

16. The World Bank, *The Assault on World Poverty: Problems of Rural Development, Education and Health*, Johns Hopkins University Press,

Baltimore, 1975, p. 215.

17.   F. M. Lappé and J. Collins, *Food First*, Abacus, London, 1982, p. 141.

18.   E. Croll, 'Production versus Reproduction: A Threat to China's Development Strategy', *World Development* 11, 6 (1983), p. 469.

19.   W. Bello, 'Aquino's Elite Populism: Initial Reflections', *Third World Quarterly* 8, 3 (July 1986).

20.   For an interesting slant on the subject, see B. Rogers, *The Domestication of Women: Discrimination in Developing Societies*, Tavistock Publications, London and New York, 1981. Rogers suggests that the decline in food production in Third World states can often be linked to sexual discrimination; women do the bulk of the work in subsistence agriculture, and there are no incentives aimed at them specifically. See also J. K. Henn, 'Feeding the Cities and Feeding the Peasants: What Role for Africa's Women Farmers?', *World Development* 11, 12 (1983).

21.   *World Bank Report*, The World Bank, Washington DC, 1978. Statistical tables reveal that almost all of the least-developed Third World states, and many of the middle-income developing states, spend more on imported food per annum than on imported fuel.

22.   For a specific example of US policy on food, see, for instance, P. Eldridge, *The Politics of Foreign Aid in India*, Weidenfeld & Nicolson, London, 1969, ch. 6; and R. L. Paarlberg, *Food Trade and Foreign Policy: India, the Soviet Union and the US*, Cornell University Press, Ithaca and London, 1985.

23.   See C. Payer, *The World Bank: A Critical Assessment*, Monthly Review Press, London and New York, 1982.

24.   Lappé and Collins, p. 114.

25.   E. Feder, 'Capitalism's Last-Ditch Effort to Save Underdeveloped Agricultures: International Agribusiness, the World Bank and the Rural Poor', *Journal of Contemporary Asia* 7, 1 (1977), p. 57. By the same author, see also 'McNamara's Little Green Revolution: The World Bank Scheme for the Liquidation of the Third World Peasantry', *Comercio Exterior de Mexico*, August 1976.

26.   For a general study, see B. Dinham and C. Hines, *Agribusiness in Africa*, Earth Resources Research, London, 1983.

27.   See D. Weir and M. Shapiro, *Circle of Poison: Pesticides and People in a Hungry World*, Food First, Institute for Food and Development Policy, San Francisco, 1981.

28.   George, *Feeding the Few*, p. 70.

29.   See G. Kent, 'Food Trade: The Poor Feed the Rich', *The Ecologist* 15, 5/6 (1985).

30.   L. Leghorn and M. Rodkowsky, *Who Really Starves? Women and World Hunger*, Friendship Press, New York, 1977.

31.   See P. Donaldson, *Worlds Apart*, Penguin, Harmondsworth, 1986, pp. 45–9. Also, see R. Chambers, 'Putting "last" thinking first: a professional revolution', in *Third World Affairs*. Third World Foundation, London, 1985.

32.   This strategy came as a result of the International Conference on

Primary Health Care, held in September 1978. See *Keesings Contemporary Archives*, Bristol, 1981, p. 31044.

33.   O. Shirley (ed.), *A Cry For Health: Poverty and Disability in the Third World*, Third World Group for Disabled People and AHRTAG, Frome, Somerset, 1983.

34.   For a case study, see A. Seedat, *Crippling a Nation: Health in Apartheid South Africa*, IDAFSA, London, 1984.

35.   T. Heller, *Poor Health, Rich Profits: Multinational Corporations and the Third World*, Spokesman Books, Nottingham, 1977; and M. Muller, *The Health of Nations*, Faber & Faber, London, 1982.

36.   For the example of the drug Lomotil, produced by the Searle Company, see C. Medawar and B. Freese, *Decoding the Conduct of a Multinational Pharmaceutical Company, and the Failure of a Western Remedy for the Third World*, Social Audit, London, 1982.

37.   S. Patel, 'Introduction', *World Development* 11, 3 (1983), p. 167.

38.   *Ibid.*, pp. 165–6.

39.   See *The Health of Nations*, Coursebook, Open University Press, Milton Keynes, 1985.

40.   L. Capo, 'International Drug Procurement and Market Intelligence: Cuba', *World Development* 11, 3, p. 221.

41.   *Ibid.*, p. 217.

42.   *Keesings Contemporary Archives*, Bristol, 1972, p. 25306.

43.   C. Medawar, 'The Disabled Consumer: How Multinational Corporations Affect the Third World', in Shirley.

44.   C. Marzagao and M. Segall, 'Drug Selection: Mozambique', *World Development* 11, 3: 207.

45.   *Ibid.*, pp. 214–5.

46.   *World Development Report*, 1982.

47.   'Report to the Expert Committee for Drugs: Bangladesh', *World Development* 11, 3: 251.

48.   *Ibid.*, p. 252.

49.   *Washington Post*, final edition, 19 August 1982.

50.   *Ibid.*

51.   See 'Report of the Expert Committee', p. 251.

52.   *Ibid.*, p. 252.

53.   For a selection of important documents, see *World Development* 11, 3: 289–328.

54.   For further details, see K. Balasubramaniam, 'The Main Lines of Cooperation among Developing Countries in Pharmaceuticals', *World Development* 11, 3 (1983), 281–7.

55.   *Ibid.*, p. 285.

56.   Patel, p. 166.

57.   For these documents, see *World Development* 11, 3.

58.   For instance, the attitude of the British government can have important ramifications in the Third World. See C. Medawar, *Insult or Injury: An Equiry into the Marketing and Advertising of British Food and Drug Products in the Third World*, Social Audit, London, 1979.

59.   See *Keesings Contemporary Archives*, Bristol, 1981, p. 31044.

6 Nuclear Weapons and the Search for Security

The issue of nuclear weapons for Third World states, as for any other states, is highly emotive. It is a cause of dissension not only between Third World states and developed states but also amongst Third World states and, indeed, within them. This chapter looks at the international regime which governs the acquisition of nuclear weapons, and at the attitudes of Third World states towards it. While a majority of Third World states have accepted the regime developed by the great powers of both East and West, their reasons for this do not always stem from their belief in its inherent worth. They may be the product of a realistic assessment of the price to be paid for defiance of the wishes of the superpowers, or conversely, the spin-off benefits to be gained from compliance. Moreover, of those states which have chosen not to comply with the nuclear non-proliferation regime, several have either already developed nuclear weapons or are very well on the way to having the capability to do so. In this chapter the difficulties which the non-proliferation regime poses for Third World states are examined, with special attention being paid to such problems as the definition of proliferation itself and the associated problem of contending interpretations of the significance of Article 6 of the Non-Proliferation Treaty (NPT), fulfilment of which by the superpowers is regarded as crucial by Third World states. The case put for the acquisition of nuclear weapons by one Third World advocate, Ali Mazrui, and one First World advocate, Kenneth Waltz, are outlined briefly. Finally, the question of the 'near-nuclear' or 'nuclear threshold' states is addressed, for they represent a successful

Third World challenge to the rules developed and sustained in concert by the original nuclear powers, the UK, the US and the USSR, in an area which the latter regard as vitally important.

THE NUCLEAR NON-PROLIFERATION REGIME

The NPT forms the cornerstone of the nuclear non-proliferation regime.[1] The treaty was signed first in London, Washington and Moscow on 1 July 1968 and came into force on 5 March 1970. This unusual unity in the policies of East and West is significant. For once, the superpowers perceived a mutual interest in establishing common rules to govern a particular aspect of international relations that was considered to be of the utmost importance to both. Even now, sixteen years later, 'the NPT continues to be one of those rare areas of international politics in which the superpowers see eye to eye'.[2] The treaty encompasses three main points: first, that nuclear-weapon states should not transfer nuclear weapons or nuclear explosive devices to other states; second, that non-nuclear-weapon states should not seek to obtain nuclear weapons; and third, that the International Atomic Energy Association (IAEA) should administer safeguards, or in other words, it should check that parties to the treaty are complying with its demands. The treaty also contains a number of carrots for non-nuclear states, in the form of Article 4 and Article 6. Under the former, the non-nuclear states party to the treaty are entitled to material, scientific and technological help for the development of nuclear energy for peaceful purposes. Article 6 states that 'Each of the Parties to the Treaty undertakes to pursue in good faith on effective measures relating to cessation of the nuclear arms race at an early date and to nuclear disarmament, and on a treaty on general and complete disarmament under strict and effective international control.'[3] Unlike most other international regimes governing areas such as money and trade, this particular regime has been instituted for a limited lifespan, whereas the others are open-ended. In 1995 a conference will be convened to decide on whether it should survive, and if so, in what form and for how long.

The basic problem for Third World states is that the treaty

seems to institutionalise inequality, since it is characterised by unequal rights and obligations. As D. Keohane has remarked, 'That the principal institution established to prevent the spread of nuclear weapons ... is discriminatory between States possessing and those without nuclear weapons, is difficult to deny'.[4] Some states are allowed to have nuclear weapons, while others are not. How far the USSR and US planned this hegemony together is a matter of some dispute. Millar, for example, regards the NPT as a 'deliberate or implicit attempt at condominium by the two super-powers'.[5] The hierarchy of states established there does seem set to stay, and critics argue that the treaty and the regime which it represents are nothing more than a direct reflection of the power hierarchy in the international political system.[6] In other words, any discussion of the position of the Third World within the context of the non-proliferation regime parallels a discussion of their position in the international political system. Keohane, however, seems less convinced of deliberate and concerted efforts at condominium by the superpowers.[7]

An understanding of the contending conceptions of proliferation held by the original nuclear powers and the Third World states goes far to explain the dissatisfaction of the latter with the perceived intransigence of the US, USSR and UK regarding the NPT in general, and Article 6 in particular. A succinct example of the definitional problem illustrates this:

In US parlance, proliferation means the spread of the ability to build nuclear weapons in countries that do not now have them; nonproliferation involves a variety of measures designed to block that spread. Most Third World countries and other states that do not possess nuclear weapons consider proliferation and nonproliferation in terms of another, even more important dimension, which is vertical. It involves the piling up and ever more devastating refinement of nuclear armaments by the nuclear weapons states.[8]

When considered from the standpoint of Third World states, it does seem remarkable that the superpowers, who are the very states which have been proliferating at a rapid pace, are worried about the possible acquisition of a few nuclear bombs by a handful of relatively weak states. One Third World analyst has remarked that 'Nuclear proliferation is essentially a problem relating to those countries which are multiplying nuclear weapons rapidly both in qualitative and quantitative terms. It is an abuse of the English language to term acquisition of a few nuclear weapons by a new country as proliferation.'[9] The reason for superpower concern that these weapons should not spread may have much to do with their respective perceptions of their dominant role in the international system, and the challenge to their superiority that may confront them if they do not have a monopoly on these weapons. In their congruent attitudes here the primary motivation of each springs from their common great-power status and probably only secondarily from any ideological concern. Fear of the destructive potential of these weapons may not necessarily play the major role, since if it were considered to be of overwhelming importance the superpowers would surely check their own proliferation. As Nye points out, however, the superpowers regard the 'relative risk' of increasing their own arsenals as smaller than the risks posed by non-nuclear states obtaining nuclear weapons.[10] To many non-nuclear states, especially in the Third World, such an attitude appears arrogant. Some comments on the respective attitudes of the USSR and US to the NPT are appropriate here.

One prominent US writer on the NPT has analysed US policy thus:

Avoidance of the spread of nuclear weapons has occupied a central role in US strategic and foreign policy since the dawn of the atomic age. Nuclear weapons proliferation has been viewed as incompatible with US security interests, and with the goal of maintaining a peaceful world order. It has been regarded as a threat to alliance cohesion and credibility; as a potential source for the enlargement and intensification of local and regional conflict; and as a generally complicating factor in the management of international politics.[11]

It can be seen from this quotation that US advocacy of the treaty is a product of its perception of its own national security which is closely bound up with the vision of its dominant role in world affairs and its desire to be the manager of those affairs. There is no hint that for the US the treaty was a stop-gap measure to discourage further horizontal proliferation while the US, USSR and UK proceeded to dismantle their own nuclear arsenals. While a cursory reading of the treaty might suggest that that was the purpose, especially on account of

Article 6, it now seems that such action may not have been seriously contemplated by the original formulators; if it was, it has long since been forgotten. The implication is that nuclear weapons are only safe in the hands of the original proliferators, the US, the UK and the USSR. Yet this argument does not stand in practice, for China and France, which developed the weapons in the 1960s, have so far acted 'responsibly' in as much as they have not put them to military use. While it is true that the nuclear-materials sales policy of both, especially France, have come under attack, it is equally true that the original three have apparently done nothing effective to hinder or prevent the development of nuclear weapons by a state like Israel, even though at least one of them, the US, has been in a good position to do so if she desired.[12]

Literature on the Soviet position, as compared with the US, is not prolific here in the West, and hence its stand is largely a matter for deduction. One Soviet author, Zheleznov, has put forward some fairly dubious arguments against proliferation:

the threat of nuclear war would be much greater if non-nuclear states were involved in the process of developing and stockpiling nuclear weapons. One can easily imagine the outcome of developments if nuclear weapons were also in the arsenals of conflicting parties. All this means that the further spread of nuclear weapons must be checked once and for all.[13]

This is a strange statement for a number of reasons. First, it assumes that non-nuclear states would not be as sensible as nuclear states in dealing with these weapons of mass destruction. While the superpowers may believe that they themselves have a monopoly on common sense, many Third World statesmen would disagree. Second, nuclear weapons are already in the arsenals of several conflicting parties, yet those parties have not resorted to their use. The USSR and US are in a state of perpetual conflict. Relations between the USSR and China have long been strained, and China and India have had several border clashes. Third, it is surprising that given the stated level of the threat of nuclear weapons, why is no mention made of the need to check vertical proliferation? It seems that the desire of both superpowers to retain nuclear weapons within an exclusive club is motivated less by fear of the potential of those weapons than by a desire to retain their position within the international hierarchy of states. Zheleznov's comments mirror the official Soviet government line. Speaking at the 1978 UN Special Session on Disarmament, Foreign Minister Gromyko said that 'Nuclear weapons, if they get into the hands of states in conflict with their neighbours, may become the detonator of a worldwide nuclear clash. We are tirelessly drawing attention to this danger to universal peace.'[14] There is no mention of the threat posed to world peace by superpower proliferation. Time and time again Soviet writers highlight the dangers of horizontal proliferation without due consideration of the vertical dimension of the problem. S. I. Kislyak says that 'The danger of nuclear catastrophe would increase enormously if a gradual increase of nuclear weapons on our planet occurred simultaneously with the acquisition of these weapons by new countries'.[15] The fact of the matter is that the nuclear arsenals of the superpowers have increased at a very *rapid* pace. Such statements do little to ease the anxiety of the non-nuclear states.

One thing that can be concluded from the American and Soviet attitudes outlined above is that for them the treaty represents an attempt to check horizontal nuclear proliferation; it is an *arms control* agreement. For the non-nuclear states who have become party to it, however, it represents an *arms reduction* agreement. These are two very different things. This profound difference in interpretation of course has far-reaching effects on an assessment of the implementation of the treaty. This can be seen clearly in the starkly different attitudes towards Article 6 on the part of the USSR, US and UK on the one hand, and the non-nuclear states, especially but not solely of the Third World, on the other.

COMPETING CONCEPTIONS OF ARTICLE 6

Differing attitudes toward Article 6 are revealed in the literature of the various states. Soviet writers often refer to this article, and attempt to refute Third World charges of Soviet non-compliance. Writers from the US and UK tend to ignore Article 6, concentrating on technological discussions rather than the fundamental political questions raised by non-compliance. Third World writers emphasise their perception of the crucial role of Article 6 in the NPT.

Referring to Article 6, the Soviet author Y. Tomlin has remarked that:

some of the signatory states . . . have been levelling sharp criticism at some of its [the NPTs] provisions. They tend to take a maximalist stand, ignoring or failing to reckon with the important fact that any international agreement has to take account of the views of a broad range of states. From the standpoint of one state or another, the Treaty may perhaps have some flaws, but it was elaborated to express, to a certain extent, the wishes of the whole community of states, and to be a kind of common denominator in the solution to the problem.[16]

It seems that when non-nuclear states ask nuclear signatories to the NPT to keep their side of the bargain, they are charged with being 'maximalist' or unreasonable. This is not surprising, since the three original nuclear powers see the treaty in terms of a mechanism to stop horizontal nuclear proliferation, and not as an arms-reduction agreement to control vertical proliferation. Yet invoking the numbers argument, as Tomlin does implicitly in his reference to the 'whole community', does nothing to strengthen the Soviet case. For the majority of states would welcome a halt to the superpower nuclear arms race. Later in the same article, Tomlin becomes more explicit in defence of Soviet compliance with Article 6, arguing that the Soviet Union has offered several types of reductions but the US or other states have failed to agree to mutual steps. He cites as examples Brezhnev's offer in 1974 to stop all underground nuclear-weapons tests, and his suggestion that the US and USSR withdraw ships and submarines carrying nuclear weapons from the Mediterranean. There is no mention of the possibility of unilateral action with regard to Article 6: either mutual concessions are negotiated by the superpowers, or none at all. (Indeed, this was reiterated explicitly by Foreign Minister Gromyko in 1978, when he suggested that the production of all types of nuclear weapons be ended, and that the production of new types of conventional weapons be banned. He added the proviso that talks concerning this, however, 'must be held with the participation of all the nuclear powers; such a complex problem cannot be resolved on a selective basis'.)[17] In a contradictory fashion, Tomlin goes on to state that 'there is no reason to agree with the assertions that Article 6 of the Treaty on Non-Proliferation is not being implemented. This kind of groundless tendentious criticism can do nothing to strengthen the Treaty or to promote any further progress on the talks on disarmament'.[18] This comment is highly surprising, given the preceding remark concerning the lack of enthusiasm with which Soviet overtures under Article 6 have been met by other nuclear powers. Is this compatible with progress?

While the Soviets have done little substantively to fulfil the requirements of Article 6 they do at least acknowledge its importance rather than dismiss it out of hand in the manner of the Americans and the British. Hence, S. I. Kislyak remarks:

The majority of states, including the Soviet Union, believe that the interests of world security and strict compliance with and the strengthening of the nonproliferation regime would be met by the adoption of practical measures to curb the nuclear arms race and bring about nuclear, in accordance with article 6 of the treaty, disarmament.[19]

From the point of view of the non-nuclear states, however, actions on the part of the nuclear powers, including the USSR, would surely speak louder than words.

American and British writings on Article 6 are noteworthy by their absence. The most usual approach on the rare occasions when the article is mentioned or alluded to at all, is to make reference to it either at the outset or at the conclusion of an essay. For example, one author remarks in the opening of his essay that 'until the superpowers can achieve substantial self-denial with respect to nuclear weapons, American efforts to dissuade other countries from acquiring nuclear weapons capabilities—or from at least reserving that option for themselves—will be less than fully convincing'.[20] The article rarely warrants any real discussion. One reason for this is that many of those writing in the field tend to be bureaucrats or government appointees; hence debate on the fundamental political problem is not something that they are eager to entertain or even perhaps think is important.[21] Again, the perception of the major nuclear powers of the treaty as an arms control agreement is influential here. When the political dimension *is* brought up, it may directly reflect the specific interpretation of the word 'proliferation', which depends largely on whether the author comes from a state which has the weapons or one which does not. Hence Charles Van Doren begins a paper arguing that 'the greatest challenge of non-proliferation policy is the political one of fostering and preserving the judgement by non-nuclear-weapon states that the acquisition of nuclear weapons would not be in their best interests'.[22] Evident here is the belief that the treaty should deal first and foremost with the problem of horizontal rather than vertical proliferation. While this is what one would expect to hear from someone who comes from a leading nuclear-weapon state, to be fair to those writers like Van Doren who are committed to peace, it must be stated that horizontal proliferation may be more destabilising than vertical proliferation since arms control thereby involves more governments.

Some authors are dismissive of Article 6. For Nye:

the Non-proliferation Treaty rests on more than just Article 6 . . . the Non-proliferation Treaty rests on a fairly firm basis that goes beyond the rhetoric over Article 4 and Article 6. That does not mean we do not have to be careful about Article 4 and 6, and indeed try to conform our behaviour better to them, but it means that we should also keep in perspective that there is a difference between rhetoric and underlying political reality.[23]

Hence the attitudes of the non-nuclear-weapon states, the majority of which are Third World states, are insensitively categorised as mere rhetoric; they are not something to be taken seriously. Political reality means that any consideration of them in superfluous.

Interestingly, the Soviets have been critical of the US attitude towards Article 6. Potter has suggested that the first signs of the USSR distancing itself from the US on account of this came in January 1984: 'The Soviets explicitly charged the US with failing to honour its article 6 NPT obligations'.[24] The Soviets are more sensitive than the US to their public image in the Third World.

In some ways the USSR is more stringent about the application of the treaty.[25] While neither have fulfilled their obligations under Article 6 to a satisfactory extent, the case against the US is somewhat stronger. For instance, Potter has drawn attention to the lack of progress on nuclear disarmament in general, but also specifically to the 'reluctance of the US to ratify the Salt II Treaty, the Threshold Test Ban Treaty, and the Peaceful Nuclear Explosion Treaty'.[26] Strong criticism can be levelled at both superpowers. One fairly neutral observer, Emeritus Professor Joseph Rotblat, has commented:

Article VI is the main bone of contention between many NPT members and the nuclear weapon States party to the Treaty. . . . The history of the nuclear arms race over the past 15 years throws very serious doubt on the good faith, as well as on the capability of the super-powers to fulfil their obligations, caught as they are in the action–reaction syndrome. Because of this, even during the 'on-periods' of negotiations on arms control, very little progress has been achieved and . . . the very few measures agreed to were dwarfed by the qualitative and quantitative intensifications of the arms race.[27]

Rotbalt points out that this was the main cause of the breakdown of the 1980 Review Conference to monitor the progress of the NPT. He adds that the incentive for the non-aligned countries to remain within the NPT diminishes when 'they can see no validity in a treaty systematically violated by its "privileged" members.'[28] He argues that the Third World states have a legitimate reason for concern with the lack of progress towards nuclear disarmament, for if a nuclear war occurred in the northern hemisphere, its effects would be felt in the southern hemisphere also.

Rotblat's views reflect accurately the views of many Third World statesmen. The vital status accorded to Article 6 is echoed in the words of a former president of Venezuela, Carlos Andrés Pérez:

Neither the Soviet Union nor the United States has pursued 'negotiations in good faith on effective measures relating to cessation of the nuclear arms race at an early date' as Article VI of the NPT states. The Soviet Union which in 1970, when it signed the Treaty, had 2,000 nuclear weapons now has 9,000 and the United States which then had 4,000 now has 11,000. The latter, in the face of universal protest, is assuming the responsibility of starting an accelerated arms race in outer space. Meanwhile, in the developing countries thousands of children are dying daily of hunger, pneumonia or enteritis while the world is spending a million and a half dollars in arms each minute . . . we are not resigned to hoping that the two super-powers reach an agreement on nuclear disarmament. We know that both have made solemn declarations on their objectives to eliminate nuclear arms. However, we also know that this formulation of objectives has no time limit. The world is looking for tangible results. This is a struggle for the right to life, which belongs to all nations, all peoples, those of today and those of the future.[29]

Extreme anger is evident in this statement. The moral and developmental arguments do not hold much sway in the calculations of the superpowers. However, the time-factor argument is more tangible to *all* parties involved. While on the surface Article 6 seemed to be a concession by the original nuclear powers, the lack of specific detail or time framework for its achievement have made it easy for the latter to evade fulfilment of their obligations under it. The patience of many non-nuclear states who were happy with the NPT fifteen years and more ago is wearing thin. Clearly, the superpowers do not themselves provide a very good example to Third World states who are considering nuclear proliferation, nor even those who might simply consider withdrawal from the treaty as a protest measure.[30] It is pertinent at this point to look at various arguments that have been forwarded to justify horizontal nuclear proliferation.

SECURITY THROUGH PROLIFERATION: A THIRD WORLD JUSTIFICATION

The most provocative Third World advocate of nuclear weapons for those states is surely Professor Ali Mazrui. Here attention is paid to his case for nuclear weapons for the black African states of Nigeria and Zaire, and looking into the future, a black-ruled South Africa (i.e. Azania). His ideas, however, can be applied more generally to the Third World.

Mazrui regards the NPT as a system 'designed to minimise the number of countries that have a nuclear weapon capacity, and ultimately intended especially to discourage Third World countries from going nuclear', and says that it can be regarded 'as an extension of the old philosophy of 'imperialism as a monopoly stage of warfare.'[31] There is no doubt in Mazrui's mind that the NPT represents superpower domination of the Third World:

From a Third World point of view, I do not believe the treaty is worth the
paper it is written on. And if I were to become president of a Third World
country, I would not hesitate to withdraw from it. Imperialism in the nuclear
age is the monopoly stage of nuclear technology.[32]

Both in response to this situation, and to make the
superpowers see sense and be shocked into halting the arms
race, Mazrui advocates a Third World challenge: the
nuclearisation of non-alignment. This would mean 'not only
using nuclear power for peaceful purposes, but using that
power to reduce the danger of East–West convulsion'.[33] He is
not blind to the problems, not least the likelihood of sub-
imperialism within the Third World. He compares the impact
of the atom on the Third World now to its impact on the
international system a few decades ago: it creates or reinforces
a hierarchy. Yet he believes the global benefits would outweigh
the regional costs. To go down the nuclear road is a political
decision for Mazrui: it has little to do with military strategy,
and much to do with the politics of dependency.

Dealing with the concept of a 'nuclear-free zone', Mazrui
suggests that the time for such a thing in Africa, and by
implication the rest of the Third World, has passed. He argues
that it made sense in the early 1960s, when France was
conducting nuclear tests in Africa. At that time, Nigeria, led by
Sir Abubaka Tafewa Balewa, broke off diplomatic relations
with France on account of those tests in the Sahara Desert.
Ghana under Kwame Nkrumah's leadership had gone so far as
to freeze French assets in protest at her violation of African
soil.[34] Mazrui advocates that now the time is ripe for key
African states to move towards the possession of nuclear
weapons as a means of raising Africa's peripheral position in
world affairs. The motivation is not primarily
military/strategic, despite the threat posed by South Africa's
military capability; the motivation for Mazrui at least is
primarily political (Edem Kodjo, outgoing secretary-general of
the Organisation of African Unity in 1983, speaking at the
Addis Ababa Summit in June of that year, advocated the
acquisition of nuclear weapons by black African states but
specifically to counter the physical threat to those states of the
South African nuclear capability, which, he argued, could only
be used against *them*. Indeed, he claimed that it was 'the duty of

those who are able to embark on the nuclear path'.[35]) Mazrui believes that the superpowers will only seriously undertake nuclear disarmament when they realise that they cannot prevent other states from acquiring them.

Mazrui's language is literary and emotive. He calls going nuclear 'a rite of passage' and a 'recovery of adulthood' for states which have suffered colonisation: 'No longer would the great powers be able to say that such and such a weapon is not for Africans and children under 16.'[36] Such language is little understood, and even less appreciated, in the US, UK and probably in the USSR as well. Only those states which have undergone the humiliation of colonisation could relate positively to it. However, what cannot escape even the least sympathetic observer is the presentation of the problem in highly political rather than the narrow, neutral, technological terms often favoured by the superpowers. The latter, especially the US and UK, tend to pose the problem in terms of technical constraints and so forth.

Ideas such as Mazrui's have thus been much criticised by the superpowers. Professor Anatoly Gromyko of the Soviet Union has argued:

The idea that the nuclear arms race can be halted if more countries participate in it is an extremely dangerous delusion. If new States acquire a few nuclear weapons and systems for their delivery, or even dozens of them, this cannot have a decisive impact on the global balance of nuclear arsenals that contain thousands of such weapons. On the contrary, this would make nuclear arms control more difficult, increase the global impact of the factor of uncertainty, breed distrust and mutual suspicions in international relations, and, I would say, would further strain the already tense 'nervous system' of nuclear politics.[37]

While some of the claims here are true, the statement is marred by a total lack of understanding of the Third World states' attitudes towards the NPT in general, and in particular the reasons why some may take the road of horizontal proliferation. Mazrui is not urging such proliferation in order to affect the overarching East–West military balance in favour of one side or the other; far from it. He is urging it to improve the political position of Third World states in the international system. The actions of Third World states are not always to be measured in terms of the East–West balance; they have indigenous desires, aims and requirements which cannot be interpreted within the boundaries of a simple East–West framework. Moreover, distrust and suspicion are bred not only by horizontal proliferation but by vertical proliferation also, and it is certainly the case that many non-nuclear states are becoming distrustful of the superpowers' commitment to the NPT as a whole. Of course, Gromyko's statement is self-serving; it stresses the superpowers' perceptions of why non-nuclear states should refrain from going nuclear, without even a mention of the negative aspects of the superpowers' own proliferation.

There are some writers from the developed world, however, who advocate the spread of nuclear weapons, but these are few in number. One among them, Kenneth Waltz, has written a much-cited monograph entitled 'More May Be Better'.[38] There Waltz concludes that 'the gradual spread of nuclear weapons is better than no spread and better than rapid spread.'[39] On American security guarantees, he says:

We are wisely reluctant to give guarantees, but we then should not expect to decide how other countries are to provide for their security. As a neighbour of China, India no doubt feels more secure, and can behave more reasonably, with a nuclear-weapons capability than without it. The thought applies as well to Pakistan, India's neighbour. We damage our relations with such countries by badgering them about nuclear weapons while being unwilling to guarantee their security. Under such circumstances they, not we, should decide what their national interests are. Nations attend to their security in ways that they think best. The fact that so many more countries can make muclear weapons than do make them says more about the hesitation of countries to enter the nuclear business than about the effectiveness of American policy. . . . No one policy is right for all countries. We should ask what our interests in regional peace and stability require in particular instances. We should ask also what the interests of other countries require before putting pressure on them. . . . The measured selective spread of nuclear weapons does not run against our interests and can increase the security of some states at a price they can afford.[40]

Waltz's arguments for horizontal proliferation are of a very different kind to those of Mazrui. While they may not find support among US policy-makers, they will at least be comprehensible to them. Waltz's case is based on a very realistic assessment of the current extent of nuclear know-how throughout the world, which cannot be confined within territorial borders, and on a similar assessment of the current pace of horizontal proliferation with and without the acquiescence of the superpowers (especially the US), and also of the political value of sovereign equality. Indeed, it is on the importance of the value of sovereignty that Mazrui and Waltz share common ground. While the argument of one is based on emotional, political and ethical grounds, and that of the other on pragmatic grounds, the fundamental beliefs which inform each are very similar. For the superpowers, such convictions find a place in rhetoric but rarely in practice.

HOLDOUTS FROM THE NON-PROLIFERATION TREATY

About one-quarter of the states in the international political system have not accepted the NPT. Almost all of these are in the Third World. France's position is exceptional: a developed nuclear-weapon state which is not party to the NPT. The only other self-confessed nuclear-weapon state not party to the treaty is China. However, it is common knowledge that Israel and South Africa have nuclear weapons, even though the public position of each is very ambiguous, with neither having directly admitted possession. Neither has signed the treaty. It may also be the case that India, which has held out against signing the NPT, has a nuclear bomb. Apart from these, there are a significant number of states which are on the verge of being able to produce a nuclear weapon. These are Argentina, Brazil, Pakistan and Spain, and along with Israel, South Africa and India they are categorised as 'near-nuclear' or 'nuclear threshold' states. As well as these states, there are a large number of Third World states who have shown no interest in developing nuclear weapons but who have still refused to sign. The Third World states that are financially strong are noteworthy by their absence from the NPT. An important factor contributing to their refusal is the threat they perceive to Islam via Israel. Hence the Gulf states of Oman, Qatar, Saudi Arabia and the United Arab Emirates have not signed. There are others which have not signed because they regard the NPT as institutionalising the prevailing power hierarchy in the international system and infringing sovereign rights. Thus it is politically unacceptable for states such as Algeria, Tanzania, Mozambique, Zimbabwe, Zambia, Niger and Malawi to join the NPT. The states with which we are most concerned here are the threshold group, since they pose the greatest challenge presently to the non-proliferation regime and hence to what they regard as the explicit designs of the superpowers.

The main motivation of the threshold states for going along the nuclear road is without a doubt political. Goldblat and Lomas, who have undertaken the production of a highly informative volume on the subject,[41] deal with the threshold states in pairs, and with each pair they find politics to be at the root of the desire for proliferation. The reader may not find this surprising, for states are after all at bottom political beings. However, it is this political imperative on the part of other states that the nuclear-weapon states have failed to be cognisant of (or perhaps they understand it all too well, and hence the NPT!). Goldblat and Lomas put their point across succinctly:

> The policy of rejecting international control over Argentina's nuclear programme appears to express more a desire to inflate the country's international prestige than the need to safeguard its security. . . . from the point of view of national security, there seems to be no justification for a Brazilian nuclear bomb. . . . given the geopolitical circumstances in the Middle East, nuclear deterrence is hardly likely to be a trump card over the long term. . . . South Africa is under no threat of external aggression. . . . there is the danger of mass insurgency. . . . but nuclear weapons would hardly be useful in dealing with such a danger.[42]

All of these examples suggest that there can be very compelling domestic, regional and global reasons why states are unwilling to forgo the nuclear-weapon option. Their paper outlines some of the domestic and regional reasons, such as the prestige of the military within a country, or the status of a country within a region, or sectoral prestige, as with the idea of an Islamic bomb,[43] and so forth. On the global level, many reasons come into operation. There is the strong sense in which the non-proliferation regime is perceived as being cut in the same mould as so many of the other regimes governing activities such as money and trade, but this one is special because it arose as a result of the collusion of the two superpowers and it has been sustained by their continued cooperation on this matter. Third

World states have charged the IMF, as the linchpin of the international monetary regime, with enhancing international security at the expense of the national security of Third World states. Their charge against the NPT, as the cornerstone of the non-proliferation system, is that it protects international security, as defined by the superpowers, while discriminating against the security needs of the non-nuclear, especially those of the Third World. What follows is a more detailed analysis of the attitude of one Third World nuclear-threshold state, India, to the acquisition of nuclear weapons.

The Indian position is interesting. Girilal Jain, editor of the *Times of India*, has explained India's position on the nuclear issue thus:

India's nuclear policy must be seen as the product of tensions between modernization, and the external technological dependence it involves, and Indian nationalism, hostile to external restrictions on the country's decision-making processes, as well as between the technocratic plans of Nehru and the philosophy of Gandhi, in which over time the former have proved victorious.'[44]

At the time of the NPT negotiations, opinion was far from unanimous in India. Advocates of the nuclear bomb for India, such as K. Subrahmanyam, director of the Institute of Defence Studies and Analyses, argued that only through nuclear weapons would India be able to have a credible defence posture against nuclear-weapon states.[45] Such a position was supported by the fact that China and India had experienced military conflict in the autumn of 1962, and China had held her first nuclear tests in October 1964. Hence many in India believed that China, a hostile neighbour, would soon be a nuclear weapon state. Indian opponents to the nuclear road framed their arguments in terms of the prohibitive cost for a country in such need of economic development and increased social welfare.[46] A few added the thought that a nuclear India might provoke a similar response from Pakistan, and hence another type of arms race would occur. R. D. Jones has argued that neither of these two lobby groups predominated, since most support was forthcoming for the position that India should retain the nuclear-weapon *option*, which amounted to neither an acceptance of the bomb, nor a rejection of it, but placed significant obstacles in the way of India signing the NPT.[47]

During the 1960s India had played a formative role in the international debate on nuclear weapons. She joined the Partial Test Ban Treaty in 1963, which prohibited atmospheric testing, and championed a comprehensive nuclear-test ban. The Indian position through the mid-1960s was that nuclear weapons were inherently evil, and that there was no difference between peaceful nuclear explosions and nuclear-weapons tests. Technologically, this is correct. If there is a difference, then it is one of intention, but of course an interpretation of intention rests, like beauty, in the eye of the beholder. India made several initiatives on the nuclear proliferation issue at the UN General Assembly and UN committees during this period, and she was always striving for the most stringent controls.

The Chinese nuclear test in 1964 undoubtedly had a profound effect on Indian thinking on the nuclear issue. After that date Indian representatives pushed harder for a freeze on the production of weapons by the nuclear states, and gradually India came to present the first and fundamental step in any non-proliferation treaty as action by the nuclear states to stop production and then to reduce their nuclear arsenals. Chakravarty, who represented India at the UN Disarmament Commission, said in 1965 that 'some countries may find it necessary, in the interests of their own security, to acquire nuclear weapons, if proliferation is allowed to go on.'[48] Another Indian representative, Trivedi, developed this argument at other UN committees later that year. 'Opposition to the concept of nuclear monopoly or privileged club-membership is thus our fundamental response in any examination of a draft treaty or a convention on non-proliferation.'[49] India's perception of the proposed NPT at the time was becoming increasingly sharpened by the inherent inequalities between nuclear and non-nuclear states, made more acute for her on account of developments in China. These developments made her own security dilemma all the more difficult, especially given her uneasy relations with that state. To that, however, was added the perception of grave injustice by a major Third World state which had not all that long ago won the struggle for political independence and now perceived itself as being asked to accept the institutionalisation of a power hierarchy in which it saw itself severely disadvantaged. This was politically unacceptable.

India gave several explicit reasons for rejecting the NPT at the UN in 1968, and interestingly, most of them revolved around the inequality argument. The treaty was unacceptable because it failed to prevent vertical proliferation; because its obligations were unbalanced and institutionalised discrimination between nuclear-weapon haves and have-nots; because the clause on disarmament had no specific requirements or time framework; because technical dependence was heightened by the fact that safeguards would apply to non-nuclear-weapon states but not to nuclear-weapon states regarding peaceful uses of nuclear energy; and because China's proliferation, a particular problem for India, was not constrained at all.[50] In Jones's words, 'India wished to (a) refuse acceptance of second class status; (b) avoid international controls on indigenous nuclear activities that did not apply to all states; and (c) hedge against uncertainties about the intentions and capabilities of an adversary, namely, China.'[51] Clearly, the case for respect and recognition of sovereign equality was uppermost in the Indian government's attitude to the NPT in 1968. India's physical size and weight of numbers, its relative scientific and technical expertise, as well as its leadership role among the newly independent states, enabled that state to defy the wishes of the superpowers in a manner in which many very small, weak, sparsely populated states of the Third World would find difficult. For many of them, demonstrations of sovereign authority would bring few tangible results, while joining the NPT might bring with it advantages. States like Bhutan, Chad, Gabon, Gambia, Cameroon and Burkina Faso could not conceivably develop their own nuclear weapons. The Third World states like India, which are classified as near-nuclear, also tend to be the states which by Third World standards have relatively large indigenous pools of technological expertise. South Korea and Taiwan also have such assets, and indeed, while neither are officially classified as nuclear-threshold states, and while both have joined the NPT, some question-marks have remained over how far their nuclear developments have taken them along the road to the construction of weapons.[52] Their commitment to the NPT has come into question, particularly in the South Korean case.

By not joining the NPT, India has kept open the *option* of developing nuclear weapons, and this has been as much— probably more—a political manoeuvre than a military one. Ever since 1968 she has maintained her commitment to nuclear disarmament. Yet publicly the explosion of a nuclear device underground in the Rajasthan desert in 1974 has resulted in a certain ambiguity in Indian policy and intentions. The US and USSR have been highly critical of the action. It was the first nuclear explosion to emanate from a peaceful nuclear energy programme rather than one designed for weapons production. It caused alarm because it demonstrated that 'as nuclear power programs spread, much of the capability to generate nuclear weapons spreads with it.'[53] Moreover, the context of the push for more nuclear power generation which would probably follow from the increased oil prices of 1973, heightened concern. Perhaps greatest indignation was caused by the fact that 'any such poverty-stricken, aid-receiving country of brown-skinned people should seek to make its way into the 'nuclear weapons club'' '.[54] Indian defiance of superpower designs was of great political significance, both for her, for them and for the Third World. Yet this demonstration of independence was not met by any effective sanctions from the superpowers; indeed, Spector has remarked that 'India has enjoyed cordial and expanding relations with East and West since 1974.'[55] He says that this is in line with the US attitude to other potential or real proliferators, especially Israel, which has probably been able to make nuclear weapons since the late 1960s or early 1970s, and South Africa since 1977.[56] In their response to these developments, the superpowers have to take account not only of their desire for horizontal non-proliferation, but also other priorities. Thus, if Pakistan were to develop nuclear weapons, while technically under US law the US would immediately have to cut off aid, in practice her response might well be very different. For, as Nye has remarked, 'You cannot pretend that you are never going to play with Pakistan again, so long as Pakistan is located where it is and so long as there are countries like India, Afghanistan and the Soviet Union.'[57]

CONCLUSION

From the point of view of Third World states (even those who have joined the NPT), the nuclear non-proliferation regime in its present form institutionalises inequality between nuclear-weapon states and non-nuclear-weapon states. Several important Third World states have refused to join the NPT, and unlike most other international regimes governing vital areas of national policy, key states have been successful in their defiance of the superpowers' wishes. While their motivations have been primarily political, the spread of nuclear weapons will increase the military-security input in their defiance. However, concentration on the near-nuclear states should not allow us to forget that a full quarter of the world's states are not party to the NPT, and most of these are not on the verge of developing nuclear weapons. Moreover, both these, and the threshold states, and many non-nuclear states party to the NPT, have long championed the idea of a comprehensive test-ban which would prohibit all nuclear-weapons testing in a universal and non-discriminatory fashion. The superpowers, particularly the US, have been unwilling to agree to such a measure. Lewis Dunn, assistant director of the US Arms Control and Disarmament Agency, has remarked that:

Making a complete nuclear test ban the litmus test of arms control diverts energies away from the negotiation of deep and meaningful arms reductions. Only those reductions are the true first step towards a world in which the threat of nuclear war no longer exists and towards the elimination of the discrimination between nuclear-weapon States sought by Article VI.[58]

Yet the truth of the matter is that not even these arms reductions have been achieved by the superpowers, and the latter have displayed little evidence of commitment to *all* the clauses in the NPT. Some states are more equal than others in the NPT, and some clauses are also more equal than others! It is not only Third World states who are dissatisfied with this situation. Olaf Palme, former prime minister of Sweden has urged that 'If authority is to remain with the Treaty . . . the nuclear-weapon states should live up to the spirit and letter of their obligations . . . [they] have the key to progress in the work to prevent both horizontal and vertical proliferation of nuclear arms.'[59]

On 28 January 1985 the New Delhi Declaration went out to the superpowers in particular and the world in general.[60] The declaration represented the maturation of ideas resulting from an initiative in May 1984 by Prime Minister Indira Gandhi and five other world leaders. Following her assassination, her son Rajiv took her place among these leaders from four continents—Nyerere of Tanzania, de la Madrid of Mexico, Raul Alfonsin of Argentina, Andreas Papandreou of Greece and Olaf Palme of Sweden—to call for an immediate ban on the testing and production of nuclear weapons and to halt their deployment in outer space.[61] Gandhi stated that while India had exploded a nuclear device in 1974, it had done so for peaceful purposes, and it had no intention of developing nuclear weapons. He urged the superpowers to follow suit and undertake *serious* talks in Geneva to eliminate nuclear weapons. These leaders stood by the belief that security for the majority of states in the world was more likely to be protected by a comprehensive test-ban than by an unequal treaty which seemed to provide greater security for a privileged few than for the majority. The New Delhi Declaration by implication highlighted the fact that ultimately security is not the product of the fulfilment of a particular military equation. Arms alone will never be enough to protect any state. Arbatov has written that 'the problem of security, political by nature, can be solved only by political means'.[62] Arms that increase one state's security, decrease the security of other states, and a vicious circle is established. In their attitude towards the nuclear non-proliferation regime, Third World states which are party to the NPT and those who are not, clearly acknowledge the importance of this political dimension. They now await the time when the superpowers' actions show that they too have recognised this. The criticisms voiced by the Third World of the non-proliferation regime and their efforts to change that regime stand out among the battles they have fought for regime change, particularly since here they oppose a relatively united front of East and West, of US and USSR. In this particular battle they see themselves fighting not only to improve their own security but to increase the security of mankind.

NOTES

1. For the treaty, see J. Goldblat, (ed.), *Non-Proliferation: The Why and the Wherefore*, Taylor & Francis for SIPRI, London and Philadelphia, 1985, Appendix 1, pp. 247–50.
2. J. Goldblat, 'The Third Review Conference of the Nuclear Non-Proliferation Treaty', *Bulletin of Peace Proposals* 17, 1 (1986), p. 13.
3. Goldblat, *Non-Proliferation*, p. 249.
4. D. Keohane, 'Nuclear Non-Proliferation', *Yearbook of World Affairs*, 1981, p. 11.
5. T. B. Millar, 'The Nuclear Non-Proliferation Treaty and Superpower Condominium', in C. Holbraad (ed.), *Superpowers and World Order*, Australia National University Press, Canberra, 1971, p. 64.
6. A. K. Ray, 'Third World Perspectives on Security', in J. Simpson, (ed.), *The International Non-Proliferation Regime in the 1990s*, Proceedings of the Sarnia Symposium, 17–20 March 1986, Cambridge University Press, Cambridge, 1987.
7. Keohane.
8. R. F. Goheen, 'Problems of Proliferation: US Policy and the Third World', *World Politics*, January 1983, p. 194.
9. K. Subrahmanyam, 'The Link Between Horizontal and Vertical Proliferation', in S. A. Khan, (ed.), *Nuclear War, Nuclear Proliferation and Their Consequences*, Proceedings of the Fifth International Colloquium organised by the Group De Bellerive, 27–9 June 1985, Geneva, Clarendon Press, Oxford, 1986, p. 136.
10. J. Nye, 'Prospects for Nonproliferation', in R. W. Jones, C. Merlini, J. F. Pilat and W. C. Potter (eds.), *The Nuclear Suppliers and Nonproliferation: International Policy Choices*, Lexington Books, Lexington and Toronto, 1985, p. 220.
11. L. Scheinman and J. Pilat, 'Toward a More Reliable Supply: US Nuclear Exports and Non-Proliferation Policy', paper presented at the Sarnia Symposium on The International Nuclear Non-Proliferation Regime in the 1990s, Guernsey, 17–20 March 1986.
12. L. Spector, 'Proliferation: Silent Spread', *Foreign Policy* 58 (Spring 1985), pp. 57–61.
13. R. Zheleznov, 'Atomic Power and Non-Proliferation of Nuclear Weapons' *International Affairs* (Moscow), (February 1977, p. 50.
14. Reprinted in *Survival* 20, 5 (September–October 1978), pp. 224–6.
15. S. I. Kislyak, 'A Soviet Perspective on the Future of Nonproliferation', in Jones, Merlini, Pilat and Potter, p. 211.
16. Y. Tomlin, 'Nuclear Non-Proliferation', *International Affairs* (Moscow), December 1974.

17. Statement by A. Gromyko, reprinted in *Survival* 20, 5, (September–October 1978), pp. 224–6.
18. *Ibid.*, p. 35.
19. Kislyak, p. 217.
20. Goheen, p. 194.
21. See, for instance, most of the edited volumes cited in this chapter. International conferences on the international nuclear non-proliferation regime have often hardly warranted a mention of, let alone a paper on, Article 6 and its crucial political dimension. Yet for the majority of states in the world, that article is as important for the credibility of the regime as the horizontal spread of nuclear weapons—perhaps more important.
22. C. Van Doren, 'The Outlook for Safeguards and Technical Constraints', in Simpson.
23. J. Nye, 'Prospects for Nonproliferation', in Jones, Merlini, Pilat and Potter, pp. 222–3.
24. W. C. Potter, 'US–Soviet Cooperative Measures for Nonproliferation', in Jones, Merlini, Pilat and Potter, p. 12.
25. This is especially the case in their attitude towards the supply of materials to non-nuclear weapon states for peaceful purposes. The Soviets have pushed, to no avail, for 'full-scope safeguards', which would mean that all nuclear facilities of the recipient state would come under inspection, not simply the facility for which the material is intended. Only this, they maintain, would safeguard the complete nuclear fuel cycle in non-nuclear states, and ensure that no weapons were being developed. The Soviets would like to see full-scope safeguards applied to any recipient, not simply recipients who are party to the NPT. It is not only the intentions of the governments of non-nuclear states which they fear—it is also the intentions of big business. Zheleznov has expressed such a fear:

Unfortunately, far from all the exporters of nuclear materials and equipment share this approach [i.e. the need for full-scope safeguards]. Any indulgence with respect to control over nuclear exports would play into the hands of the capitalist monopolies, which willy-nilly help spread nuclear weapons in their drive for superprofits. . . . The task is, however, to replace the rivalry involved in marketing atomic materials and equipment by reliable cooperation in the peaceful uses of atomic energy, backed up with the necessary guarantees against uncontrolled use of this great achievement of the human mind.

See Zheleznov, p. 52.
26. Potter, pp. 11–12.
27. J. Rotblat, 'The Foundations for a Strengthened Non-Proliferation Regime', in Khan, p. 65.
28. *Ibid.*
29. C. Perez, 'The Nuclear Arms Race: A View from the South', in Khan, p. 305.

30. Oye Ogunbadejo, 'Africa's Nuclear Capability', *Journal of Modern African Studies* 22, 1 (1984), 22.
31. Ali Mazrui, 'In Search of Pax Africana', *The Listener*, 13 December 1979, p. 77.
32. Ali Mazrui, *The African Condition: A Political Diagnosis*, London, 1980, p. 122.
33. Mazrui, *the Listener*, 13 December 1979, p. 77.
34. Ogunbadejo, p. 21.
35. See *Keesings Contemporary Archives*, Bristol, 1983, p. 32420.
36. Mazrui, *The Listener*, 13 December 1979, p. 79.
37. Anatoly Gromyko, 'A Soviet Perspective', in Khan, p. 129.
38. K. Waltz, *More May Be Better*, Adelphi Paper no. 171, IISS, London, 1981.
39. *Ibid.*, p. 28.
40. *Ibid.*, p. 28–9.
41. Goldblat, *Non-Proliferation*.
42. Goldblat and Lomas, 'The Near Nuclear States in 1995', in Simpson.
43. On the Islamic bomb, see Z. Khalilzad, 'Pakistan and the Bomb', *Survival*, 21 (1979).
44. G. Jain, 'India', in Goldblat, *Non-Proliferation*, p. 89.
45. For K. Subramanyam's view on contemporary proliferation, see his article 'The Link Between Horizontal and Vertical Proliferation', in Khan.
46. For a discussion of costs, see Bhabani Sen Gupta, *Nuclear Weapons: Policy Options for India*, Sage, New Delhi, 1983, ch. 1.
47. R. W. Jones, 'India', in Goldblat, *Non-Proliferation*, p. 105.
48. Quoted in Jones, *ibid.*, p. 103.
49. *Ibid.*
50. *Ibid.*, p. 104.
51. *Ibid.*
52. Joseph Yager, 'South Korea', in Goldblat, *Non-Proliferation*, pp. 197–206. See also George Quester, 'Taiwan' in Goldblat, *Non-Proliferation*, pp. 227–34.
53. Goheen, p. 196.
54. *Ibid.*, p. 197.
55. Spector, p. 59.
56. *Ibid.*, p. 53.
57. Nye, p. 225.
58. L. Dunn, 'The Non-Proliferation Treaty: An American Perspective', in Khan, p. 387.
59. O. Palme, 'The Threat of Proliferation', in Khan, p. 25.
60. John Elliot, 'Gandhi Hosts Six Nation Nuclear Arms Talks', *The Times*, 29 January 1985.
61. The Declaration is quoted at length in Khan, p. 304.
62. Arbatov, in Khan, p. 320.

7 Jamaica and the Search for Security in the 1970s

The purpose of this chapter is to demonstrate the great problems facing Third World states when they try to increase their security by exercising the sovereign right to choose domestic economic, social and political systems and foreign policies. The Jamaican example presented here shows the intricate and intimate relationship between the domestic and international spheres of policy for such states, and the denial by external actors of the rights inherent in sovereign statehood. During the period under review, Jamaica's search for the expression of sovereignty and for increased security was constrained, and in some ways even controlled, by external agents—not only states, but multinationals, international institutions, the market and even the weather. An independent course of action by Jamaica would be no small feat in such circumstances.[1]

In October 1980 Michael Manley was heavily defeated in a national election that he himself, as prime minister, had called eighteen months before it was constitutionally due. Manley had been elected to office first in 1972 and then again in 1976. By 1980 Jamaica was in a state of economic collapse, and social tensions revealed themselves in the mounting tide of violence overcoming Jamaican society. Manley had decided to go to the people and present them with two clear-cut alternatives. The first was that of voting-in the Jamaican Labour Party (JLP), under Edward Seaga, which in effect would mean an acceptance of IMF policies and all the social, economic and political consequences that carried with it. In contrast, the second was that of re-electing the People's National Party

(PNP), led by Manley himself, which would mean a rejection of IMF policies and the adoption of a new, largely untried road to economic development with all the inherent uncertainties that involved. In the event, 58 per cent of the electorate opted for the JLP, and only 41 per cent for the incumbent PNP.[2]

Primary attention is thus paid in this case study to the relationship between the IMF and Jamaica in the 1970s, in order to discern how far the IMF influenced the domestic economic and by implication, socio-political, face of Jamaica. However, the context is much wider, and as the story unfolds, the influence of other actors becomes apparent. The chapter is divided into five parts, each of which can be read as a self-contained unit; together, they are intended to form a fairly comprehensive picture of the range of problems contributing to Jamaican insecurity and of the difficulties facing the two democratically elected Manley governments in trying to decrease Jamaica's vulnerability. The first part presents an overall survey of the Jamaican economy, focusing specifically on the fate of her main export earners. The second part looks at Manley's response to the very poor economic situation, in terms of his general strategy or ideology: democratic socialism. The third section deals in detail with the governments' fiscal policies, concentrating specifically on its relationship with the IMF. The fourth section assesses the significance of the general election result of 1980 for national attitudes towards the IMF and democratic socialism. The fifth and final part, from a consideration of all the above, offers some suggestions as to whether the IMF was guilty of illicit intervention in Jamaica, disregarding her sovereignty, and draws some general conclusions about the possibility of Third World states making themselves more secure in the international political system.

THE JAMAICAN ECONOMY: A GENERAL SURVEY

This section looks at the major foreign-exchange earning industries in Jamaica in the 1970s. A recurrent theme is that the problems besetting them were very largely outside government control. Consequently, the room for manoeuvre of the two governments during this period was very limited, and their achievements inevitably few.

When Manley first became prime minister in 1972, he inherited an economy which, in comparison with other Third World states, seemed fairly promising. Over the previous decade, GDP had risen from 252 million pounds sterling to 516 million, and per capita income had risen from 137 pounds to 232 pounds per annum.[3] However, these figures were deceptive.

Apart from the structural weaknesses besetting most developing economies as producers of primary products, the Jamaican economy was struggling in the face of certain particular problems. For example, the trading deficit, which had increased from 15 million pounds to 85.6 million in the 1962–71 period,[4] was worsening at an alarming rate when Manley took up office. This was due in part to the drying up of large capital inflows in the form of foreign investment in the bauxite and alumina industry. The Shearer government had not planned for the extension of such inflows. An additional factor was the size of the food import bill, which Jamaica could ill afford and which to a certain extent was unnecessary.[5] Unemployment in Jamaica had reached sizeable and chronic proportions (around 25 per cent), and hence there existed a ready pool of labour which could be channelled into agricultural development. Consumption was by far outrunning production, and the general economic picture was one of despondency and gloom rather than the optimism suggested by the figures quoted earlier.

The economic history of Jamaica over the period 1972–80 provides an excellent example of how the ruinous vagaries of fate can afflict those countries reliant on the production of primary products. Throughout this period, natural factors compounded with those of the world market to disrupt severely the production of sugar and bananas, two of Jamaica's biggest export earners. In the case of bauxite and alumina, a slackening of demand in the US market and the calculated action of the multinationals added to the natural problems involved in maintaining the competitiveness of a product whose occurrence was widespread rather than restricted to one or a few states.

The Banana and Sugar Industries
In the case of bananas, drought fluctuated with floods to devastate the main exporting parish of St Mary's.[6] National output fell from around 180,000 tons per annum in the mid-1960s, to 70,000 tons in 1974,[7] thereby substantially inflating the level of overheads per ton. These climatic problems were compounded by problems of quality control, which to a large extent were due to the nature of the terrain and the poor transportation infrastructure. Market factors, such as the dumping of bananas from the Ivory Coast, Surinam and Martinique by Fyffes in late December 1972, led to a massive price slump in Britain, Jamaica's largest market, of West Indian bananas from 102 pounds sterling to 72 pounds a ton.[8] By 1974 the Jamaican Banana Board was losing 20 pounds on every ton shipped to Britain.[9]

The story of the sugar industry is similar. Natural disasters played a major role in the fall of output from 500,000 tons in 1966,[10] to 290,000 tons in 1977,[11]—the lowest figure in thirty years. Whereas drought hampered the development of the crop, heavy rains resulted in a reduction in the sucrose content. No sugar was exported to Canada after 1966, nor to the US after 1973, because of the shortfall. Moreover, that exported to Britain at the beginning of 1974 under the Commonwealth Agreed Price of 61 pounds sterling a ton, was being sold at one-tenth of the world market price.[12] While charges of inefficient management have been levelled at the government which owned the sugar estates, it should be noted that the estates were uneconomic when operated by the multinationals. This was a major contributory factor in their decision to sell to the government. The sugar industry was in need of complete modernisation, and this would be a costly affair. Moreover, additional labour was needed in the industry, yet despite high, rising unemployment, it was difficult to attract. There were two main reasons for this. First, there was still a stigma attached to the industry as a hangover from the days of slavery. Second, conditions of employment in the industry were very bad; wages were low, hours long and employment insecure. Moreover, the cane-cutters who were syphoned off into the US labour pool found wages there much higher, and after cutting cane in Florida they had no inclination to cut in Jamaica. They returned with their new-found wealth, albeit temporary, and with changed expectations of their job's worth.

The Bauxite and Alumina Industry

The one promising light in the Jamaican economy was the bauxite and alumina industry. However, even this example is a testimony to the very limited amount of control that Third World states can exert over their own economies, and how much is left to fate and the market, and the owners of capital.

When Manley came to power, the bauxite and alumina industry accounted for more than 40 per cent of Jamaica's foreign-exchange earnings[13] and employed over half of those people working in Jamaica. The industry had been developing for over twenty years in the hands of multinationals, mainly from the US. These companies owned upwards of 80 per cent of the known bauxite reserves in Jamaica.[14] While they held such a tight grip on the Jamaican economy, they were unwilling to encourage local participation in the running of the industry.

In 1974 Manley decided to renegotiate the contracts with these companies to the advantage of Jamaica. This decision was prompted by the massive increase in the import bill expected in 1974, which to all intents and purposes was unavoidable. The increase was due mainly, but not exclusively, to the rise in the price of oil. Jamaica's oil bill for 1974 was expected to be at least 100 million US dollars more than it had been in 1973.[15] The import of oil could not be cut back because the operation of the bauxite and alumina industry depended on this fuel. Such increased costs would be devastating for a problem-ridden Third World economy like Jamaica's. Moreover, it was not only oil that resulted in a rise in the import bill: wheat costing 78 US dollars per metric ton in December 1972, cost 243 dollars per metric ton by December 1973[16] (partly due to the wheat deal between the US and the USSR), and this was a staple food in Jamaica. Hence, foreign reserves standing at around 150 million US dollars in 1972, dropped to well below 100 million dollars in 1974.[17]

The bauxite levy called for by Manley was a direct response to the anticipated massive increase in the 1974 import bill. It was also regarded by Manley as a duty, since it was incumbent upon him as prime minister to assert Jamaica's sovereign authority and independence, and to ensure that the wealth of Jamaica was enjoyed by Jamaicans, in Jamaica, and not channelled abroad. Justifying his stand, Manley stated, 'The renegotiation of contracts with aluminum companies is not only a necessity and a right of a sovereign nation but an obligation to the people. These considerations outweigh the sanctity of contractual agreements.'[18] The measure was a demonstrative act of sovereign authority, and directly reflects the arguments and values soon to be formally established in the Charter of Economic Rights and Duties of States.

Before imposing the levy, Manley visited Kissinger in March 1974 to inform him of the pending bauxite negotiations and of Jamaica's objectives. Jamaica did not want a monopoly price for bauxite, merely a fair price. The US government had an interest in the success of the forthcoming negotiations, since its Overseas Private Investment Corporation had a 470 million dollar guarantee covering US investment in Jamaica, should expropriation occur.[19]

The bauxite companies put up a stiff vocal resistance, but there was little they could do. They argued that the contracts prohibited an increase in the taxes charged to them, or in the levies paid, unless the government and the companies were in agreement.[20] Alcoa, Kaiser and Reynolds lodged protests at the World Bank's International Centre for the Settlement of Investment Disputes[21] and asked for arbitration; but that body was powerless in the face of the Jamaican government's refusal to submit counter-memorials. Twenty million pounds sterling was paid by the six companies as the levy for the first quarter of 1974.[22] David Coore, the finance minister, hoped that the levy would bring in up to 200 million US dollars in 1974,[23] and thereby offset the increase in import costs. Kaiser was the first company to reach an agreement with the government, (possibly because it was most dependent on Jamaica for procuring bauxite), in November 1974.[24] The Jamaican government was to get a 51 per cent share in the company's operations in Jamaica, and a 7.5 per cent production levy was imposed,[25] based on the US market price of an aluminium ingot.

On the face of it, the Jamaican government had scored a resounding victory; yet it was not long before there sounded a hollow ring. By October 1975 bauxite production in Jamaica was reduced to only 75 per cent of the rated capacity.[26] The Revere company cited a cutback in demand for aluminium in the US market and announced that it would temporarily suspend bauxite production in Jamaica.[27] This decline came as a blessing in disguise for Revere, since its Jamaican plant was uneconomical anyway. Strikes over wage negotiations led production figures to plummet and resulted in the closure of a 1.2-million-ton plant operated by the Aluminium Parties of Jamaica.[28] Since bauxite was Jamaica's major foreign-exchange earner, the decline of the industry in 1975 contributed very largely to a negative growth rate of 2 per cent that year.[29]

With this decline in view, 1976 witnessed another increase in the bauxite levy, which it was estimated would bring in an extra 13 million US dollars in revenue for the government.[30] The government continued its stated policy of taking over a majority holding in the companies, and in 1977, Reynolds Mines was taken over.[31] The outlook in the industry was somewhat brighter in the early months of 1977, as a recovery in the US market for alumina augured well for an increase in bauxite production in Jamaica. However, even this hope did not hold up, for in that year the multinationals still produced only 75 per cent of the rated capacity of 16 million tons of bauxite, and only 71 per cent of the rated capacity of 3 million tons of alumina.[32] Moreover, Jamaica's share in the US market fell from 25 per cent to 17 per cent over the 1974–7 period.[33] This represented a percentage drop far out of proportion with the drop in demand. It represented a definite turn away from Jamaica to other sources. It is reflected also in a breakdown of percentages for various companies. For example, Alcoa relied on Jamaica for 70 per cent of its bauxite in 1974, and only 38 per cent in 1976.[34] The implications for Jamaica were great and can be demonstrated by reference to a few simple statistics. If the companies had operated at 95 per cent of capacity (which they did in 1974), the additional export earnings generated would have wiped out the 1977 trade deficit completely and reduced the government deficit by as much as one-third as well.[35] Some authors, such as Mark Figueroa, have argued that this cutback constituted economic sabotage by the companies.[36] The situation deteriorated to the point where in June 1979 the Jamaican government had to agree to cut the levy if the companies promised to sustain a fixed level of production.[37] The levy was to be halved on all production over 13 million tons. Only a month previously, the government had sought a rise in a levy. Its bargaining power was extremely small, given the weakness of the Jamaican economy as the country plunged deeper into debt.

The example provided by the bauxite and alumina industry in Jamaica is another illustration of how difficult it is for Third World states to capture control of their own economies while they have no control over the market, and while they do not have monopoly control of a primary product that is not subject to substitution in the developed world.

The Tourist Industry

After the bauxite industry, tourism was the next biggest foreign-exchange earner for Jamaica. When Manley assumed office, it was responsible for around 20 per cent of the foreign-exchange earnings per annum.[38] This industry provides yet another example of how external factors can have a crucial and often detrimental effect on the industries of vulnerable Third World states. The tourist industry was dependent mostly on vacationers from North America, who readily acknowledged Jamaica as one of the most beautiful holiday spots in easy reach. English was the language spoken, which was an advantage, and prices were relatively low.

As the cost of living began to escalate dramatically for Jamaicans in the 1970s, so too did the cost of holidays in Jamaica. However, this was not the only reason for the decline in the tourist trade, which by 1976 had almost collapsed. A contributory factor was the image attributed to Jamaica by the US media.[39] Especially after Manley's announcement in 1974 of a policy of democratic socialism (see next section), the US press portrayed Jamaica as a country teetering on the brink of communism. Relations with Cuba were latched upon as evidence that Jamaica was turning red and was falling into the arms of the communist camp. The extent and location of violence in Jamaica was also misrepresented. Jamaica *was* a violent society, and violence was on the increase during the

1970s; but holiday resorts were not nearly so affected by this as Kingston. So Jamaica was left with thousands of hotel beds empty, and with vastly diminished foreign-exchange earnings, plus increased unemployment.

THE IDEOLOGICAL SETTING

Manley and his government responded to the deteriorating economic situation from a very definite ideological standpoint. Having been swept to power in 1972 with 56 per cent of the vote[40]—the largest mandate to that date in Jamaican history— Manley was determined to adopt a new approach to tackling Jamaica's social and economic problems. He believed that development should be undertaken *only with regard to* the social and economic needs of the majority of the population, and *not regardless* of them, as he thought had been the case in Jamaica up till then. Hence he advocated a move away from the Puerto Rican model[41] of development, which had been tried in Jamaica in the 1950s and 1960s, and he called for development with a more humane face. In accordance with this approach, he announced the policy of democratic socialism in 1974. In the domestic context this amounted to a call for a mixed economy, with the government playing a more creative role than it had done in the past. It stood for a redistribution of income and the development of a social-welfare system to cope with the immense problems confronting Jamaican society. Democratic socialism was opposed to capitalist exploitation in Jamaica, and it represented a desire to curb dependence on foreign capital and to increase Jamaica's self-reliance. In the international context the policy was expressed in Manley's desire to make Jamaica an independent sovereign state, bound to no particular great power and no power bloc. Hence Jamaica pursued a policy of non-alignment.

The policy of democratic socialism came under attack both by the domestic opposition, the JLP, and some external powers, especially the US. Opponents represented the policy in terms of Marxist dogma; yet Manley's democratic socialism included none of the class antagonism which is an integral part of Marxist theory.

In December 1976 a national election was held five and a half months before it was constitutionally due. The PNP fought the election under the banner of democratic socialism and won a sweeping victory, capturing 56.8 per cent of the vote.[42] Manley's party won forty-eight seats out of a possible sixty.[43] Of interest here is the fact that the JLP fought and lost the election on the issue of a communist threat from Cuba, and claimed that the policy of democratic socialism was taking Jamaica down a path which would doubtless turn her into a second Cuba. The bogey of communism was rejected by a majority of the electorate; the JLP suffered its worst electoral defeat in Jamaican history.

Manley regarded the election result as a mandate to continue the policy of democratic socialism, especially since it was given in a time of increasing unemployment and inflation. He saw the election result as a demonstration of hope and faith in the path he was adopting for Jamaica. What did democratic socialism mean in practice?

Democratic Socialism and the Domestic Environment
In the domestic setting, democratic socialism provided the government with a framework in which to analyse and evaluate problems and projects; and it provided the government with a set of goals and priorities.

A main aim of the government was to bring important industries and public utilities under its control. We have already seen how the government set about this in the bauxite and alumina industries by renegotiating contracts with the multinationals. A similar practice was followed in the sugar industry, where foreign-owned estates were bought up. In 1975 the government took over the Jamaican telephone company, acquiring 68 per cent of its shares.[44] The Jamaican government agency for public information described this measure as being 'in keeping with the government's policy to own public utilities that are essential to national development.'[45] The foreign-owned omnibus service had already been nationalised. In 1975 Barclay's Bank was nationalised as part of an attempt to create a commercial banking sector under public ownership. Confiscation was never the method of acquiring foreign-owned concerns in

Jamaica; compensation was always given. There was still a place for foreign investment in Jamaica, but it had to be consistent with, and responsive to, Jamaica's own needs. Foreign investors had to be prepared to move towards the situation whereby worker participation extended beyond a role in decision-making to a share in profits and even ownership.

Out of the philosophy of democratic socialism there evolved a policy on land reform which was present earlier in embryonic form. In 1973 Manley brought in farm legislation stipulating that any unused land had to be sold, leased or directly developed by the owners. In practice the idea turned out to be more significant than the reality. Dissatisfied with the slow pace of government reform, some PNP youths took part in illegal land-seizures in 1972. The 1973 legislation did little to speed up the process. Manley was well aware of this. In his budget speech in 1975 he remarked that 53 per cent of the land in Jamaica was in the hands of one thousand people. 'Project Land-Lease', as his land-reform programme was called, hardly amounted to a radical socialist measure. One survey suggested that in 1975, 18 per cent of new land-lease tenants already owned, rented or leased over five acres of land before becoming involved in government's project.[46] Most of the land leased, too, was idle government land. These criticisms aside, it should not be forgotten that some people certainly did benefit from the project. By August 1977 at least 24,000 farmers had become involved in the scheme,[47] and ten state farms had been established on over 3,000 acres of land.

The humane face of democratic socialism was reflected in the employment policies introduced by Manley's governments. In 1975, 25,000 jobs were created for street cleaners in Kingston.[48] For the first time, a small weekly state payment was instituted for unemployables.[49] In a country where unemployment had passed the 25 per cent mark, such measures revealed real government concern. There was no system of social security or welfare in Jamaica to protect the poor, and Manley wanted to alleviate the worst injustices of the situation. In the sugar industry, year-round employment was guaranteed for the first time. A minimum wage of 20 Jamaican dollars was instituted in October 1975, and at the same time, in several of the poorest localities rents were rolled back to the 1971 level.

One field which experienced notable success was that of literacy. When Manley assumed office, five million Jamaicans were unable to read or write. Whereas 60,000 children attended primary school, only 9,000 progressed to further education due to the lack of facilities. Moreover, the majority of these came from families which could afford to pay. The literacy project was launched in 1973, and by 1975, there were 49,000 people in classes and 18,000 had already learned the basics.[50] Special radio and TV programmes were put out to aid the campaign against illiteracy. Having instituted free secondary education on a competitive basis, the government decided that those who graduated should perform two years of National Youth Service. Introduced as a voluntary measure in 1973, this was made compulsory in 1974. By 1975 there were 9,000 youths working under the scheme in 190 different occupations. Many of them became teachers on the literacy programme.

Democratic Socialism and the External Environment

The philosophy of democratic socialism informed the government's external stand. Unfortunately, it was marred by misrepresentation, both at home and abroad. Basically, the Manley government wanted to develop links with any state, regardless of ideological colour or the power-bloc to which it belonged (by choice or otherwise). Manley saw this as necessary not only to demonstrate the independent exercise of sovereignty but also because as a Third World state functioning in an economic structure that was heavily biased against it, Jamaica needed all the help she could get—whatever the source—to increase her security. Thus, under Manley's guidance, Jamaica was to move in just a few years from a well-entrenched position in the Western camp to a position of prominence in the non-aligned movement. Manley identified Jamaica firmly with the Third World.

Many observers failed to realise that far from rejecting friendship with the US and the rest of the Western world, Manley extended the hand of friendship to them and beyond. He rejected the notion that in accepting one state as your friend, you accept automatically its enemies as your own. In 1973 he made the following statement: 'the opposition has done its best to paint a middle of the road administration in the most lurid colours'.[51] The fact that he had announced in late November 1972, that Jamaica would seek to establish closer trading links with Cuba (which, after all, was another developing country situated just 90 miles away), and also that Jamaica would recognise the People's Republic of China, had sent shock waves of horror reverberating through the JLP opposition and the Western world. Manley's acceptance of a lift to the Algiers Non-Aligned Summit in 1973 in Castro's Russian-built jet, was seen as evidence that Jamaica was slipping irretrievably into the communist camp.[52]

If the general philosophy behind isolated examples had been considered, then reactions would have been less alarmist. In July 1975, for example, Manley visited Cuba, and later that year technical and economic agreements were signed in Kingston. Cuba was to donate a 500-place secondary school to Jamaica. (This was later converted into a military establishment by Seaga's government.) In 1976 Manley stated that there were eighty Cubans in Jamaica, excluding the diplomatic staff. Twenty-one were working on microdam projects; nine were constructing 400 houses on the north coast; and fifty were preparing to build the secondary school.[53] There was no evidence of the 250 Cubans that Seaga had told *Newsweek* would be working on the housing project.

Similarly, in March 1976 the JLP and the US made much noise about the fact that Cuban aid was being given to train the Jamaican security forces. They forgot that for the most part this training was provided by British, Canadian and US forces, and that Cuban aid in this field amounted to the training of eight of Manley's personal bodyguards.[54] The Cuban role was exaggerated and misrepresented.

Saul Landau reported in the *International Herald Tribune* on 28 August 1976 that 'The charge that Jamaica is a satellite of Cuba has no basis in fact or logic'. Rather, he saw it as the product of an irrational fear in the minds of men who were not willing to allow Jamaica to follow the path of non-alignment and democratic socialism. Manley's support of Cuban involvement in Angola was seen as the act of one already in the communist camp and under Soviet control rather than as the decision of an independent actor. Moreover, as far as Jamaica's friendship with Cuba was concerned, the actual development of economic relations between the two countries took place at an extremely slow pace, and on close inspection could not in any way have been seen as a potentially important phenomenon.

Manley's overall objective was the exercise of independent sovereign authority by Jamaica in an attempt to break the ties of dependence with the US and UK, to diversify trading links in the cause of self-reliance, and thereby to enhance Jamaica's security. In 1975 he made a significant political statement which amounted to a classic liberal stand: 'The independence of a country cannot be bestowed by others but actively achieved by one self'.[55] His actions were decided with this end in view. Hence, as well as traditional trading partners (the importance of which Manley certainly did not underestimate), he pursued links with a wide variety of countries belonging to both the Eastern and Western blocs and the non-aligned group. He was particularly interested in realising the potential that existed for intra Third World help in the form of the transfer of expertise, and so on. He saw India in particular as playing a major role here. Dudley Thompson, as foreign minister, visited India in February 1975 and stressed his hope she would provide technical help to other Third World states.

While Jamaica's policy of non-alignment produced alarm and displeasure, especially in the US and UK, it should not be forgotten that her early flirtation with other countries, stemming back to 1973, was prompted in part by the UK's entry into Europe. This disrupted Jamaica's most important export market.

An Assessment
All in all, the ideological setting of Manley's governments displayed definite traces of socialist attitudes. Yet the distance—and the difference—between democratic socialism as Manley espoused it and Marxist-Leninist doctrine, was vast. Manley did not try to institute a one-party state in Jamaica (although the JLP maintained that such a one-party system on Tanzanian lines was a logical implication of democratic socialism). In 1972 he made a speech claiming that Jamaica was 'deeply, permanently, and above all, naturally committed to the democratic process'.[56] It is a pity that his democratic

socialism was portrayed in a garb that did it little justice and so much harm.

To a large extent, both Manley and his governments must shoulder responsibility for this. Without doubt, they misread both the domestic and the external situations. Or perhaps they were simply not adept at the art of politics. An outright statement of political beliefs and social and economic preferences which goes against the tide of power and convention is rarely met with understanding by the adherents of the status quo. Despite the sweeping victory in the 1976 election, prudence was required in the application of domestic policies due to the nature of the opposition, and the violent nature of Jamaican society. Externally, in asserting Jamaica's sovereign right to independence and in expressing this right by developing links with the communist world and other symbolic gestures, Manley acted in a manner which offended Western— especially US—sensitivities. Given that these links existed more at the level of rhetoric than reality, the price paid for them was all the heavier. Had he been more politic in his behaviour, then he may not have so conclusively lost the chance to get what he wanted for Jamaica. His emotional attachment to the morality of the Jamaican cause—and for that matter, the cause of all other Third World states—seemed to blur his vision of the possible in regard to Jamaica's international and domestic situation. In the last resort, he seemed to be unconversant with the rules and reality of the political game, and a little naïve in his attempt at playing it. Hence, his credibility as a political leader was eroded both at home and abroad.

An illustration of this is that while the social aspects of his domestic policy were given so much prominence, other elements, such as the promotion of the private sector, were not awarded such rhetorical importance. Many people both within and outside Jamaica concluded that this sector was being disregarded totally. It will be shown later that this was not the case. The dilemma of the Manley governments—like that of any governments elected in a competitive party system, and trying to alter fundamentally the socio-economic structure of a state—was that they had to attempt the implementation of long-term goals by short-term policies since their life was limited. In attempting to create a more just and equitable society in Jamaica, Manley's governments gave the impression to those who did not delve below the surface that they were neglecting the very sectors on which the Jamaican economy relied—at least in the immediate term—to survive.

THE FISCAL POLICIES OF THE MANLEY GOVERNMENTS, AND THE RELATIONSHIP WITH THE IMF

The fiscal policies adopted by the Manley governments to alleviate the deterioration in the Jamaican economy, which was reflected in the growing shortage of foreign exchange, are examined here. It was mentioned earlier that statistics indicating the rise in GDP and per capita income during the 1962–71 period threw false light on what was actually a very bad situation before the PNP came to power. This was made all the more acute in the early years of Manley's rule due to the massive rise in oil and wheat prices. On top of this, bauxite production was dropping, due partly to a fall in demand for alumina in the US; the banana and sugar industries were hampered by inauspicious natural conditions and dumping, and tourism was in decline. Given that Manley was eager to help in particular the poorer sectors of society, the situation confronting the government was extremely difficult. With unemployment running at 25 per cent in 1972, and increasing during the decade, the two successive Manley governments were anxious to make the richer elements in society take the brunt of new measures. The reality was very different from the theory, however, and the aims seemed to escape achievement.

Problems and Policies in the Early Years

Manley began by imposing a total import ban on fifty-six items, and he restricted the import of fifteen others.[57] In 1971, 9 million pounds sterling had been spent on cars, and this was something that Jamaican society as a whole could not afford.[58] The limited foreign exchange available was to be spent on essentials. In line with this, Manley took some measures to try to stop the drift from the land and to encourage farming. Spending foreign exchange on imported food was a waste when that food could be produced at home. Some pioneer state farms were set up accordingly.

Throughout 1972 the drying up of large capital inflows into the bauxite and alumina industry meant that the trading deficit grew worse. Hence the decision was taken in January 1973 to devalue the Jamaican dollar by 6.5 per cent, and to peg it to the US dollar[59] in an effort to halt the rapid erosion of Jamaica's foreign reserves. The Shearer government had kept a tight control on prices before the election of 1972, and this situation could not continue indefinitely. The problems faced by the Manley government in its first term of office, therefore, were not all of its own making. Like any new government, it had to cope with problems left over from the previous administration, and to a certain extent it had to carry the can for them also.

By 1974 Jamaica was facing acute problems trying to pay for her imports. Foreign exchange earned from tourism was declining; oil price rises were potentially crippling for the Jamaican economy; food imports were becoming more expensive; it was uneconomic to export sugar and bananas to Britain (traditionally the main market), at current prices. We have seen how the bauxite and alumina contracts were renegotiated to offset the increased oil bill. Other measures included the repatriation of overseas assets, and further reductions in the import of consumer goods. All this must be seen against the background of rising inflation and unemployment. The increased cost of imports, while the government was curbing them, resulted in the side-effect of a 20 per cent rise in the cost of living in 1974.[60] Foreign reserves fell to 100 million US dollars in the same year.[61] During 1975 Jamaica managed to attract loans from diverse sources. A 38 million US dollar loan was arranged under the lead of the First Chicago Bank. A syndicate of twenty international banks put up the loans for capital expenditure in agriculture and forest development, the improvement of roads, the domestic water supply and the expansion of airports. The terms were over five years.[62] Other institutions provided more funds, for example, the Inter-American Development Bank, the World Bank and AID. In September, Jamaica negotiated a 50 million US dollar Euromarket two-tranche loan.[63] Here the lead was taken by Citicorp International. Thirty million US dollars were offered for seven years maturity, and 20 million for five years. The fact that so much of the money raised in 1975 was channelled into non-productive infrastructural projects meant that its effectiveness in curbing the downward spiralling foreign reserves' figures was small; it did little to increase domestic productivity.

In October 1975 Manley introduced a prices-and-incomes policy to help cut inflation from 21 per cent to a target of 16 per cent over the next 12 months.[64] The import ceiling was lowered to 900 million Jamaican dollars (480 million pounds sterling).[65] In the first six months of 1976, the deficit sank to 130.6 million Jamaican dollars, and so in July, the import ceiling was lowered yet again to 820 million Jamaican dollars.[66]

Other major problems which the government had to face were sabotage from within and the attractions of other states. By the end of 1976, local businessmen had illegally exported an estimated 200 million US dollars.[67] Also, professional expertise had flowed out of the country. By May 1977, Coore, the deputy prime minister, estimated that 2,000 out of a total of 10,000 professional people had emigrated.[68] The loss of one-fifth of the professional body was indeed acutely damaging, especially since it occurred when the need was greatest for professional technicians and managers to cope with the ever-growing problems besetting the economy. This raises the interesting and difficult question of whether developed countries have a responsibility to help stop the brain drain, and whether their failure to do so can be represented as interference in the domestic affairs of developing countries. The North is depriving the South of one of the latter's major development resources—expertise. In this sense, emigration can be seen as sabotage, and participation in this act by developed countries might be seen as an interference. On the other hand, of course, the Jamaican government must shoulder some responsibility, for its rhetoric did little to allay the fears of the business community.

The period 1974–6 saw the development of a gloomy trend, as the borrowing necessary to keep Jamaica afloat was given under increasingly harsh terms. Three-year terms were fast becoming the order of the day, and 12 per cent interest was average. With commercial borrowing becoming more difficult on the scale that Jamaica required it, there was little recourse left now except to turn to the IMF.

Jamaica and the IMF: The Early Phase

Jamaica's previous history with the IMF was short and uncomplicated. Within seven months of gaining independence in August 1962, Jamaica joined the IMF. She became a first-class member under Article 8, agreeing to pay contributions in the manner of a developed country and entitled to support on the same basis.[69]

Four months after joining the Fund, Jamaica entered into a stand-by arrangement, under which she was allowed to draw into the second credit tranche of her quota.[70] At this time, her balance-of-payments position was relatively comfortable, and the arrangement can be regarded in Robichek's words as, 'a precautionary move to assure foreign creditors and investors that independence had in no way increased the risks they were taking in Jamaica.'[71] In other words, the arrangement was concluded by Jamaica not out of immediate financial need but rather out of a desire to obtain the IMF's stamp of approval for her economic policies. It was hoped and expected that this would result in an easier flow of capital from the commercial lenders. Conditionality did not become an issue as adjustment was not called for.

It was not until June 1973 that Jamaica entered into another stand-by arrangement with the Fund,[72] the intervening years being marked for the most part by balance-of-payments surpluses or very small deficits. This stand-by agreement, also encompassing borrowing in the first two credit tranches, was negotiated out of financial need, and not merely to obtain the IMF's seal of approval. The IMF-imposed performance tests were met, and the agreement was fully utilised by Jamaica. At this stage the relationship between the two parties remained cordial.

On completion of this one-year agreement, Jamaica decided to make use of the low conditionality facilities available in the Fund, instead of negotiating another stand-by agreement. The government preferred to avoid a situation whereby the continued provision of funds remained dependent on the fulfilment of economic policies and targets stipulated by the

IMF. Jamaica drew on the oil facility and the compensatory finance facility during the period 1975–6, thereby avoiding the constraint on policy of having to follow IMF advice. Despite the 32.8 million US dollar loan taken up in March 1976 from the oil facility,[73] by the end of August foreign-exchange reserves had fallen to minus 43.3 million Jamaica dollars.[74] In November, Jamaica obtained a 13.5 million SDR loan under the compensatory finance facility.[75]

On the granting of the November loan under the compensatory finance facility, Jim Morrell notes that 'the major industrial countries' representatives vied with one another in scolding President Michael Manley's government for slapping on unauthorised import licensing restrictions and otherwise breaking their promises to the Fund.'[76] For the time being, however, scolding was the full extent of their ability, since the facility had as its only condition that the 'member cooperates with the Fund in an effort to find appropriate solutions for any payments difficulties.' In criticising the Manley government's policies, these industrialised states did not feel that it was necessary to refer to, or in any way make allowances for, the difficult domestic situation. For them, domestic social or political factors in no way present extenuating circumstances. Representatives of the Third World, however, more conversant with the type of problems overcoming Jamaican society, found it easier to lend a sympathetic ear. Thus Festus G. Mogae, representing a group of sixteen African states, maintained that 'The social and political conditions were such that they could not be ignored'.[77] By the time of the granting of this loan, it was becoming clear that Jamaica would very soon need extensive financial assistance which, given the circumstances, could only come from the IMF.

During these years and earlier even, the IMF had been keeping a watchful eye on Jamaica's economic performance, as it does with all its members. Dissatisfaction had been voiced at the rate of wage inflation (contracted wage increases reached, on average, between 50 and 60 per cent in late 1974 and throughout 1975), the fiscal deficit, monetary expansion and restrictions on trade and prices. While Jamaica maintained positive foreign reserves, it was possible for Manley's government to turn a deaf ear to the murmurs of discontent emanating from the Fund. However, when these reserves became negative, as they did in March 1976, the government became more vulnerable to pressure from the Fund.

The IMF Call for a 40 Per Cent Devaluation, and the Government's Response

An election had been set for December 1976, and before it took place, Fund officials, in conjunction with government representatives, worked out a two-year stand-by arrangement in outline. The IMF suggested a massive 40 per cent devaluation of the Jamaican dollar, and a sharp cutback in government expenditure. Unaware as yet of its future status, the PNP government decided to discuss the matter after the election, should it be victorious. When the new cabinet was formed following the PNP electoral victory, the idea of a 40 per cent devaluation was thrown out as unacceptable. The price in human terms would be phenomenal. The cost of living would rise steeply, and government cutbacks would inevitably eat into those very programmes designed to help the poor.

It was in their attitude to the poorer sections of society that the argument between the Fund and progressive elements inside Jamaica found its most acute expression. It was noted above that in criticising Jamaica during the granting of the compensatory finance facility loan in November 1976, the representatives of the industrialised states at the Fund lamented the government's unwillingness to cut wages and social services for the poor. They had been concerned primarily—indeed, exclusively—with Jamaica's failure to adhere completely to the basic theoretical principles of free trade, and had attacked specifically her import restrictions. Their emphasis derived from their main interest, which was that of maintaining the smooth functioning of the international trade and monetary systems, regardless of specific national consequences.

In the Fund's recommendations to the new Manley government, the same emphasis—and the same lack of concern—were evident. Having been elected by a sweeping majority on the platform of democratic socialism, Manley's new government would have a difficult time explaining and justifying policies which displayed such little regard for the needs of the poor. As Girvan, Bernal and Hughes point out, many people in Jamaica believed that 'the adoption of the proposed agreement would be inconsistent with the political mandate that the PNP had freshly secured.'[78] Immediately following the PNP triumph, the voices of progressivism grew louder. Elements both inside and outside the PNP including trade-union activists and academics, as well as those in the mainstream of Jamaican electoral politics, pressed for a greater adherence to the democratic-socialist platform pledges. They argued that this was the time to move forward in the direction indicated by the mandate; this was not the time for retrenchment or even simple consolidation. The left wing of the PNP, in particular, denied the validity of the Fund's call for a 40 per cent devaluation, and questioned the basis of a resort to the Fund. Manley has written that this group believed that 'an IMF programme for adjustment and recovery meant delivering Jamaica into a trap'.[79] They believed that the Fund's traditional policies were designed to cure the typical ailments of developed capitalist economies; as such they failed to do justice to the Third World states in either an economic or a social sense. While arguing that developed countries were far better equipped than the developing to offer comprehensive welfare services to protect the poor from the adverse effects of IMF adjustment programmes, they also pointed to weaknesses in the IMF analysis on economic grounds. For instance, they believed that devaluation, far from increasing exports by making them cheaper, would have no influence on some of them. The reason for a fall in exports of bananas and sugar had nothing to do with their price, but rather with problems within those industries which led to shortfalls in production, and to market factors. Similarly, if devaluation were to result in less foreign-exchange earnings from bauxite, the situation for Jamaica would be catastrophic.

In this climate the differences prevalent within the PNP became more acute. It is pertinent at this point to take a brief look at the structure of the PNP in an attempt to understand the crystallisation of different factions within the party on the IMF issue.

The Background to the Division Within the PNP

The PNP was founded in 1938, its primary *raison d'être* at that time being to struggle for independence. It stood for universal adult suffrage within a democratic system. Around these central issues, the party attracted people from many different social backgrounds and walks of life. In 1940 the PNP made a commitment to socialism, and as such it divorced itself from some oligarchic elements which had joined its ranks. Its supporters came mainly from the industrial workers, small businessmen, the white-collar middle class, the professionals and the intelligentsia. The agricultural policies introduced by Manley on gaining office in 1972 resulted in the swelling of PNP ranks with agricultural labourers and small farmers.

When Manley formed his first government in 1972, he encouraged the National Executive Council of the PNP to discuss the subject of socialism, with a view to hammering out a definite ideology.[80] Since the party was in theory committed to socialism, there was a need to arrive at a consensus on what this meant given the party's vision of Jamaican society and Jamaica's role in the international environment. In Manley's own words, 'This provoked immediate controversy within our ranks.'[81] For the PNP, ideological differences were long-standing; the present controversy was nothing new. As far back as the 1940s, right and left wings had emerged, and in 1952, four leaders of the Left had been expelled following an in-house inquiry on the teaching of Marxism in secret cells. Over the years, the ideological argument had never really been resolved; as Manley comments, 'It merely went underground'.[82] The campaign for the 1967 election led to the resurfacing of old struggles, with the left wing under Manley's leadership coming out on top—but only just. The 1967 PNP election campaign was weak, largely due to the lack of central direction which resulted from the opposing viewpoints within the party. The PNP narrowly lost the election. On gaining office in 1972, Manley was determined that a PNP consensus on ideology should be arrived at so that the government, the party and the people of Jamaica would all have a clear vision of where the country was heading under PNP rule.

Intensive discussions took place at all levels of the party on the basis of a working document drawn up by a committee chosen by the NEC. Following on from this, in October 1974, Manley outlined the PNP concept of democratic socialism to the nation. The elucidation of this policy, far from uniting the party and establishing a general consensus, seemed to make the division more acute. Members polarised around divergent interpretations of, for example, the role of the public sector in the mixed economy. In 1975 Manley convened another committee on policy following bitter internal wranglings and the suspension of a political education programme. This committee faltered along, with no real results. It was after the 1976 election that matters came to a head, crystallising on the question of relations with the IMF. As mentioned earlier, in this major battle the left wing of the PNP won out. Hence, while never formally breaking off negotiations with the IMF, the government rejected the 40 per cent devaluation, and embarked on an attempt to mobilise resources elsewhere.

The PNP Government Chooses an Alternative Path

The aim was to redirect the national effort to save the economy, while maintaining the highest possible level of independent decision-making within the hands of the government. Clearly, the well-being of the economy was not the only thing at stake; so too was the health and stability of the tension-ridden society. The government hoped to restructure Jamaican society and to make the state less dependent on external powers, thereby making it more secure.

Manley was well aware that this alternative route would necessitate a national effort of massive proportions, yet he remained defiant *vis-à-vis* the IMF. For him, the matter extended far beyond pure economics and hit at the heart of the issue of sovereignty. In his speech to the nation on 5 January 1977, he said in reference to the IMF's terms, 'this government, on behalf of our people, will not accept anybody anywhere in the world telling us what to do in our country. We are the masters in our house and in our house there shall be no other master but ourselves.'[83] Manley perceived the problem in terms of a struggle to maintain Jamaica's political integrity as an independent actor while this independence was under attack from the IMF as a representative of the international capitalist system. He wanted to make it clear to the public that decisions affecting Jamaicans would be made by Jamaicans in Jamaica and would not be imposed from outside.

On 20 January 1977 Manley made an economic policy statement in the Jamaican parliament. This contained six main clauses:[84]

1. An immediate price and wage freeze till July.
2. A 600 million Jamaican dollars import ceiling (compared with the 1976 target of 820 million, which had been overreached by 20 million), and this was to include external debt repayment.
3. The tightening of exchange controls, which meant that commercial banks could only deal in foreign exchange as agents of the Bank of Jamaica.
4. An increase in surtax from 60 to 70 per cent on incomes of 30,000 Jamaican dollars per annum; and to 80 per cent on incomes of over 30,000 Jamaican dollars per annum.
5. An increase in the price of petrol.
6. No capital was to be made available to expatriates and dependants abroad.

While some of these measures, such as the wage freeze and tax increases, were in keeping with the previous IMF recommendations, there was no devaluation of the dollar, and this of course had been strongly advocated by the IMF. While the IMF believed that such a measure would stimulate exports and cut domestic consumption, Manley believed it would achieve little but an increase in inflation.

1977 was labelled the 'Year of the Economic Emergency' in Jamaica. A people-based 'Production Plan' was worked out. Manley has remarked that this 'represented the first attempt at economic mobilisation in Jamaican history'.[85] Communities right down to the village level identified projects and production plans. Manley believed firmly that 'Authorship should provide a better foundation for commitment than the platitudinous exhortations in which governors general and other ceremonial heads of state specialized.'[86] A new Ministry of National Mobilisation undertook the task of increasing national unity in an effort to see Jamaica through this trying period. Given the tense and violent nature of Jamaican society, the need for this to be successful was all the more acute.

The problems besetting the Jamaican economy were so serious and deep-rooted that these measures could do little to rectify them, especially the shortage of foreign reserves. However, the value of foreign exchange had to be weighed against the cost of obtaining it, and this was a constant theme in Manley's speeches. In February he remarked, 'It is true that Jamaica needs foreign capital. But we will not seek to attract it if the price which we have to pay is the unbridled exploitation of our human and natural resources.'[87] He outlined the government's strategy thus: 'The deficit has to be reduced, but this has to be done in a way which will not generate additional unemployment or the removal of any of the people's programmes which the government has introduced. Indeed, our goal is to streamline and strengthen these programmes.'[88] Manley seemed to have set himself an enormous task here. The stated goals, priorities and policies of the government were to be adhered to despite the inauspicious economic circumstances. In February he banned another 128 items by placing them on the list of prohibited import commodities.[89] The object was twofold: to stimulate domestic production and to save foreign exchange. Of the 600 million Jamaican dollars allocated for foreign imports, 210 million was set aside for petrol and petrol products; 200 million for raw materials; 75 million for capital goods; and 115 million for food and consumer product.[90] In April the government introduced a two-tier exchange-rate system and temporarily closed all foreign-exchange markets.[91] The new rate was established for areas where local production needed stimulation; the old rate was retained for food imports and bauxite dealings. In effect, the new exchange-rate system represented a partial devaluation of 37.5 per cent.

During the first six months of 1977, therefore, Jamaica tried to get by without help from the IMF, but negotiations with that institution were never broken off. Since commercial lending bodies often took their cue from the IMF, Jamaica did not find it easy to obtain loans. The few loans that were obtained, such as 53 million US dollars from the European Development Fund for the banana industry, were totally inadequate; and her foreign reserves were almost exhausted. Jamaica seemed to have little alternative but to go to the IMF once more.

Jamaica Returns to the IMF Fold, Summer 1977

On 12 July a loan agreement was announced,[92] and in August, a two-year stand-by arrangement came into operation. It was rumoured at the time that the price to be paid for the IMF loan was a currency devaluation and cuts in social programmes. These were the two stipulations that had previously resulted in deadlock in negotiations with the IMF. In effect, the two-tier exchange rate represented a partial devaluation, and perhaps this concession was enough. For after the announcement of the deal, Manley rebuffed any idea that he had acceded to the IMF's demands.

In a press release on 11 August, the IMF outlined the policies that it recommended Jamaica pursue. With the aim of reducing borrowing requirements and building up foreign-exchange reserves, Jamaica was exhorted to 'increase domestic production; to tighten further its demand management policies; to follow a restrained incomes policy; to pursue a flexible exchange rate policy; to eliminate existing payment arrears; and to liberalise the exchange and trade system.'[93] In effect, the IMF got what it wanted in terms of a tight incomes policy and a high degree of fiscal restraint, while the Jamaican government got what it wanted in terms of limited exchange adjustment. The stand-by arrangement provided for loans to Jamaica over the next two years totalling 74 million US dollars; that is, the equivalent of 64 million SDRs, or 121 per cent of her quota. The loan was divided into two tranches: 44 million dollars was to be made available in 1977, and another 30 million in 1978.[94] Available immediately, in August 1977, was 22.4 million dollars. The continued availability of these funds over the two-year period naturally depended upon the fulfilment of the quarterly tests. Failure would result in an interruption of the loan. Thus, while the agreement resembled a compromise, the IMF held the trump card. Once the IMF loan was announced, the way was paved for loans from a variety of sources, such as Venezuela, the Netherlands and many commercial banks.[95] A total of 190 million US dollars was sought in external loan finance in 1977, and the IMF's loan represented only a small part of this.

The news of the IMF loan in July 1977 did not really come as a shock to many Jamaicans. As early as the April/May edition of the *West Indies Chronicle*,[96] it had been reported that the Jamaican government had earmarked the greater part of the extra foreign exchange expected to be obtained from the IMF and other sources to make available more raw materials for the private-sector export industries. (The import ceiling meant that many industries were operating well below capacity due to a shortage of materials.)

The question of the private sector raises some interesting points. It was maintained by the JLP that Manley was attempting to wipe out the private sector and bring everything under public control. His claim that democratic socialism stood for a mixed economy went unheeded. What exactly was the attitude of the Manley governments towards private industry? First, it must be remembered that the welfare aspects of Manley's ideological framework had not found expression in Jamaica before, and hence, having declared his intentions, Manley had to be seen from the outset to be implementing welfare policies. In the case of the private sector, which was already well-entrenched, the need for vocal attention was not so urgent. There was nothing new about the private sector, other than its location within the framework of a mixed economy. Its exclusivity had gone, but it remained very important. Manley put his finger on this point when he wrote:

Who says that 'deeds speak louder than words'? Our 'deeds' to the private sector were the most eloquent testimony to our sincerity with respect to the mixed economy. To these deeds were added countless words of categoric, official reassurance. Against this were ranged some cases of irresponsible comments from our side and a ceaseless stream of provocative, manipulative, and patently dishonest propoganda from the opposition. It was obvious that the private sector chose to assume the worst presumably because we were challenging the system in the pure form which they prefer. They were not prepared to accept the entirely honourable place which they were being offered in a modified system.[97]

What deeds did the PNP government perform in relation to the private sector? One notable deed was the choice of persons for the post of industry minister, which reflected a real concern to appoint people 'with good business sector credentials'.[98] For example, Danny Williams and William Isaacs were chosen, and both were acceptable in terms of their past involvement in the business community. Second, in almost all of Manley's major speeches concerning the economy made since 1974, he tried to reassure the business sector. His budget speeches to parliament are a testimony to this.[99] Third, the Manley governments did much to help the private sector at a time when it, like all other sectors, was under severe pressure. Manley states that:

Special loan funds were earmarked; an export credit facility was introduced in April 1974; Bank of Jamaica loans were available at special interest rates for exports; the Jamaican Export Credit Insurance Corporation was created to provide guarantees for exporters on as much as 80 per cent of the value of their exports; accelerated depreciation rates were arranged for private enterprises operating two or more shifts; tax rebates were provided for training workers required for expansion or production; the consolidation of group profits and losses was permitted where companies were 100 per cent owned by the same group; credit facilities through the Jamaican Development Bank were expanded.[100]

It cannot be said, therefore, that the Manley governments disregarded the private sector and failed to give it any concessions or encouragement. What is more, even without government help (which was indeed forthcoming), the private sector was still influential in Jamaican society at least in terms of political leverage. This was demonstrated in the early months of 1977, for example, when many manufacturers convinced their workers to picket the office of the trade administrator in an effort to have the supply of import licences increased. The manufacturers knew that they stood to gain if an agreement was reached with the IMF, for that would lead to an influx of commercial loans from which they would benefit directly. They threatened the government with massive layoffs if more money was not forthcoming and they encouraged workers to strike.

Manley's problem was that he was trying not just to get the economy moving again, but to achieve that goal within the framework of a new social structure. The creation of the latter absorbed much time, money and energy. Had these been directed instead to restoring the economy to equilibrium, then the latter may have been achieved, but only as the result of a trade-off: an increase in human misery. As it happened, Manley's policy fell between two stools because he had neither the time, the money, nor the support to give it a chance to succeed. Ironically, those people who Manley intended to help the most, suffered the most.

In December 1977 Jamaica failed the IMF's quarterly test. Hence the 74 million US dollar agreement announced in July 1977 was interrupted. Only the first tranche of 22 million had been drawn on 10 October. The second tranche of 11 million, due on 15 December, was not forthcoming. The IMF had stipulated a set of four conditions for continued drawings: targets were set for public expenditure, for public borrowing from the banking system, for foreign-exchange holdings and for domestic credit expansion. David Coore, the finance minister, has remarked that Jamaica very narrowly failed the final test concerning domestic credit expansion though it had passed the rest. On 15 December the net domestic assets of the Bank of Jamaica failed to be below the IMF-imposed ceiling of 335 million Jamaican dollars by just 9 million dollars, or 2.6 per cent.[101] The Jamaicans were angry not only because of the marginality of the shortfall but also because they believed that it was due partly to the fact that certain foreign loans had failed to materialise. As far as the IMF was concerned, this excessive expansion in domestic credit had financed the fiscal deficit which now reached 16.3 per cent of GDP instead of the targeted 9.1 per cent, and had increased wage–price pressure. The IMF concluded that the end result was a further decrease in Jamaica's external competitiveness. At a time when the Bank of Jamaica estimated official reserves to be running at a net deficit of 170 million US dollars, Jamaica could ill-afford this new misfortune. For the loss was not limited to the actual IMF loans but extended much further, for many loans—such as a 32 million US dollar package from a commercial banking consortium—were dependent upon a continued IMF agreement to assist Jamaica. The disbursement of a newly negotiated 30 million US dollar World Bank loan was also prevented.

Jamaica Renegotiates with the IMF, 1978
So dire was Jamaica's position that no feasible alternative was open but to renegotiate with the IMF. Such was Jamaica's need, and such was the IMF's power, that the organisation was able to demand a total weighted devaluation of 10 per cent as a

precondition even for negotiations. The government believed that the 10 per cent devaluation was much higher than what was needed to protect the Jamaican economy, yet it had no choice but to implement the policy. The IMF also stipulated that the linking of the wage rate to the exchange rate was to be the basis of a framework for a new programme. In a speech to the nation on 14 January 1978, Manley remarked that 'we would have preferred a smaller adjustment, but in the end the fundamental consideration is that we must have access to foreign exchange in the future.'[102] He was admitting that in its control over foreign exchange, the IMF had ultimate control over a theoretically 'sovereign' country. Manley had no choice but to concede to the IMF's demand. However, in an attempt to cushion the poorest sectors of Jamaican society from the effects of the devaluation, the minimum wage was increased from 20 to 24 Jamaican dollars. Food subsidies were also increased.[103] These measures were very small, but they were better than nothing.

The new package took five months to sort out. The Jamaican team was led by Eric Bell, who had replaced David Coore as finance minister. (Coore had to take political responsibility for the failure of the December test, and thus was removed from the job.) There was much bad feeling because of the belief that Jamaica had been singled out by the IMF for harsh treatment. It was widely believed in Jamaica that the IMF was putting that country in its place because it had fought vehemently over the terms of loans before and had flouted its authority in the past, and because it had encourged Canada and Britain to exert political pressure in the Fund to get a loan on modified terms.[104] (The Labour government in Britain had suffered at the hands of the IMF too, and hence Britain had taken a sympathetic attitude towards Jamaica's predicament.) Jamaica had not always followed IMF directives to the letter. In September 1977 she devalued the special exchange rate by 2.5 per cent instead of moving 50 million US dollars' worth of imports from the basic to the special exchange rate, arguing that the effect on the weighted exchange was the same. Such claims, of course, are intangible and cannot be verified. However, they certainly created an unfavourable atmosphere in which to negotiate.

The three-year extended fund facility loan concluded in May 1978, represented a 240 million US dollar package (i.e. a massive 270 per cent of Jamaica's quota). Manley described it as 'one of the most savage packages every imposed on any client government by the IMF.'[105] The finance minister, Bell, took a more moderate, yet still critical, stand: 'Some of the conditions on which they [the IMF] have been insisting appear to us to be unduly harsh.'[106] The package completely overturned the government's previous economic policies, with the private sector being given the major role in the country's economy and with state control being pared down. Free-market forces were to be given full rein, and export-led growth was to be the direction of development. Social and political costs and consequences were disregarded.

The two-tier exchange rate was abolished, and there was an immediate devaluation of 15 per cent on the lower-level unified rate. This devaluation was the fourth in only fifteen months. It followed on the tail of the closure of the foreign-exchange market for an indefinite period. Moreover, this was merely the beginning. A 'crawling peg' arrangement was demanded by the IMF whereby the Jamaican dollar would be devalued a further 2.5 per cent every two months for the next year, thus reaching the target of a 30 per cent devaluation. The IMF also insisted on a massive tax package, the most demanding in Jamaica's history—180 million dollars' worth of new taxes were announced, with cigarettes, alcohol and petrol being particularly hard hit. The Fund demanded also that teeth be put into the wages policy, and so increases were limited to 15 per cent of an employer's total existing expenditure on wages. The objective was that funds released should find their way into savings to boost fixed investment from the current level of 12 per cent of GDP up to 21 per cent by 1980.[107] This target was considered to be in line with self-sustained growth. An 11 per cent decline in the percentage of GDP pre-empted by consumption, from 91 per cent to 80 per cent in two years, represented a drastic reallocation of resources. Given that Jamaica's consumption was so far outrunning production, the IMF considered this to be a reasonable demand. Cutting consumption and increasing exports were the two main motivating factors behind the IMF policies.

Much of the 240 million US dollar loan was to be devoted to helping the export industry by financing raw materials and machinery needed by Jamaican industry and agriculture. The 1977 trade deficit amounted to 206.3 million Jamaican dollars,[108] and this had to be reduced. The remainder of the money would be used for debt-servicing. In a situation where local demand was acutely dampened by the repercussions of other policies contained in the package, the prospect of recovery in the local private sector was slim. It was in the export sector that the IMF expected strides to be made. There, however, the general world recession would take its toll.

The local reaction to the package was unfavourable. The Left of the PNP saw its acceptance as a grave mistake, believing that Jamaica should have continued in her search for alternative finance. The JLP considered the terms to be far too harsh, and called for a renegotiation. The trade-union movement was overcome with shock and bitterness. Wage-rise limits of 15 per cent seemed worthless in the circumstances of crawling peg devaluation, a reduction in the price controls on twenty-six basic items, and the restrictions on the activities of the State Trading Corporation (another IMF demand).[109] Positive action by the unions was unforthcoming because of their fragmented nature. There was no central trade-union organisation; rather, the unions followed party lines, with the Bustamente Industrial Trade Union supporting the JLP, and the National Workers Union supporting the PNP. There existed twenty-seven other small unions also.

On 27 November 1978 the journalist Michael Leapman commented in *The Times*:

The story of Jamaica's decline into brutal austerity is an example of how little freedom of political manoeuvre can be enjoyed by theoretically independent countries which rely on overseas investment. The foreign exchange crisis which forced the government to seek IMF help was caused by the oil crisis of 1973 and by an abrupt halt in overseas investments from 1974, because investors mistrusted the intention of Mr Manley's government.

Speaking of Manley, Leapman continues: 'To keep Jamaica afloat, he has been forced to adopt policies which hit hardest the poor people he so eloquently champions ... it is an unhappy irony that the advocate of the new economic order has fallen victim to the old IMF squeeze.' Manley has always maintained that he had no choice but to go back to the IMF in 1978. An alternative route had been attempted but had proved unsuccessful, at least in the very short time it was given to prove itself. The policies which Manley had to accept on returning to the IMF not only went against the ideological grain but also did not seem to make sound economic sense to him either. Technically, the IMF cannot order specific policy changes, but in practice it does not lend money unless it is happy with a country's programme; that is, the country must accept its advice. In the case of Jamaica, the Fund team, led by David Finch, and the Jamaican team, under Bell's leadership, were in fundamental agreement on many of the policies for adoption. These included the need for tighter control of imports, the reduction of the government deficit by an increase in taxes, and the need to keep a tight rein on government expenditure. The two parties were in fundamental disagreement, however, on the need for a massive devaluation, and also on the government's plans to use the State Trading Corporation for all importing. The Jamaican team believed that the devaluation made many of the other policies which had been agreed upon morally untenable in a society where basic needs went unfulfilled. Manley believed that a technical fallacy underlay the IMF's approach to Third World economies in general. The remedies suggested by the Fund were, in his opinion, far more suited to rectifying imbalances in developed economies. The IMF asks for devaluation because this reduces the demand for imports by making them more expensive and it stimulates exports by making them more competitive. It also asks for tax increases and/or a reduction in government expenditure to make less spending money available to the domestic economy, which has the result of forcing producers to look for external markets. The achievement of both goals is made easier by the tight wage ceiling. Yet, as Manley points out, developing countries do not have the productive capacity necessary for the policies imposed to produce the required effect; nor do they have adequate welfare provisions to protect the poor from the repercussions of these rigorous policies. Moreover, even details like the quarterly tests made no sense in Third World states when they failed to take into account the seasonality of production and earnings.

In the Jamaican case, the cost of imports could not have been significantly reduced, because the oil which ate up over one-third of Jamaica's export earnings was vital for bauxite production. Also nearly one-quarter of her imports were essential capital goods, and devaluation would make them more expensive. Moreover, Norman Girvan, head of the National Planning Agency, has remarked that devaluation could not stimulate Jamaica's two main exports.[110] The price of sugar sold to Europe was fixed in foreign-currency terms, and sales to the US were on a quota basis. In the case of bauxite, the alumina companies argued that Jamaica would still be uncompetitive even after devaluation. Hence they urged the government to reduce the levy or face a continuing decline in production. The situation in Jamaica was compounded by the fact that the foreign capital which the IMF advocated did not flow in despite IMF approval. Having borne the austerity consequent upon IMF demands, Jamaicans found that their country made little, if any, noticeable economic progress. Manley has commented that, 'the population is subjected to severe pressure in pursuit of benefits that are unattainable.'[111]

It is surprising to note that despite the hardships incurred, and despite opposition from both the PNP and the JLP, support for the IMF's policies did not completely trail away amongst the general population. A poll published by Carl Stone in September 1978[112] showed that 46 per cent of Jamaicans favoured the loan, while 40 per cent opposed it. By early 1979 the climate of opinion was changing, but the irony is that it was becoming anti-Manley, rather than anti-IMF.

1979: Austerity Does Not Pay Off; Jamaica Fails the December Test

In January 1979 a 13-cent increase in the price of petrol sparked off demonstrations in Kingston. Manley said that this measure was required under the IMF terms, so he had no choice but to impose it. Social tensions were increasing. Yet on paper, at least, economic austerity seemed to be paying off in early 1979. The reserves in the monthly trading accounts showed a slight improvement at that time, narrowing the budget deficit. This small success was not translated into tangible benefits for the Jamaican people; the only tangible things for the average Jamaican were the increased cost of living, higher taxes and wage ceilings.

The rest of 1979 did not witness a sustained improvement. Although in the quarterly assessment of June, the IMF noted that Jamaica had brought down inflation to somewhere in the 15–20 per cent range, by September the external debt totalled 877 million US dollars and foreign-exchange reserves stood at only 47 million dollars.[113] In September the government failed in its bid to renegotiate foreign loans totalling 450 million US dollars with a consortium of US banks.[114] The economy had shown no sign of sustained growth since 1974, and Jamaica was not considered to be a good bet. The government did manage to obtain a 180-day credit from the Export–Import Bank to help local exporters. This was worth about 100 million US dollars[115]—a significant amount in the short term for a country whose cash-flow problems were as acute as Jamaica's.

The search for commercial funding was hampered in the autumn by an ill-timed statement made by Manley at the Non-Aligned Conference in Havana. On 1 October he spoke out against the US blockade of Cuba, and championed a more independent Puerto Rico.[116] Eric Bell was at that very moment attempting to negotiate a loan package from a group of international bankers. Needless to say, Manley's remarks sent waves of fear through those sensitive actors in the commercial world, and the bogey of communism was raised yet again. Predictably, Bell's efforts were in vain. A few days later Manley remarked that 'Commercial banks are not designed for bad weather';[117] Manley's ill-timed and imprudent speech at Havana provides another illustration of how he misread the external situation through political naïveté.

The Jamaican case became something of an embarrassment to the IMF because it indicated that the policies expounded by that institution did not always have the expected results. It appears that during 1979, with IMF approval, some of the tough constraints were loosened and more money was provided to ease the poor foreign-exchange situation. The monthly currency devaluations were suspended on condition that wage awards were moderated and the financial targets were revised to allow higher current and overall government deficits than had previously been stipulated. This latter measure was an attempt to ensure adequate imports to stimulate economic growth. The hope was probably still held out by the Fund that the economy would correct itself given time. Larosière, the new president of the Fund, was thought to be more responsive than his predecessor to Jamaica's needs, because he realised the implications of failure in the Jamaican case for the confidence of the entire developing world. By June 1979 Jamaica was the largest per capita borrower from the Fund, having been told that she could draw up to 338 million US dollars over the next two years.[118]

The outlook seemed bleak for Jamaica as the December tests drew nearer and failure was anticipated. On 19 December the cabinet and some junior ministers resigned. It was hoped that a new team would encourage the Fund to act mildly with Jamaica. The Fund had set the foreign-reserves limit of the Bank of Jamaica at 370 million US dollars for 31 December, but the expected figure was 500 million dollars.[119] The government was hoping that the IMF might bend the rules and provide some emergency aid. It would plead oil price rises, inflation, the collapse of growth and stagnant exports with this aim in mind. The predictions proved correct, and, exceeding the December target by 117 million US dollars, Jamaica forfeited the 40 million dollar tranche due in mid-January.[120]

Major differences existed between the government and the IMF analyses of why the December test was failed. On a very general level the Fund attributed the failure to factors under the control of the Jamaican government, while that government pointed to factors outside its control. An IMF economist, Russel Kincaid, while not denying the existence of exogenous factors, points to Jamaica's fiscal policy as the main reason for the non-fulfilment of the quantitative December test.

Two major factors—greater than agreed wage increases granted to the public sector employees and inability to contain other expenditures—led to a recurrent budget deficit of 4.0 per cent instead of a balance, and contributed to the overall public sector deficit expanding to 13.7 per cent of GDP, compared with the target of 8.9 per cent. The deficit was financed primarily by domestic credit expansion, with Bank credit to the government growing by three and a half times the amount envisaged in the financial programme. Excess demand pressures led to a widening of the current account deficit to

6.8 per cent of GDP, an increase in the overall external deficit, and a doubling of international payments arrears from their mid-year level.[121]

The Jamaican economist, Norman Girvan, offers a different explanation. He urges that 'internal and external factors beyond the control of Jamaica were responsible for 60 per cent or 120 million US dollars . . . of the breach.'[122] He claims that higher oil price rises than had been expected added 33 million dollars to the oil bill. Also, international inflation exceeded 14 per cent, though Fund and government officials had estimated that it would run at 8.5 per cent. This meant an extra 18 million dollars. Domestic factors beyond governmental control, included severe flooding, which resulted in a loss of 20 million dollars in export earnings. Girvan denies that there was any overspending by the government up to 31 December; rather, he looks to shortfalls in revenue consisting of 40 million dollars in foreign loans, 40 million in domestic non-bank financing and 20 million in tax revenue to explain the 117 million dollar failure to meet the fiscal target.

Both Kincaid and Girvan have a vested interest in establishing that the responsibility did not lie with their respective institutions. It is extremely difficult for an observer to determine where the blame really lies. There is probably an element of truth in both analyses. Certainly, many factors beyond the control of the government played a large part in the failure to meet IMF conditionality; however, the government could have made a greater effort to meet the IMF wage targets, for example, but the political price for doing so may have appeared unacceptable.

February 1980: Manley Breaks with the IMF

Negotiations continued with the IMF in the hope of achieving a waiver of the December tests. However, they reached an impasse in early February, when the Fund wanted wage-rise limits of 10 per cent and demanded public spending cuts of 38 million pounds sterling.[123] Manley maintained that 20 million pounds was the limit. He estimated that to meet IMF requirements, his government would have to lay off at least 11,000 workers,[124] abolish the few remaining food and transport subsidies and close down the adult-literacy programme. Alternatively, he could have closed down some hospitals. Neither option was acceptable to him. He believed that there was a basic level that could not be disregarded in terms of the provision of services to the poor—which in Jamaican terms meant most of the population.

While the *Daily Gleaner* (the daily newspaper with the largest circulation in Jamaica), regarded the IMF as 'the greatest friend of Jamaica',[125] Beverley Manley regarded that institution as one of Jamaica's greatest enemies: 'The IMF is not there as any friend in need for developing countries. All over the world people are speaking out against the oppressive terms and conditions of the IMF loans.'[126] The IMF was demanding an estimated 323 per cent drop in real expenditure in Jamaica over the 1980–1 period, and this would have entailed a massive job displacement. Public and social services would have been slashed, with grave consequences for the 26 per cent unemployed. Moreover, the political repercussions would be vast in a society where unemployment in the 15 to 29 years age-group was running at 40 per cent.[127] Such factors held no place in the IMFs formulation of a package.

In early February, Manley announced that he had decided to call an election on the issue of the IMF, in an attempt to settle an economic path for Jamaica once and for all. Addressing the nation, he said:

I believe that the country needs to settle and decide its economic strategy and that when it is settled it will be easy to understand what part the IMF should play, or whether it should play any part at all. What must be brought to an end is the present state of confusion, because the country has to settle on a path and understand the efforts, the discipline and the sacrifices that are necessary to that struggle.'[128]

The National Executive Council of the PNP, meeting in March, decided that Jamaica should break with the IMF immediately.[129] The decision to do this was carried by 103 votes to 45, with 4 abstentions.[130]

The Jamaican government was faced with two immediate problems: the first was that of obtaining funds from other sources; the second was that of educating the people of Jamaica—and especially the PNP—politically, to understand democratic socialism and its implications, and to engender in them in a few short months the feeling of unity, purpose, courage and determination necessary for the pursuit of a self-reliant policy should the PNP win the election.

Whichever party won, and whichever economic path was followed, the way ahead would be hard. The PNP route, in that it was new and filled with so many uncertainties, was perhaps the more daunting of the two to the population at large. The alternative path, advocated by the JLP under Seaga's leadership, was to turn wholeheartedly to the IMF and to accept sharp adjustment, regardless of the social cost; it was considered a necessary evil if Jamaica wanted to remain within the international capitalist system. The problems of this route were at least familiar.

THE 1980 ELECTION

On 30 October 1980 the PNP suffered a resounding defeat at the national polls. Of the million people who had registered, 86.9 per cent voted. Of these, 58 per cent opted for the JLP and only 41 per cent for the PNP.[131] The record turnout at the election lent weight to the result.

On the face of it, the election result can be interpreted as a green light for IMF borrowing and the policies this implied. For the electorate had been presented with a clear-cut, polarised choice: a continuation of democratic socialism and the search for self-reliance which the PNP now saw as the only possible solution to Jamaica's economic and social problems; or, alternatively, a return to the IMF and the continuation of the measures already tried with the aim of achieving economic improvement regardless of the immediate social cost.

What must be considered here is whether the electorate actually saw the contest in those terms, and hence whether it *was* actually giving a mandate for a return to the IMF. Did the vote in reality represent something else? For it is rather surprising that after the sweeping victory of 1972, and the even greater victory in 1976 on the platform of democratic socialism, the PNP had lost so much ground on this very same platform by 1980. Conditions in Jamaica had been adverse for the majority of people in 1976; the deterioration by 1980 was the continuation of a trend, rather than something new. It is contended here that to interpret the election result as a victory for the IMF supporters in the JLP is to over simplify the case. There are several reasons for this claim.

First, for much of Manley's second term in office, IMF policies had been followed, and despite the sacrifices made, the economy did not improve. The policies did not seem to be working. Some estimates suggest that the standard of living dropped by 50 per cent in the two years preceding the election.[132] It is unlikely that the electorate would have voted for policies which had already added greatly to the burdens of daily living. Moreover, the economic intricacies of the case would have been difficult for the average person to grasp. What is likely is that, aware of the tangible problems which they faced as consumers, the electorate might well have reasoned that the party in power, if not responsible for the problems, was incapable of solving them. It is here that the lack of attention devoted by the PNP to the political education of Jamaicans—especially among their own supporters—was most costly in the final analysis. Especially with the introduction of democratic socialism in 1974, the opportunity was missed for familiarising the populace with the goals and priorities of the PNP, and for mobilising them for their achievement. After this, as sacrifices increased, there was no clear idea in people's minds of the direction in which Jamaican society was moving, and hence there was no general understanding of the cause for which these sacrifices were being made. Hence people lived from day to day, coping with each new price rise, tax increase or food shortage as it arose; there was no compelling faith or ideology to justify the sacrifices.

Therefore, when the PNP asked the electorate to vote for the path of democratic socialism, it was not at all clear to many Jamaicans what they were calling for. It was this that was the PNP's greatest stumbling block in the domestic context, and it was this that was perhaps its greatest lost opportunity while in office. Whereas a slogan may have sufficed in 1976, it was inadequate in 1980. Conditions had worsened and the feeling of despair and hopelessness had increased. To a large extent, therefore, the electorate voted for a change. They had no more overriding faith and trust in the IMF than they had in democratic socialism. What is more, by voting-in the JLP, Jamaicans were voting for a continuation of the policies adopted by the Manley governments, but without the human face.

A second element also figured in a key role in the election result: the huge increase in violence in Jamaica experienced progressively during Manley's years in office. Large areas of Kingston were unsafe to walk in at any time of the day or night. The city was divided along party lines, and gang warfare was the norm. Many particularly vicious incidents occurred, perpetrated by both sides. 1976 seemed to be a turning point, whereupon the violence increased substantially to the point where the Jamaican security forces chiefs noted that it had gone beyond party political violence and showed signs of external organisation and planning.[133] There was even a rumour that the US was backing a destabilisation campaign.[134] The Emergency[135] was extended beyond the election, and over 400 people were detained at some point. The Home Guard, set up in early 1976, was expanded as the years passed by. Its duty was to function as a community-based militia, and to prevent members of one party from entering the territory of the other party. In 1979 the numbers of the Home Guard were bolstered till they equalled those of the police and the National Defence Force combined. By the time of the 1980 election, fear was instilled in the minds of many Jamaicans, who believed the violence had reached uncontrollable proportions. Thus, apart from the economic situation, Jamaicans responded in their voting to the perception that the violence in their society had got out of hand. Manley's Heavy Manners slogan of a few years earlier, which had referred to his party's intention of coming down hard on violence and crime, had seemingly held out false hope, and the JLP was in part looked to to bring some security and order to the confusion.

DID THE IMF VIOLATE JAMAICA'S SOVEREIGNTY?

The charge that the IMF intervened in the domestic affairs of Jamaica, violating her sovereignty, is a difficult one to defend. For the obvious and technically correct response is that

Jamaica chose to join the IMF, and that membership entails acceptance of conditions on drawings. Hence, when she made the decision to go to the IMF to borrow money, she went in the full knowledge that conditions would be attached to the loan.

While this is true, it presents the issue in a clear-cut fashion which obscures the real nature of the problem; that is, the question of what conditions are acceptable. This is not the place for a discussion of the suitability of quarterly tests based on quantitative economic indicators derived from IMF models of national and international economies. Arguments for and against the validity of such tests baffle economists and laymen of all schools of thought. What concerns us here is whether the IMF has the right to disregard the domestic aspirations of a government—especially a freely elected one which has gained the support of a majority of the population who choose to exercise their democratic right.

In 1976 the Manley government was returned to office on the platform of democratic socialism by a sweeping majority. It is reasonable to assume that this gave the government a mandate to attempt to continue and develop that policy, which represented a long-term vision of a restructured society in Jamaica based on a more equitable distribution of wealth with the state accepting responsibility for the provision of basic needs.

Whether the government had chosen to adopt the Puerto Rican model of economic development, or the democratic socialist one, it would have been compelled to go to the IMF. The control Jamaica could exercise over her own economy was marginal; its well-being was significantly dependent on the policies of OPEC, a fickle international demand for bauxite, the contrary behaviour of the multinationals, EEC policies, the price of wheat on the world market and even the weather. Foreign exchange was needed desperately in the short term to provide basic essentials, and in the long term to develop the economy. The commercial banking world looked to the IMF for a stamp of approval before lending to developing countries, and so an unwillingness to negotiate with that institution would result in difficulties in obtaining loans from the latter. (Indeed, it has been shown that Jamaica found that not even this stamp of approval was enough to win favour with the commercial banks.)

On going to the IMF, Manley found that institution particularly insensitive to his government's priorities and goals. The IMF packages to Jamaica in his second term of office were fundamentally inconsistent with the goals and instruments of democratic socialism, and as such they jeopardised not only the achievement of those goals but also the life of the government and the stability of strife-ridden Jamaican society.

The conflict arose due to divergent interests. The IMF recommended policies which were motivated by the desire to ensure the smooth functioning of the international systems of money and trade. The Jamaican government, on the other hand, wanted to implement policies which it believed would be most beneficial for a long-term restructuring of the Jamaican economy, away from its peripheral dependent position within the international capitalist system, to a less vulnerable, more self-reliant and generally more secure position. The IMF, perceiving itself as an agent supplying technical economic remedies for ailing economies, paid no attention to the social and political cost of policies. Indeed, there are many people who believe, as Michael Leapman does, that 'it is not up to the IMF to take account of the political consequences of the economic measures it demands'.[136] The government, however, was very concerned about the repercussions of economic policies. Manley believed that it was unacceptable—indeed, immoral—to expect people who do not have the basic necessities of life, such as food, health care, education and housing, to take further cuts in their standard of living. The IMF did not recognise any 'basic needs' criteria in its formulation of country packages. It did not differentiate between standards of living in different countries when it formulated policies. This disregard shown for the social cost of economic policies borne by the poor was the greatest point of contention between Manley and the IMF. For Manley, no economic policy could be implemented in a social and political vacuum.

Predictably, the consequences of the implementation of IMF packages led to a loss of faith by Jamaicans in Manley's government. It seemed to be reneging on its election promises. The decline in, and eventual near-eradication of, social programmes in the fields of housing, education, health care and food subsidies, made inflation and wage ceilings all the more stinging. The IMF stop on government job-creation projects, coupled with the lack of new investment in the private sector, meant that the unemployment situation continued to deteriorate. For the average Jamaican, by 1980 there was no visible sign of improvement in his or her personal economic situation. There was much hostility towards the IMF in Jamaica, but at its peak it was associated with, and directed against, Manley's acceptance of the harsh conditions—hence the JLP's slogan, *It's Manley's Fault*. It is rather ironic that after labelling Manley as the culprit in this way, the JLP then fought the 1980 election under the IMF banner, while the PNP rejected it.

The Jamaican case points to the fact that it is questionable whether a freely elected democratic-socialist government could ever survive—or, at least, carry out its stated goals and pursue its stated priorities—while borrowing from the IMF. It has been commented that any centre-left government, while carrying out IMF policies, becomes 'the apologetic messenger with perpetually bad news and the exposed neck.'[137] The policies implemented by such governments at the request of the IMF seemed to hurt most the people who can least afford it. Moreover, these are the very people that such governments purport to champion. The situation can eaily arise where the ideological stand which the government claims as its own is seen as being incapable of bringing about the gains its advocates promised. In the Jamaican case, those people who came to blame democratic socialism for the country's ills were distorting the situation. For, even if in the long run it may have been the case that democratic socialism would have perpetuated and/or intensified Jamaica's economic problems, in the time period in which Manley attempted to put it into practice, this was not the case. As he himself remarked in the fifth Annual Conference of PNP Youth, in July 1978, 'The blame cannot be laid on socialism because Jamaica is not a socialist country.'[138]

It has been claimed that 'While the IMF seeks to punish no

country for the political and social system it chooses to adopt, some kinds of government find it tougher to meet IMF conditions than others.'[139] It is contended here that while the latter claim is true, the former is false. The IMF advocates orthodox economic policies which derive from a definite political philosophy. The policies it asks social-democratic governments to follow are policies which it knows in advance the latter cannot implement and still save face. It is a fact that governments of the right usually find it easier to meet IMF conditions because their populations have less opportunity to protest. In a situation where the population is highly politicised and active in the domestic political process, an elected government could not implement such policies with ease unless it had signifcant backing from the electorate. In the case of Jamaica, the participative sector of the population was significant both for its size and also for the fact that it was highly 'tribalised'. Definite territorial demarcations were drawn between the two major parties, and gang warfare between opposing parties was the norm. In such a highly charged political environment, unwelcome policies could not be implemented without expressions of discontent. It is argued here, therefore, that in a situation such as Jamaica's, the IMF's inaction—in terms of its unwillingness to consider the priorities of the elected government and the lack of consideration shown for the social and political consequences of its policies—must at best be regarded as disruptive insensitivity regarding the domestic political process, and at worst be considered as blatant, calculated interference in that process.

The argument up to now has focused on demonstrating insensitivity on a very broad, general level. However, there is one very specific point regarding the IMF and intervention in Jamaica which must not be overlooked. In September 1980 Hugh Small, the finance minister, asked the IMF to comment on reports that the opposition leader, Seaga, had already begun negotiations with the Fund in anticipation of an election victory. According to a letter from the Jamaican government to Larosière, president of the Fund,[140] released in late October, these negotiations dated as far back as June. Small called it 'interference in the political life'[141] of Jamaica. Eric Williams, the president of Trinidad and Tobago, also protested vehemently to the Fund about this. The fact that the IMF had held talks with the opposition leader can be seen as distasteful in itself, yet necessary. However, Small's accusation of interference was valid because the JLP election manifesto included figures about the financing of the foreign-exchange gap which could only have been known as a result of discussions with the IMF. The JLP made its ability to obtain the foreign exchange necessary to close the gap a major plank in its election platform. This could amount to nothing less than an infringement of sovereignty and an interference in the domestic political process of Jamaica.

In the final analysis it is argued here that the IMF took advantage of Jamaica's position of acute economic weakness and the fact that the country had no choice but to go to the Fund and accept its terms if it was to have access to much-needed foreign exchange. It paid no respect to the stated goals and priorities of a democratically elected government, and imposed on the country economic policies which were an anathema to the government. The IMF decided, against the wishes of the Jamaican government, the economic course which the country should take. It forced Jamaica to move back from the mixed economy which the government was trying to create, in the direction of a capitalist economy where the government did not assume responsibility for the provision of basic needs for its people. While no bank can be expected to lend money without expectation of repayment, there must be limits also to what can be expected of a sovereign government. The IMF exceeded those limits when it violated Jamaica's right as a sovereign authority to make its own decisions and policies, and imposed policies and priorities at odds with those favoured by the government. Given the lack of alternatives open to Jamaica, it seems fair to say that the IMF took advantage of the situation and coerced Jamaica into following a particular economic path which carried with it distinct social consequences, disapproved of by the government. The Charter of Economic Rights and Duties of States, approved by the UN General Assembly in December 1974, maintains that 'Every state has the sovereign and inalienable right to choose its economic system as well as its political, social and cultural system in accordance with the will of its people, without outside interference, coercion or threat in any form whatsoever.'[142] Clearly, the IMF acted against the dictates of this charter, and its behaviour amounted to interference in the domestic affairs of Jamaica.

NOTES

1. For an excellent account of Jamaica during these years, see E. H. Stephens and J. D. Stephens, *Democratic Socialism in Jamaica: The Political Movement and Social Transformation in Dependent Capitalism*, Macmillan, London, 1986.
2. M. Manley, *Jamaica: Struggle in the Periphery*, Writers and Readers, London, 1982, p. 207.
3. *Financial Times*, London, 6 September 1972.
4. *Ibid.*
5. See *Sunday Telegraph Magazine*, London, 27 October 1972.
6. *Financial Times*, 22 August 1974.
7. *Ibid.*, 12 March 1975.
8. *The Guardian*, 9 January 1973.
9. *Financial Times*, 12 March 1975.
10. *Ibid.*, 20 September 1977.
11. *Ibid.*, 11 May 1978.
12. *Daily Telegraph*, 9 November 1974.
13. *New York Times*, 17 May 1974.
14. *Financial Times*, 17 May 1974.
15. *Christian Science Monitor* (London edition), 23 May 1974.
16. *Ibid.*
17. *Ibid.*
18. *New York Times*, 17 May 1974.
19. *New York Times*, 3 June 1974.
20. *International Herald Tribune*, 19 June 1974.
21. The ICSID is a centre for arbitration between nationals (i.e. companies) of one state and the government of another. It is powerless to take action in the face of intransigence by members. While Jamaica did not withdraw from that body, she simply refused to communicate on the issue.
22. *Financial Times*, 26 June 1974.
23. *Christian Science Monitor* (London edition), 23 May 1974.
24. *New York Times*, 21 November 1974.
25. *Ibid.*
26. *Financial Times*, 1 October 1975.
27. *Ibid.*, 22 August 1975.
28. *Ibid.*, 4 May 1976.

29. *Ibid.*
30. *Hsinhua*, 20 June 1976. This would be true, provided that production remained at the 1975 level of 11.3 million tons, which had resulted in 153 million US dollars in tax.
31. *Financial Times*, 29 March 1977.
32. *The Morning Star*, 5 July 1978.
33. *Ibid.*
34. *Ibid.*
35. *Ibid.*
36. *Ibid.*
37. *Financial Times*, 20 June 1979.
38. *New York Times*, 17 May 1974.
39. For example, in the *New York Times*, 13 May 1976, it was reported that the CIA attributed violence in Jamaica to left-wing groups. For more details, see M. Kaufman, *Jamaica Under Manley*, Zed Books, London, 1985, pp. 121–2.
40. *The Guardian*, 21 June 1976.
41. See Manley, pp. 28–38. Under this model, Jamaica aimed primarily at developing the manufacturing sector through the import of foreign capital. However, very few new jobs were created and little attention was paid to social welfare. Manley believed that no economic policy could be chosen without regard to its social implications. He believed that the social costs of the Puerto Rican model were too high.
42. Kaufman, p. 125.
43. *The Guardian*, 17 December 1976. In the previous parliament there were fifty-three seats, out of which the PNP had won thirty-five.
44. *Hsinhua*, 18 September 1975.
45. *Ibid.*
46. *The Morning Star*, 5 August 1975.
47. *Hsinhua*, 3 August 1977.
48. *Sunday Times*, 11 May 1975.
49. *Ibid.*
50. *New York Times*, 16 May 1975.
51. *Financial Times*, 18 January 1973.
52. Manley, p. 108. Manley points to the double standards of people who 'had watched De Gaulle put France on a course which set the example of détente to the world: who had lived through the Ostpolitik of West Germany under Willy Brandt; who had seen peaceful co-existence unfold into détente and were to watch Kissinger and Nixon set up their marriage of convenience with China', become hysterical on hearing that Manley was to travel with Castro.
53. *Financial Times*, 23 April 1976.
54. *Daily Telegraph*, 22 March 1976: also, *Christian Science Monitor* (Weekly International Edition), 5 April 1976.
55. *Hsinhua*, 31 May 1978.
56. *The Guardian*, 7 December 1972.
57. *Observer Foreign News Service*, 24 November 1972.
58. *The Daily Telegraph*, 11 November 1972. This recalls to mind the

viewpoint of Nyerere in Chapter 3. The IMF's attitude is that if a government does not want citizens to spend money on luxury items, then those items should be taxed heavily; but their import should not be banned. Nyerere's position was that in a state as poor as Tanzania, any precious foreign exchange wasted on these goods was too much. They simply should not be available.

59. *Financial Times*, 18 January 1973.
60. *Christian Science Monitor* (London edition), 23 May 1974.
61. *Ibid.*
62. *Financial Times*, 6 June 1975.
63. *Ibid.*, 26 September 1975.
64. *Ibid.*, 10 October 1975.
65. *Ibid.*, 12 October 1975.
66. *Ibid.*, 15 July 1976.
67. *The Guardian*, 7 July 1976.
68. *Daily Telegraph*, 31 May 1977.
69. See *IMF Annual Report*, Washington DC, 1963, pp. 12–13. Jamaica joined the Fund on 21 February, and on 28 February the Fund received notification that she had accepted the obligations of Article 8, sections 2, 3 and 4. This rendered her currency convertible. For details of this article, see J. K. Horsefield (ed.), *The IMF, 1945–65*, IMF, Washington DC, vol. 1, pp. 195–6.
70. See *IMF Annual Report*, IMF, Washington DC, 1964, p. 11. Jamaica negotiated a stand-by arrangement with the IMF covering the period 13 June 1963 to 12 June 1964. Under this agreement 10 million US dollars was the amount of drawings allowed. See Chapter 2 for details of stand-by borrowing.
71. See W. E. Robichek, 'The IMF's Experience in Facilitating Adjustment in the Commonwealth Caribbean', presented at the Seminar on Adjustment Policies, Malborough House, London, 27–30 April 1982.
72. See *IMF Survey*, Washington DC, 11 June 1973, p. 167. This agreement allowed Jamaica to purchase currencies up to the equivalent of SDR 26.5 million over the next year. She was expected to fulfil a set of fiscal, monetary and external debt-management policies.
73. *Financial Times*, 24 March 1976.
74. *Ibid.*, 28 September 1976.
75. *Ibid.*
76. J. Morrell, 'Behind the Scenes at the IMF', in *The Nation*, Washington DC, 16 September 1978.
77. *Ibid.*
78. N. Girvan, R. Bernal and W. Hughes. 'The IMF and the Third World: The Case of Jamaica, 1974–80', *Development Dialogue*, Sweden, no. 2, 1980.
79. Manley, p. 153.
80. *Ibid.*, p. 120.
81. *Ibid.*, p. 121.
82. *Ibid.*

83. Girvan *et al.*, p. 123.
84. See *Keesings Contemporary Archives*, Bristol, 1977, p. 28220.
85. Manley, p. 154.
86. *Ibid.*
87. *The Times*, 4 February 1977.
88. *Keesings Contemporary Archives*, Bristol, 1977, p. 28531.
89. *Hsinhua*, 13 February 1977
90. *Ibid.*
91. *Financial Times*, 26 April 1977.
92. *Ibid.*, 14 July 1977.
93. *Keesings Contemporary Archives*, Bristol, 1977, p. 28682.
94. *Financial Times*, 14 July 1977.
95. *Ibid.*, 27 September 1977.
96. *Keesings Contemporary Archives*, Bristol, 1977, p. 28531.
97. Manley, p. 135.
98. *Ibid.*, pp. 243–4.
99. See Manley, Budget Debate Speech, 27 May 1975, Agency for Public Information, Kingston, e.g. p. 59, pp. 64–7. Also, see Manley, *The Private and Public Sectors in our Economy*, Ministry Paper No. 16, Kingston, April 1977: 'The philosophy of Democratic Socialism has at its core full acceptance of the principle of a mixed economy.'
100. Manley, p. 135.
101. Girvan *et al.*, p. 125.
102. *Ibid.*, p. 126.
103. *Financial Times*, 19 January 1978.
104. Manley, p. 156, and Kaufman, p. 141.
105. Girvan *et al.*, p. 160.
106. *Ibid.*, p. 126.
107. *Financial Times*, 19 May 1978.
108. *Ibid.*
109. The State Trading Corporation had been set up in late 1977, and it was responsible for the import of all basic commodities into Jamaica. The JLP had opposed its establishment.
110. *New York Times*, 9 October 1979.
111. Manley, p. 164.
112. *The Guardian*, 6 September 1978.
113. *The Guardian*, 16 July 1979.
114. *Financial Times*, 25 September 1979.
115. *Ibid.*
116. *New York Times*, 1 October 1979.
117. *New York Times*, 9 October 1979.
118. *Ibid.*
119. *Financial Times*, 21 December 1979.
120. *Ibid.*, 5 February 1980.
121. R. Kincaid, 'Conditionality and the Use of Fund Resources', *Finance and Development*, Washington DC, June 1981, p. 20.
122. Girvan *et al.*, p. 129.
123. *The Guardian*, 5 February 1980.

124. *The Morning Star*, 6 February 1980.
125. *Observer Foreign News Service*, 26 February 1980: 'The JLP position is being waged with missionary fervour in the *Daily Gleaner*'.
126. *The Observer*, 9 March 1980.
127. *The Guardian*, 17 March 1980.
128. Kincaid, p. 20.
129. This led to the resignation of Eric Bell, who wanted to get an interim agreement with the IMF until the general election. See *Financial Times*, 25 March 1980.
130. Manley, p. 189.
131. Manley, p. 207.
132. For example, *Sunday Times*, 28 December 1980, which quotes a leading US banker who believes that the standard of living dropped by 50 per cent in eighteen months.
133. *Financial Times*, 14 May 1976.
134. *Ibid.*, 3 June 1976.
135. The Emergency was established on 19 June 1976 to cope with the violence that was increasing daily as the election drew nearer. On 28 October it was further extended till February. It was finally lifted on 6 June 1977.
136. *Times*, 6 June 1980.
137. *Observer Foreign News Service*, 27 March 1979.
138. *Morning Star*, 28 July 1978.
139. *Times*, 6 June 1980.
140. *Financial Times*, 29 October 1980.
141. *Ibid.*
142. See *Keesings Contemporary Archives*, Bristol, 1975, p. 26954.

General Conclusion

The Jamaican case study illustrates the great constraints, even controls, on Third World states in the international capitalist system when they try to exercise their sovereign right to an independent foreign and domestic policy. (The lessons learned are instructive in many respects even for those few Third World states which operate instead as part of the world socialist economic system under Soviet leadership. Recent economic policies in Vietnam are testimony to the constraining/controlling influence of Soviet hegemony). It appears, therefore, that the chance of an independent policy by Third World states is extremely low, since the leading Western powers (especially the US), are almost incapable of interpreting Third World activities, desires, problems and developments in anything other than an East–West framework. Little respect is paid to the viability of indigenous ideologies, social, economic and political preferences, while too much emphasis is placed on perceived indigenous folly which is often portrayed as the root cause of economic chaos. Hence situations arise whereby states which are trying to increase their security by extending links with other states of all political persuasions, are seen to be moving from one of the two recognised 'camps' into the other. Very few Third World states have managed successfully to distance themselves from both blocs—revolutionary Iran, with its *na gharb na sharg*[1] slogan being a notable exception. Post-revolutionary Nicaragua began life pleading for help from all sides, and is slowly being pushed into the Eastern bloc by repudiations from the US. This is a position that neither Nicaragua, nor probably the Soviet

Union, welcome. India is an example of a Third World state which perceives itself as belonging to neither camp, yet even in this case the West, especially the US, often perceives it as being pro-Soviet. In such irrational, ideologically based judgements there is no room even for calculation of the possible regional *raison d'état* of the individual state concerned.

The outlook for Third World states remains bleak. While it is very far from true to suggest that everything that happens to them is a result of external factors, it is fallacious to believe that indigenous factors play the most influential role most of the time. The Jamaican example illustrates all too clearly the influence of the developed states in the Western camp, most particularly the US; the international institutions such as the IMF and the World Bank, which the US largely controls; the power of multinationals; the salience of the market; of private international banks, and even the weather. It illustrates also the tremendous difficulties involved in creating a different type of society, especially when trying to do this through the operation of a Westminster-style democracy in a young state which has no real conception of nationhood. Populist and clientelist policies are almost inevitable, and sometimes these can be highly destabilising. Pragmatism and piecemeal change seem to be the only realistic possibilities, yet these are not the type of policies which can bring a rapid redistribution of national wealth and opportunities. In the final analysis, it seems that most Third World states find their efforts to pursue an independent domestic or foreign policy at minimum constrained, and at maximum controlled, by the preferences of the world's strongest states and the systems which they respectively lead. In exceptional cases, such as that of China, which is so vast, Third World states have a greater chance to be master of their own fate. This remains the privileged position of the few.

As a final word, a brief discussion of the specific role of the US for Third World international relations is in order. Virtually all the themes illustrated in this book indicate that the majority of Third World states have to function within a framework of rules created by the European states, and/or developed and imposed more recently by the US. The USSR's close relationship with a small number of Third World states stands in marked contrast to the relationship of the US with Third World states. While the US has a close military relationship with several of them, such as Taiwan, Pakistan and Guatemala, it is able to influence so many other aspects of the total existence of the vast majority of Third World states because of its position of pre-eminence in international economic rule-making and management; in other words, because of its role as leading capitalist state. The USSR has no such world-wide economic clout. The US, much more so than the USSR, exerts real preponderant power in regard to Third World states generally. Moreover, certain recent trends and developments in US policy under Reagan have led to the specific exercise of that power. For instance, its staunch perception of the East–West confrontation as the central characteristic of contemporary international affairs has determined its attitude towards Third World states. The latter are categorised as either pro-Soviet or pro-US. They receive financial, military and technological help in accordance with their status under this classification. Such a conception leaves little room for radical Third World states which are not party to the Soviet cause. (Iran is an exception, but this may be due more to the particular nature of the revolution there than to a foresighted US policy). Caught in this perceived web of all-encompassing global East–West rivalry, several Third World states have found themselves the target of economic, diplomatic and paramilitary weapons originating in, or sustained by, the US. Nicaragua is a case in point. The Contras are hailed as freedom-fighters while the Nicaraguan government is said to be composed of terrorists. Perhaps more disturbing, many Third World states which are friendly with the US find themselves facing domestic political difficulties due to the economic austerity championed by the US. Recent conditions attached to IMF loans to Costa Rica and Egypt are a case in point here: the cutting of subsidies to farmers in the case of the former, and the elimination of food subsidies in the latter, threaten domestic stability. This suggests a lack of pragmatism on the part of the US, which seems to be driven on by its ideological view of national and international events. On the other hand, of course, certain Third World states have benefited from the US's ideological conception. Hence the newly-industrialising countries of South East Asia have portrayed themselves as bastions against communism, located at the sharp end of the East–West struggle, even though their developmental success has to a large degree depended on disregard of free market principles in favour of strong government intervention.

All this goes to underline the rich diversity of states which form the Third World grouping. As a final note it is emphasised here that while in general terms Third World states have been able to do little to increase their security in a significant way, on particular issues the relative ability of individual Third World states to improve their security varies through time and space. This can be seen clearly on the issues of food and health. With the massive projected increases in population by the end of the twentieth century, it is imperative that Third World governments exploit their room for manoeuvre on such issues, however small it may be. Looking no further than the implications of the demographic factor, it is clear that the search for security by Third World states has only just begun.

NOTE

1.   Neither East nor West.

Bibliography

Abdalla, I.-S. 'The Inadequacy and loss of Legitimacy of the IMF', *Development Dialogue*, 2 (1980).

Adam, H. (ed.) *South Africa: The Limits of Reform Politics, Journal of Asian and African Studies*, Special Issue, 18, 1–2 (January–April 1983).

Africa Research Bulletin, 'SADCC: Nkomati's Shadow', *African Research Bulletin*, 31 May 1984.

Albright, D. E. *The USSR and Sub-Saharan Africa in the 1980s*, The Washington Papers, 101, Georgetown University, 1983.

Albright, D. E. *Africa and International Communism*, Macmillan, London, 1980.

Ali, T. *The Nehrus and the Gandhis*, Pan Books, London, 1985.

Allsin, M. and Helger, G. 'Turmoil and the Politics of the Third World', *Yearbook of World Affairs*, 1981.

Almond, G. A. and Coleman, J. (eds.) *The Politics of the Developing Areas*, Princeton University Press, Princeton, 1960.

Almond, G. 'A Developmental Approach to Political Systems', *World Politics* 17 (1965).

Aluko, O. *The Foreign Policies of African States*, Hodder & Stoughton, London, 1977.

AMEX Bank Review *Sovereign Debt Rescheduling* 4 (July 1982).

Amin, S. 'Underdevelopment and Dependence in Black Africa', *Journal of Modern African Studies*, December 1972.

Amin, S. *Imperialism and Unequal Development*, Harvester Press, Brighton, 1977.

Angel, J. 'Indonesian Foreign Policy since Independence', *Yearbook of World Affairs*, 1977.

Anglin, D. 'Economic Liberation and Regional Cooperation in Southern Africa: SADCC and PTA', *International Organisation* 37 (1983).

Anglin, D., Shaw, T. and Widstand, C. (eds.) *Conflict and Change in Southern Africa*, University Press of America, Washington DC, 1978.

Apter, D. *The Politics of Modernisation*, Chicago University Press, Chicago, 1965.

Arnold, H. M. 'Africa and the NIEO', *Third World Quarterly*, April 1980.

Arvin, S. 'NIEO: How to Put Third World Surpluses to Effective Use', *Third World Quarterly*, January 1979.

Astrow, A. *Zimbabwe: A Revolution that Lost its Way*, Zed Press, London, 1983.

Avramovic, D. *South–South Financial Cooperation*, Pinter Press, London, 1983.

Ayoob, M. 'The Superpowers and Regional Stability: Parallel Responses to the Gulf and the Horn', *World Today*, May 1979.

Ayoob, M. 'India, Pakistan and Superpower Rivalry', *World Today*, May 1982.

Ayoob, M. 'Security in the Third World: The Worm About to Turn?' *International Affairs* 60, 1 (Winter 1983/4).

Ayres, R. 'Arms Production as a Form of Import Substituting Industrialisation: The Turkish Case', *World Development* 11, 9 (1983).

Baipaj, U. S. (ed.) *Non Alignment*, Lancers, New Delhi, 1983.

Baldwin, R. E. and Kay, D. A. 'International Trade and International Relations', *International Organisation*, Winter 1975.

Becker, D. G. 'Development, Democracy and Dependency in Latin America: A Post Imperialist View', *Third World Quarterly*, April, 1984.

Benton, G. *The Hong Kong Crisis*, Pluto Press, London, 1983.

Bergmen, A. E. *Women of Vietnam*, People's Press, San Francisco, 1974.

Bergsten, C. F. Keohane, R. O. and Nye, J. S. 'International Economics and International Politics: A Framework for Analysis', *International Organisation*, Winter 1975.

Bergsten, C. F. 'The Threat is Real', *Foreign Policy*, Spring 1974.

Bernstein, H. and Johnson, H. *Third World Lives of Struggle*, Open University, Milton Keynes, 1984.

Berridge, G. 'Apartheid and the West', *Yearbook of World Affairs*, 1981.

Berstein, H. *For Their Triumphs and Their Tears: Women in Apartheid South Africa*, IDAFSA, 1975.

Bhargava, G. S. *South Asian Security After Afghanistan*, Lexington Books, Lexington, Mass., 1983.

Bhattacharyra, R. C. 'The Influence of the International Secretariat: UNCTAD and the Tariff Preferences', *International Organisation* 30 (Winter 1976).

Bienefeld, M. and Godfrey, M. (eds.) *The Struggle for Development*, John Wiley, Chichester, 1982.

Biko, S. *The Testimony to Steve Biko: Black Consciousness in South Africa*, Granada, London, 1984.

Bindert, C. 'Debt: Beyond the Quick-Fix', *Third World Quarterly*, October 1983.

Bird, G. 'Commercial Borrowing by Less Developed Countries', *Third World Quarterly*, April 1980.

Bishop, M. *In Nobodys Backyard*, Zed Press, London, 1984.

Bissell, R. 'The Ostracism of South Africa', *Yearbook of World Affairs*, 1978.

Boardman, R. 'Chinese Foreign Policy: Options for the 1980s', *Yearbook of World Affairs*, 1980.

Brandt Commission, *Common Crisis: N/S Coop for World Recovery*, Pan Books, London, 1983.

Brandt Report, *North–South: A Programme for Survival*, Pan Books, London, 1980.

Braun, Dieter. *The Indian Ocean*, Hurst & Co., London, 1983.

Brind, H. 'Soviet Policy in the Horn of Africa', *International Affairs*, London, 1984.

Bronstein, A. *The Triple Struggle: Latin American Peasant Women Speak Out*, War on Want, London, 1982.

Brownlie, I. (ed.) *Basic Documentation on African Affairs*, Oxford University Press, Oxford, 1971.

Brown, D. 'Crisis and Ethnicity: Legitimacy in Plural Societies', *Third World Quarterly*, October 1985.

Brown, W. *Black Women and the Peace Movement*, Falling Wall Press, 1984.

Brozoska, M. and Ohlson, T. (eds.) *Arms Production in the Third World*, SIPRI, Taylor and Francis, London and Philadelphia, 1986.

Brucan, S. 'The Global Crisis', *International Studies Quarterly*, March 1984.

Bruce St John, R. 'The Soviet Penetration of Libya', *World Toady*, April 1982.

Bruce, D. 'Brazil Plays the Japan Card', *Third World Quarterly*, October 1983.

Bull, H. 'The Third World and International Society', *Yearbook of World Affairs*, 1979.

Bull, H. (ed.) *Intervention in World Politics*, Clarendon Press, Oxford, 1984.

Callaghy, T. M. 'Africa's Debt Crisis', *International Affairs* 38, 1 (Summer 1984).

Calvert, P. A. R. *The Foreign Policy of New States*, Wheatsheaf Books, Brighton, 1986.

Calvocoressi, P. *Independent Africa and the World*, Longman, Harlow, Essex, 1985.

Campbell, J. 'The Middle East: Burden of Empire', *Foreign Affairs*, Special Edition, 1977.

Caporaso, J. 'Industrialisation the Periphery', in W. Hollist and J. M. Rosenau (eds.) *World System Structure*, Sage, Beverly Hills, 1981, ch. 6.

Cardoso, F. 'Dependency and Development', *New Left Review* 74 (July–August 1972).

Carroll, T. G. 'Secularisation and States of Modernity', *World Politics* 3, 4 (1982).

Cassen, R. (ed.) *Soviet Interest in the Third World*, Sage, London, 1985.

Cervenka, Z. *The Unfinished Quest for Unity: Africa and the OAU*, Friedmann in association with the Scandinavian Institute of African Studies, London, 1977.

Chaliand, G. *The Struggle for Africa*, Macmillan, London, 1982.

Cheysson, C. 'Europe and the Third World After Lomé', *World Today*, June 1975.

Chomsky, N. *Superpowers in Collision*, Penguin, Harmondsworth, 1982.

Chubin, S. 'The Northern Tier in Disarray', *World Today*, December 1979.

CIIA/BCC *Namibia in the 1980s*, CIIA/BCC, London, 1981.

Clapham, C. (ed.) *Foreign Policy Making in Developing States*, Saxon House, Farnborough, Hants, 1977.

Clapham, C. *Third World Politics*, Croom Helm, Kent, 1985.

Cline, W. 'Can the East Asian Model of Development Be Generalised?' *World Development* 10, 2 (1982).

Cohen, B. and El-Khawas, M. A. (eds.) *The Kissinger Study on Southern Africa*, L. Hill, Westport, Conn., 1976.

Coker, C. 'Reagan and Africa', *World Today*, April 1982.

Connell-Smith, G. 'The Grenada Invasion in Historical Perspective: From Monroe to Reagan', *Third World Quarterly*, April 1984.

Cooper, R. N. 'Prologomena to the Choice of an International Monetary System', *International Organisation*, Winter 1975.

Corea, G. 'UNCTAD and the NIEO', *International Affairs*, April 1977.

Cosgrove Twitchett, C. 'The NIEO: The European Community's Response', *Journal of Common Market Studies* 17, 2 (December 1978).

Cosgrove Twitchett, C. 'Towards a New ACP–EEC Convention', *World Today*, December 1978.

Cosgrove Twitchett, C. *Europe and Africa: From Association to Partnership*, Saxon House, Farnborough, Hants., 1978.

Cosgrove Twitchett, C. 'Lomé II: A new ACP–EEC Agreement', *World Today*, March 1980.

Cuddy, J. 'Third World Liquidity Needs', *Third World Quarterly*, October 1983.

Cutler, P. 'The Measurement of Poverty: India', *World Development* 12, 11/12 (1984).

Davidson, B. *The People's Cause: A History of Guerrillas in Africa*, Longman, Harlow, Essex, 1981.

Davidson, B. *Africa in Modern History*, Penguin, Harmondsworth, 1981.

Davies, M. (ed.) *Third World: Second Sex: Women's Struggles and National Liberation Movements*, Zed Press, London, 1983.

Dell, S. 'Stabilisation: The Political Economy of Overkill', *World Development* 10, 8 (1982).

De Silva, L. 'The Non-Aligned Movement and the Group of 77: Issues in Monetary and Financial Cooperation, With a Case Study of the Non-Aligned Solidarity Fund for Economic and Social Development', in D. Avramovic (ed.) *South–South Financial Cooperation*, Pinter Press, London, 1983.

Deighton, J. *et al. Sweet Ramparts: Women in Revolutionary Nicaragua*, War on Want, London, 1983.

Document 'Opposition in South Korea', *New Left Review*, 1973.

Donaldson, P. *Worlds Apart*, Penguin, Harmondsworth, 1986.

Dorfman, A. and Mattelart, A. *How to Read Donald Duck: Imperialist Ideology in the Disney Comic*, International General, New York, 1984.

Doyal, R. 'Zimbabwe's Long Road to Freedom', *Third World Quarterly* July 1980.

Doyle, M. 'Stalemate in the N/S Debate', *World Politics*, April 1983.

Dutt, V. P. *India's Foreign Policy*, Vikat, New Delhi, 1984.

Echmeta, B. *Our Own Freedom*, Shelsa Press, London, 1981.

Eckaus, R. 'Observations on the Conditionality of International Financial Institutions', *World Development* 10, 9 (1982).

Eckstein, H. 'The Idea of Political Development: From Dignity to Efficiency', *World Politics*, 1982.

Edens, D. G. 'The Anatomy of the Saudi Revolution', *International*

Journal of Middle East Studies 5 (January 1974).

Eisen, A. *Women and Revolution in Vietnam*, Zed Press, London, 1984.

Eisenstadt, S. N. 'Approaches to the Problem of Political Development in Non-Western Societies', *World Politics*, IX, 3 (April 1957).

Elios, O. T. 'The Charter of the OAU', *American Journal of International Law*, April 1965.

El-Saadawi, N. *The Hidden Face of Eve*, Zed Press, London, 1980.

Emerson, R. and Kilson, M. *The Political Awakening of Africa*, Prentice-Hall, Englewood Cliffs, NJ, 1965.

Enloe, C. *Does Khaki Become You? The Militarisation of Women's Lives*, Pluto Press, London, 1983.

Epstein, W. *The Last Chance*, Free Press, London, 1976.

Erb, G. F. and Kallab, V. (eds.) *Beyond Dependency*, Praeger in cooperation with the Overseas Development Council, 1975.

Faaland, J. (ed.) *Aid and Influence: The Case of Bangladesh*, Macmillan, London, 1981.

Fanon, F. *The Wretched of the Earth*, Penguin, Harmondsworth, 1967.

Fatouros, A. 'Satre an Colonialism', *World Politics*, 1964/5.

Faundez, S. and Picciotto, S. *The Nationalisation of Multinationals in the Peripheral Economies*, Macmillan, London, 1978.

Feinberg, R. 'The Kissinger Commission Report: A Critique', *World Development* 12, 8 (1984).

Feuchtwanger, E. J. and Nailor, P. (eds.) *The Soviet Union and the Third World*, Macmillan Press, London, 1981.

Firebrace, J. and Holland, S. *Never Kneel Down: Drought, Development and Liberation in Eritrea*, Spokesman, Nottingham, 1984.

Fortin, C. 'The Failure of Repressive Monetarism, Chile 1973–83', *Third World Quarterly*, April 1984.

Frank, A. G. 'The Development of Underdevelopment', *Monthly Review* 18, 4 (September 1966).

Frank, A. G. 'Arms Economy and Warfare in the Third World', *Third World Quarterly*, July 1983.

Fukai, S. 'Japan's North–South Dialogue at the UN', *World Politics*, October 1982.

Furtado, L. 'Rescuing Brazil, Reversing Recession', *Third World Quarterly*, July 1983.

Galbraith, J. K. 'The Causes of Poverty: A Classification, in A. Mack, D. Plant and U. Doyle (eds.), *Imperialism, Intervention and Development*.

Gauhar, A. *The Rich and the Poor: Development Negotiations and*

Cooperation—An Assessment, Third World Foundation, London, 1983.

Gauhar, A. (ed.) *The Rich and the Poor*, Third World Foundation, London, 1983.

Gauhar, A. (ed.) *South–South Strategy*, Third World Foundation, London, 1983.

Gauhar, A. (ed.) *Talking About Development*, Third World Foundation, London, 1983.

Gauhar, A. (ed.) *Third World Affairs*, Third World Foundation, London, 1985 and 1986.

Gavshon, A. *Crisis in Africa: Battleground of East and West*, Penguin, Harmondsworth, 1978.

Geldart, C. and Lyon, P. 'The Group of 77: A Perspective View', *International Affairs*, Winter 1980/1.

George, S. *How the Other Half Dies*, Penguin, Harmondsworth, 1983.

George, T., Litwak, R. and Chubin, S. *Security in South Asia: India and the Great Powers*, Gower, Aldershot, 1984.

Gilmour, D. *The Dispossessed*, Sphere Books, London, 1983.

Gilpin, R. 'Three Models of the Future', *International Organisation*, Winter 1975.

Girling, J. 'Reagan and the Third World', *World Today*, November 1981.

Girvan, N. 'Swallowing the IMF Medicine in the 1970s', *Development Dialogue* 2, (1980).

Gladstone, J. A. 'Theories of Revolution', in *World Politics*, April 1980.

Goheen, R. F. 'Problems of Proliferation: US Policy and the Third World', *World Politics*, January 1983.

Gold, J. *Conditionality*, IMF Pamphlet Series, Washington DC, no. 31, 1982.

Goldblat, J. (ed.) *Non-Proliferation: The Why and the Wherefore*, SIPRI, Taylor & Francis, London, 1985.

Goodwin, G. 'Yet Another Paradigm', *Millenium* 7, 3 (Winter 1978/9).

Goulbourne, H. (ed.) *Politics and State in the Third World*, Macmillan, London, 1979.

Griffin, K. and James, J. *The Transition to Egalitarian Development 1981*, Macmillan, London, 1984.

Griffiths-Jones, S. and Rodriguez, E. 'International Finance and Industrialisation of LDCs', *Journal of Development Studies* 21 (October 1984).

Goulet, D. 'Obstacles to World Development: An Ethical

Reflection', *World Development* 11, 7 (1983).

Gruhn, I. V. 'The Lomé Convention: Inching Towards Interdependence', *International Organisation* 30 (1976).

Guitan, M. *Fund Conditionality, Evolution of Principles and Practices*, IMF Pamphlet Series, Washington DC, no. 38.

Guitan, M. 'Fund Conditionality and the International Adjustment Process: Early Period 1950–70', *Finance and Development*, December 1980.

Guitan, M. 'Fund Conditionality and the International Adjustment Process: The Changing Environment of the 1970s', *Finance and Development*, March 1981.

Guitan, M. 'Fund Conditionality and the International Adjustment Process: A Look into the 1980s', *Finance and Development*, June 1981.

Gustafsson, B. G. 'Rostow, Marx and the Theory of Economic Growth', *Science and Society* 25 (Summer 1961).

Gwin, C. and Vevt, L. 'The Indian Miracle', *Foreign Policy* 58 (Spring 1985).

Hall, J. A. *Powers and Liberties*, Penguin, Harmondsworth, 1986.

Hall, J. A. (ed.) *States in History*, Blackwell, Oxford, 1986.

Halliday, F. *Threat from the East*, Penguin, Harmondsworth, 1982.

Halliday, F. and Molyneux, M. *The Ethiopian Revolution*, Verso, London, 1981.

Hanlon, J. *Mozambique: The Revolution Under Fire—Why Mozambique Signed the Nkomati Accords*, Zed Press, London, 1984.

Harkavy, R. *Great Power Competition for Overseas Bases*, Pergamon Press, New York, 1982.

Harris, N. 'The Asian Boom Economies and the "Impossibility" of Natural Economic Development', *International Socialism*, Winter 1978–9.

Harris, N. *Of Bread and Guns*, Penguin, Harmondsworth, 1983.

Harris, H. 'Women in Struggle; Nicaragua', *Third World Quarterly*, October 1983.

Hart, D. *Nuclear Power in India*, Allen & Unwin, London, 1983.

Hayter, T. *The Creation of World Poverty*, Pluto, London, 1983.

Helleiner, G. K. 'The IMF and Africa in the 1980s', *Canadian Journal of African Studies* 17 (1983).

Heller, T. *Poor Health, Rich Profits: Multinational Drug Companies and the Third World*, Spokesman Books, Nottingham, 1977.

Henderson, R. 'Principles and Practice in Mozambique's Foreign Policy', *World Today*, July 1978.

Hewitt, A. 'Stabex: An Evaluation of the Economic Impact over the

First Five Years', *World Development* 11, 12 (1983).

Hollick, J. 'French Intervention in Africa in 1978', *World Today*, February 1979.

Hollist, W. L. and Rosenau, J. M. (eds.) *World System Structure*, Sage Publications, Beverly Hills, 1981.

Honeywell, M. *The Poverty Brokers: The IMF and Latin America*, Latin American Research Bureau, London.

Horsefield, J. K. *The IMF, 1945–65*, vols. 1–3, IMF, Washington DC.

Hosmer, S. T. and Wolfe, T. W. *Soviet Policy and Practice Toward Third World Conflicts*, Lexington Books, Lexington, Mass., 1983.

Huntingdon, S. 'Foreign Aid', *Foreign Policy*, Spring 1971.

Husain, M. A. 'Third World and Disarmament: Shadow and Substance', *Third World Quarterly*, January 1980.

IDAFSA *To Honour Womens Day: Profiles of Leading Women in the South African and Namibian Liberation Struggles*, IDAFSA, London, 1981.

IDAFSA *Namibia: The Facts*, WAFSA, London, 1983.

IDS (Sussex) Bulletin, 'Accelerated Development in Sub-Saharan, Africa: What Agendas for Action?' *IOS Sussex Bulletin* 14, 1 (January 1983).

Ispahani, M. Z. 'Alone Together: Regional Security Arrangements in Southern Africa and the Arabian Gulf', *International Security*, Spring 1984.

Jacobson, H. *et al.* 'Revolutionaries or Bargainers? Negotiations for an NIEO', *World Politics*, April 1983.

Jeffrey, P. *Frogs in a Well: Indian Women in Purdah*, Zed Press, London, 1979.

Johnson, D. 'The NIEO', *Yearbook of World Affairs*, 1983.

Johnson, D. 'The NIEO II', *Yearbook of World Affairs*, 1984.

Johnson, H. and Bernstein, H. (eds.) *Third World Struggle*, Part 3, Heinemann and Open University Press, London, 1984.

Johnson, R. W. *How·Long Will South Africa Survive?*, Macmillan, London, 1977.

Kaldor, M. and Anderson, P. (eds.) *Mad Dogs: The US Raids on Libya*, Pluto Press, London, 1986.

Kanet, R. E. (ed.) *The Soviet Union and the Developing States*, Johns Hopkins University Press, Baltimore, 1974.

Kapur, A. 'The Nuclear Spread: A Third World View', *Third World Quarterly*, January 1980.

Kapur, A. *India's Nuclear Option: Atomic Diplomacy and Decision-Making*, Praeger, New York, 1976.

Katz, M. N. *The Third World in Soviet Military Thought*, Croom Helm, London, 1982.

Keohane, D. 'Hegemony and Nuclear Non-Proliferation', *Yearbook of World Affairs*, 1981.

Keohane, R. and Ooms, V. 'The MNC and International Regulation', *International Organisation*, Winter 1975.

Kerina, M. *Namibia: The Making of a Nation*, Books in Focus, New York, 1981.

Kesselman, M. 'Order or Movement? The Literature of Political Development as Ideology', *World Politics*, XXVI, 1 (October 1973).

Khalidi, W. 'Thinking the Unthinkable: A Sovereign Palestinian State', *Foreign Affairs*, July 1978.

Khalilzad, Z. 'Pakistan: The Making of a Nuclear Power', *Asian Survey* 17, 6 (June 1976).

Khalilzad, Z. 'Pakistan and the Bomb', *Survival* 21 (1979).

Khalilzad, Z. *The Security of Southwest Asia*, Gower, Aldershot, 1984.

King, P. *An African Winter*, Penguin, Harmondsworth, 1986.

Koo, M. 'The Political Economy of Income Distribution in South Korea: The Impact of the State's Industrialisation Policies', *World Development* 12, 10 (1984).

Korany, B. 'The Take-Off of Third World Studies? The Case of Foreign Policy', *World Politics*, XXXV, 3 (April 1983).

Kraft, J. *The Mexican Rescue*, Group of Thirty, New York, 1984.

Krasner, S. 'Oil is the Exception', *Foreign Policy*, Spring 1974.

Krasner, S. 'Third World Vulnerabilities and Global Negotiations', *Review of International Studies* 9 (1981).

Krasner, S. *Structural Conflict: The Third World Against Global Liberalism* University of California Press, Berkeley, 1985.

Krause, L. B. and Nye, J. S. 'Reflections on the Politics and Economics of International Organisations', *International Organisation*, Winter 1975.

Kumar, C. 'The Indian Ocean: Arc of Crisis or Zone of Peace?', *International Affairs*, Spring 1984.

Kuper, L. *Genocide*, Penguin, Harmondsworth, 1981.

Lall, S. 'The Emergence of Third World Multinationals: Indian Joint Ventures Overseas', *World Development* 10, 2 (1982).

Lall, S. 'Exports of Technology by NICs: An Overview', *World Development* 12, 5/6 (1984).

Landsberg, M. 'Export-led Industrialisation in the Third World: Manufacturing Imperialism', *Review of Radical Political Economics* 11, 4 (Winter 1979).

Lanning, G. and Mueller, M. *Africa Undermined: A History of the Mining Companies and the Underdevelopment of Africa*, Penguin, Harmondsworth, 1979.

Larkin, B. D. *China and Africa, 1949–70*, University of California Press, Berkeley, 1971.

Laurent, P. 'Europe and Africa, Towards Lomé III', *World Today*, September 1983.

Lefort, R. *Ethiopia: An Heretical Revolution?* Zed Press, London, 1983.

Leghorn, L. and Roodkowsky, M. *Who Really Starves? Women and World Hunger*, Friendship Press, New York, 1977.

Legum, C. 'Foreign Intervention in Africa', I and II, *Yearbook of World Affairs*, 1980 and 1981.

Legum, C. 'South Africa's Search for a New Political System', *Yearbook of World Affairs*, 1982.

Legum, C. 'The South African Crisis: The Makings of a Second Middle East', *African Contemporary Record* 15 (1982/3).

Legum, C. and Hodges, T. *After Angola: The War Over Southern Africa*, Africana Publishing Co., New York, 1976.

Leifer, M. *Indonesia's Foreign Policy*, Allen & Unwin, for Royal Institute of International Affairs, London, 1983.

Leonard, J. 'MNCs and Politics in Developing Countries', *World Politics* 22, 3 (April 1980).

Lever, H. and Huhne, C. *Debt and Danger*, Penguin, Harmondsworth, 1985.

Levi, W. 'Are Developing States More Equal than Others?', *Yearbook of World Affairs*, 1978.

Lewis, A. 'The LDCs and Stable Exchange Rates', *Third World Quarterly*, January 1979.

Lewis, I. M. (ed.) *Self-Determination in the Horn of Africa*, Ithaca Press, London, 1983.

Lobstein, T. (ed.) *Namibia: Reclaiming the People's Health*, Namibia Support Committee, London, 1984.

Love, J. L. 'Third World: A Response to Professor Worsley', *Third World Quarterly*, April 1980.

Luckham, R. 'Militarisation and the New International Anarchy', *Third World Quarterly*, April 1984.

Mahmood, R. and Singer, H. 'Is There a Poverty Trap for Developing Countries? Polarisation: Reality or Myth?' *World Development* 10, 1 (1982).

Makgetla, N. and Seidman, A. *South Africa and US Multinational Corporations*, L. Hill, Westport, Conn., 1978.

Makgetla, N. and Seidman, A. *Outposts of Monopoly Capitalism:*

Southern Africa in the Changing Global Economy, Lawrence Hill, Westport, 1980.

Mandela, N. *No Easy Walk to Freedom*, Heinemann, London, 1983.

Manley, M. 'The Third World Under Challenge', *Third World Quarterly*, January 1980.

Manley, M. *Jamaica: Struggle in the Periphery*, Writers and Readers Publishing Cooperative, London, 1982.

Mansingh, S. *India's Search for Power: Indira Gandhi's Foreign Policy 1966–82*, Sage, New Delhi, 1984.

Marsh, J. *Stop the War Against Angola and Mozambique*, SWAM, London, 1981.

Marshall, S. 'Paradoxes of Change: Culture Crisis, Islamic Revival and the Reactivation of Patriarchy', *Journal of Asian and African Studies* 19, 1–2 (1984).

Martin, D. and Johnson, P. 'Africa: The Old and the Unexpected', *Foreign Affairs*, 1984.

Mayall, J. 'Africa and the EEC: Cooperation or Neocolonial Dependency', *Millenium*, Autumn 1974.

Mayall, J. 'The Battle for the Horn, Somali Irredentism and International Diplomacy', *World Today*, September 1978.

Mayall, J. 'Africa and the International System: The Great Powers in Search of a Perspective', *Government and Opposition*, 14, 3 (Summer 1979).

Mayall, J. 'The National Question in the Horn of Africa', *World Today*, September 1983.

Mazrui, A. 'From Social Darwinism to Current Theories of Modernisation', *World Politics* 21 (1968/9).

Mazrui, A. *Africa's International Relations*, Heinemann, London, 1977.

Mazrui, A. 'Churches and Multinationals in the Spread of Third World Education', *Third World Quarterly*, January 1979.

Mazrui, A. *The African Condition*, Heinemann, London, 1980.

Mazrui, A. 'Africa's Nuclear Future', *Survival* 22 (1980).

Mazrui, A. 'Changing the Guards from Hindus to Muslims: Collective Third World Security in a Cultural Perspective, *International Affairs* 57, (Winter 1980/1).

Mazrui, A. and Patel H. (eds.) *Africa in World Affairs*, Third Press, New York, 1973.

Mazrui, A. 'Exit Visa from the World System: Dilemmas of Cultural and Economic Disengagement', in A. Gauhar (ed.) *South–South Strategy*, Third World Foundation, 1983.

Mazrui, A. A. and Tidy, M. *Nationalism and New States in Africa*, Heinemann, London, 1984.

McCall, G. 'Four Worlds of Experience and Action', *Third World Quarterly*, July 1980.

McGrew, A. 'Nuclear Revisionism: The US and the Nuclear Non-Proliferation Act of 1978', *Journal of International Studies*, Winter 1978/9.

McKenzie, G. and Thomas, S. 'The Economics of the Debt Crisis', *Economic Review*, Southampton, Spring 1984.

McLaurin, R., Peretz, D. and Snider, L. *Middle East Foreign Policy: Issues and Processes*, Praeger, New York, 1982.

Medawar, C. and Freese, B. *Drug Diplomacy*, Social Audit, London, 1982.

Mikdashi, Z. 'Collusion Could Work', *Foreign Policy*, Spring 1974.

Moffit, M. *The World's Money*, London, 1984.

Mojdehi, J. M. M. 'America and the Third World: Return to the Past', *Survival*, XXIV, 2 (March 1982).

Molyneux, M. *Women's Emancipation Under Socialism: A Model for the Third World*, IDS, Sussex, January 1981.

Moore Lappe, F. and Beccar-Varela, A. N. *Mozambique and Tanzania: Asking the Big Questions*, Institute for Food and Development Policy, San Francisco, 1980.

Mouzelis, M. *Politics in the Semi-Periphery*, Macmillan, London, 1986.

Mugabe, R. *Our War of Liberation*, Mambo Press, Harare, 1983.

Mugomba, A. 'Small Developing States and the External Operational Environment', *Yearbook of World Affairs*, 1979.

Muller, M. *Tobacco and the Third World*, War on Want, London, 1978.

Muller, M. *The Health of Nations*, Faber & Faber, London, 1982.

Muni, S. D. 'Third World: Concept and Controversy', *Third World Quarterly*, July 1979.

Munslow, B. and O'Keefe, P. 'Energy and the Southern African Regional Confrontation', *Third World Quarterly*, January 1984.

Myrdal, G. *Asian Drama: An Enquiry into the Poverty of Nations*, Vintage, New York, 1972.

Nyerere, J. Speech at Ibadan University, reported in *Africa Current* 6 (Spring 1977).

Nyerere, J. 'Third World Negotiating Strategy', *Third World Quarterly*, April 1979.

O'Brien, D. C. 'Modernisation, Order and the Erosion of a Democratic Ideal', *Journal of Development Studies* 8, 4 (1972).

O'Neill, H. 'UNCTAD V: Lessons Unlearned', *Yearbook of World Affairs*, 1981.

O'Neill, H. 'HICs, MICs, NICs and LICs', *World Development* 12, 7 (1984).

Ogunbadejo, O. 'Africa's Nuclear Capability', *Journal of Modern African Studies* 22, 1 (1984).

Onkar, M. and Schulz, A. (eds.) *Nuclear Proliferation and the Near Nuclear Countries*, Ballinger, New York, 1975.

ORBIS, 'US Policy Towards Sub-Saharan Africa', *ORBIS*, Special Issue, Winter 1982.

Oxaal, I., Barnett, T. and Booth, D. *Beyond the Sociology of Development* Routledge & Kegan Paul, London, 1975.

Pakenham, R. 'Approaches to the Study of Political Development', *World Politics*, 1964/5.

Payer, C. *The World Bank: A Critical Assessment*, Monthly Review Press, London and New York, 1982.

Payer, C. *The Debt Trap*, Penguin, Harmondsworth, 1974.

Payer, C. 'Pushed into the Debt Trap: South Korea's Export Miracle', *Journal of Contemporary Asia* 5, 2 (1975).

Payer, C. 'Tanzania and the World Bank', *Third World Quarterly*, October 1983.

Philip, G. 'The Limitations of Bargaining Theory: A Case Study of the International Petroleum Company in Peru', *World Development* 231, 3 (March 1976).

Pineye, D. 'The Bases of Soviet Power in the Third World', *World Development* 11, 12 (1983).

Poneman, D. *Nuclear Power in the Developing World*, Allen & Unwin, London, 1982.

Quandt, W. 'The Middle East Crises', *Foreign Affairs*, Special Edition, 1980.

Radetzki, M. 'Has Political Risk Scared Mineral Investment Away from Deposits in Developing Countries?', *World Development* 10, 1 (1982).

Randall, V. and Theobald, R. *Political Change and Underdevelopment*, Macmillan, London, 1985.

Rao, R. 'The Janata Government and the Soviet Connection', *World Today*, February 1978.

Riddell, A. R. *Restructuring British Industry: The Third World Dimension*, CIIR, London, 1979.

Roberts, P. 'Feminism in Africa: Feminism and Africa', *Review of African Political Economy* 27/8 (February 1984).

Rogers, B. *The Domesticisation of Women. Discrimination in Developing Societies*, Tavistock, London, 1980.

Rothstein, R. 'Regime Creation by a Coalition of the Weak: Lessons from the NIEO and the IPC', *International Studies Quarterly* 28 (1984).

Rothstein, R. 'Is the North/South Dialogue Worth Saving?', *Third World Quarterly*, January 1984.

Rothestein, R. *Global Bargaining, UNCTAD and the Quest for a NIEO*, Princeton University Press, Princeton, 1979.

Roxborough, I. *Theories of Underdevelopment*, Macmillan, London, 1982.

Ruttan, V. 'Integrated Rural Development Programmes: A Historical Perspective', *World Development* 12, 4 (1984).

Salazar, C. 'Nicaragua: 5 Years On', *Outwrite* 32 (January 1985).

Salazar, C. 'The Changes and the Challenge', *Outwrite* 30 (November 1984).

Sampson, A. *The Arms Bazaar*, Coronet Books, London, 1985.

Sauvant, K. P. *The Group of 77*, Oceana Publications, New York, 1981.

Sauvant, K. P. 'From Economic to Socio-Cultural Emancipation: the Historical Context of the NIEO and the Socio-Cultural Order', *Third World Quarterly*, January, 1981.

Sayigh, R. 'Women in Struggle: Palestine', *Third World Quarterly*, October 1983.

Schmitz, H. 'Industrialisation Strategies in Less Developed Countries', *Journal of Development Studies* 21 (1984).

Searle, C. *Grenada: The Struggle Against Destabilisation*, Writers and Readers Publishing Cooperative, London, 1983.

Seedat, A. *Crippling a Nation:* Health in Apartheid South Africa, IDAFSA, London, 1984.

Seers, D. *The Political Economy of Nationalism*, Oxford University Press, Oxford, 1983.

Seers, D. (ed.) *Dependency Theory: A Critical Reassessment*, Pinter, London, 1981.

Sender, J. and Smith, S. *What's Right with the Berg Report and What's Left of Its Critics?*, IDS Discussion Paper, Sussex, June 1984.

Sewell, J., Feinberg, R. and Kallab, V. (eds.) *Foreign Policy and the Third World: Agenda 1985–86*, Transaction Books, Oxford, 1985.

Sewell, J. W. and Zartman, I. W. 'Global Negotiations: Path to the Future or Dead End Street?', *Third World Quarterly*, April 1984.

Shafer, M. 'Capturing the Mineral Multinational: Advantage or Disadvantage?', *International Organization*, Winter 1983.

Shaw, M. 'Dispute Settlement in Africa', *Yearbook of World Affairs*, 1983.

Shaw, T. 'South Africa's Military Capability and the Future of Race Relations', in A. Mazrui and H. Patel (ed.) *Africa in World Affairs*, Third World Press, New York, 1973.

Shaw, T. 'Southern Africa: From Détente to Deluge?', *Yearbook of World Affairs, 1978.*

Sheehan, M. The Arms Race, Martin Robertson, Oxford, 1983.

Shihata, I. 'OPEC as a Donor Group', in A. Gauhar (ed.) *South–South Strategy*, Third World Foundation, 1983.

Shirley, O. *A Cry for Health: Poverty and Disability in the Third World*, Third World Group for Disabled People, Frome, 1983.

Silkin, T. 'Women in Struggle: Eritrea', *Third World Quarterly*, October 1983.

Simpson, A. 'Women in Struggle: El Salvador', *Third World Quarterly*, October 1983.

Singham The Non-Aligned Movement in World Politics, L. Hill, Westport, Conn., 1977.

Siu-Kai, L. 'Social Change, Bureaucratic Rule, and Emergent Political Issues in Hong Kong', *World Politics*, July 1983.

Sjollema, B. *Isolating Apartheid: Western Collaboration with South Africa*, World Council of Churches, Geneva, 1982.

Slinn, P. 'The Southern African Development Coordination Conference', *Yearbook of World Affairs*, 1984.

Smart, I. 'Janus: The Nuclear God', *World Today*, April 1978.

Smith, A. *State and Nation in the Third World*, Wheatsheaf, Brighton, 1983.

Smith, D. *South Africa's Nuclear Capability*, World Campaign Against Military and Nuclear Collaboration with South Africa, London, February 1980.

Smith, M., Little, R. and Shackleton, M. (eds.) *Perspectives on World Politics*, Croom Helm and the Open University, London, 1981.

Somerville, K. 'Political Development Doctrines in the American Foreign Aid Program', *World Politics*, January 1966.

Somerville, K. 'The USSR and Southern Africa since 1976', *Journal of Modern African Studies*, March 1984.

Somjee, A. H. *The Democratic Process in a Developing Society*, Macmillan, London, 1979.

Spector, L. 'Silent Spread', *Foreign Policy*, Spring 1985.

Spence, J. 'South African Foreign Policy: Changing Perspectives', *World Today*, October 1978.

Spence, J. 'South Africa: The Nuclear Option'. *African Affairs* 80, 321 (October 1981).

Spence, J. 'South Africa: Reform versus Reaction', *World Today*, December 1981.

Spero, J. *The Politics of International Economic Relations*, George Allen & Unwin, London 1978.

Stevens, C. (ed.)*EEC and the Third World: A Survey–Hunger*,

Hodder & Stoughton, with ODI and IDS, London, 1982.

Stevens, C. (ed.) *The EEC and the Third World: Renegotiating Lomé*, Hodder & Stoughton, with ODI and IDS, London, 1984.

Stevens, C. A. *The Soviet Union and Black Africa*, Macmillan, London, 1976.

Stewart, F. 'The Fragile Foundations of the Neoclassical Approach to Development', *Journal of Development Studies* 21 (1985).

Stokke, O. and Widstrand, C. (eds.) *The UN–OAU Conference on Southern Africa*, Oslo, April 1973.

Streeton, P. 'Bargaining with Multinationals' in *World Development* 4, 3 (March 1976).

Streeton, P. 'Approaches to a New International Economic Order', *World Development* 10, 1 (1982).

Streeton, P. (ed.) *First Things First: Meeting Basic Human Needs in Developing Countries*, Oxford University Press, Oxford 1981.

Stultz, N. M. 'Interpreting Constitutional Change in South Africa', *Journal of Modern African Studies* 22, 3 (1984).

Sukono, O. 'Non-Proliferation and Developing Countries', in D. Carlton and Carlo Schaerf (eds.) *Arms Race in the 1980s*, Macmillan, London, 1982.

Tanzanian Government Statement, *Africa Current* 3 (Autumn 1975).

Taylor, L. 'Back to Basics: Theory for the Rhetoric in the North–South Round', *World Development* 10, 4 (1982).

The Times, Advertisement: public letter from Angolan head of state, London, 24 November 1984.

Thomas, A. (ed.) *Third World: Images, Definitions, Connotations*, Open University Press, Milton Keynes, 1983.

Thomas, C. *New States, Sovereignty and Intervention*, Gower, Aldershot, 1985.

Tinker, H. *Race, Conflict and International Order*, Macmillan, London, 1977.

Tinker, H. 'Indira Gandhi', *Yearbook of World Affairs*, 1979.

Touval, S. 'The OAU and African Borders', *International Organisation* 21 (1967).

Turner, L. and Bedone, J. 'Saudi Arabia: The Power of the Purse Strings', *International Affairs*, July 1978.

Turner, L. 'The Oil Majors in World Politics', *International Affairs*, July 1976.

UN Yearbook 1974, 'Charter of Economic Rights and Duties of States', *UN Yearbook*, New York, 1974.

UN Yearbook 1974, 'Declaration and Programme of Action on the Establishment of an NIEO', *UN Yearbook*, New York, 1974.

Unterhalter, E. 'Women in Struggle: South Africa', *Third World*

Quarterly, October 1983.

Urdaung, S. 'Women and Development in Mozambique', *Review of African Political Economy* 27/8 (February 1984).

Verlzberger, Y. 'Democratic-Organisation Politics and Information Processing in a Developing State', *International Studies Quarterly*, March 1984.

Vincent, R. 'The Reagan Administration and America's Purpose in the World', *Yearbook of World Affairs*, 1983.

Vital, D. *The Survival of Small States*, Oxford University Press, London, 1971.

Wolfers, M. and Bergersol, J. *Angola: The Front Line*, Zed Press, London, 1983.

Walker, C. *Women and Resistance in South Africa*, Onyx Press, London, 1982.

Waltz, K. N. 'The Spread of Nuclear Weapons: More May be Better', *Adelphi Papers* 171 (1981).

Warren, W. 'Imperialism and Capitalist Industrialisation', *New Left Review* 81 (1973).

Webster, A. *Introduction to the Sociology of Development*, Macmillan, London, 1984.

Weir, D. and Shapiro, M. *Circle of Poison: Pesticides and People in a Hungry World*, Institute for Food and Development Policy, San Francisco, 1981.

Weiss, T. 'What Are the Least Developed Countries and What Benefits May Result from the Paris Conference?', *World Development* 11, 4 (1983).

White, G. and Wade, R. *Developmental States in East Asia*, IDS Research Report No. 16, Sussex, 1984.

Willetts, P. *The Non-Aligned Movement*, Pinter, London, 1982.

Williams, F. 'The US Congress and Non-Proliferation', *International Society*, Autumn 1978.

Williamson, John, *IMF Conditionality*, Institute for International Economics, Washington DC, 1983.

Winnert, R. S. 'Coping with LDC Debt', *International Affairs* 38, 1 (Summer 1984).

Wolf-Phillips, L. *Constitutional Legitimacy*, Third World Foundation, Monograph No. 6, London.

Wolf-Phillips, L. 'Why Third World?', *Third World Quarterly*, January 1979.

Wood, R. 'The Debt Crisis and N/S Relations', *Third World Quarterly*, July 1983.

Woods, D. 'Escalation in South Africa', *Yearbook of World Affairs*, 1982.

World Development Movement *The Tea Trade*, World Development Movement, London.

World Development Movement *Sugar: Crisis in the Third World*, World Development Movement, London, 1980.

Worsley, P. *The Third World*, Weidenfeld and Nicolson, London, 1975.

Worsley, P. 'How Many Worlds?', *Third World Quarterly*, April 1979.

Worsley, P. *The Three Worlds*, Weidenfeld and Nicolson, London, 1984.

Wright, C. 'Reagan Arms Policy, the Arabs and Israel', *Third World Quarterly*, July 1983.

Yoffie, D. B. *Power and Protectionism: Strategies of the NICs*, Columbia University Press, New York, 1983.

Yost, C. 'How the Arab–Israeli War Began', *Foreign Affairs*, January 1968.

Zagoria, D. 'Into the Breach: New Soviet Alliances in the Third World', *Foreign Affairs*, Spring 1979.

Zoxey, M. 'Zimbabwe: From Illegal to Legal Independence', *Yearbook of World Affairs*, 1982.

Index